On the Ambiguity of Erasing Morphisms

Vom Fachbereich Informatik
der Technischen Universität Kaiserslautern
zur Verleihung des akademischen Grades
Doktor der Naturwissenschaften (Dr. rer. nat.)
genehmigte

Dissertation

von

Johannes C. Schneider

Datum der wissenschaftlichen Aussprache: 9. Dezember 2011

Dekan des Fachbereichs: Prof. Dr. A. Poetzsch-Heffter

Promotionskommission: Prof. Dr. K. Berns (Vorsitzender)
Prof. Dr. R. Wiehagen (Berichterstatter)
Prof. Dr. F. Otto (Berichterstatter)

D 386

Abstract

Ambiguity of morphisms is a very basic and fundamental phenomenon that can occur every time when *different* morphisms are applied to the *same* word. A morphism h is called *ambiguous* for a word w provided that there is another morphism g which satisfies $g(w) = h(w)$. If such another morphism does not exist, h is called *unambiguous* for w. Furthermore, there are different types of restricted ambiguity which make additional demands on the other morphism g. One such type is called *moderate ambiguity* which requires that every symbol in the word is always mapped to a word covering a certain factor at a fixed position in the resulting morphic image. In our setting, we examine the ambiguity of morphisms $h : \mathbb{N}^* \to \Sigma^*$, mapping words over the infinite alphabet $\mathbb{N}$ to words over a (possibly finite) target alphabet Σ.

The examination of the ambiguity of morphisms is not only of intrinsic interest, but, due to the simplicity of the concept, also shows various connections to other topics in theoretical computer science and discrete mathematics, such as equality sets (and, thus, the Post Correspondence Problem), pattern languages and various other concepts as, for example, fixed points of morphisms, avoidable patterns and word equations.

In Freydenberger et al. (*International Journal of Foundations of Computer Science* 17, 2006), those words are characterised for which there exists an unambiguous *nonerasing* morphism. In Reidenbach (*Logos Verlag, Berlin,* 2006), a characterisation of words with a moderately ambiguous nonerasing morphism is given. However, only little is known on the ambiguity of erasing morphisms, i. e., morphisms that are allowed to map symbols in the word to the empty word.

This thesis is the first comprehensive study of the ambiguity of *erasing* morphisms, including moderate ambiguity and unambiguity. As our main results, we give a characterisation of words with a moderately ambiguous morphism and characterise the ambiguity of morphisms with an infinite target alphabet Σ, additionally showing that the respective decision problems are NP-complete. Concerning finite target alphabets Σ, we observe that the question if, for a given word w, there exists an unambiguous erasing morphism with target alphabet Σ strongly depends on the size of Σ, which is a novel phenomenon in the theory of ambiguity of morphisms.

During our presentation, we develop numerous methods to investigate the ambiguity and unambiguity of morphisms, including the concept of so-called ambiguity partitions (a strong tool to discover that a morphism is ambiguous and, finally, the key to characterise moderate ambiguity) and some sufficient criteria to determine when there exists an unambiguous morphism with a finite target alphabet and when it does not exist. Furthermore, the phenomenon that words can have only a finite number of unambiguous morphic images is discovered and discussed. Several classes of example patterns without an unambiguous morphism are given and examined. Finally, we present the extension of the concept to terminal-preserving morphisms, so-called substitutions, show connections to nonerasing multi-pattern languages and demonstrate another point of view to the subject of this work.

Acknowledgements

First of all, my most sincere thank goes to my supervisor, Prof. Rolf Wiehagen. As a person with a comprehensive research career himself, truly appreciating fundamental research, he provided me with an excellent environment and very comfortable atmosphere for my research. Very open-minded about my newest insights and results, he always gave me good and constructive advice when I needed it, ever highlighting that his advice is meant as a suggestion, not as an instruction. From this help, my research and especially this thesis have benefited greatly.

I am most thankful that Prof. Friedrich Otto was willing to review this thesis. I really appreciate his reliability during the review process and the fine attention to detail with which he read this thesis, resulting into the correction of many small errors. Furthermore, I would like to thank Prof. Karsten Berns for chairing the doctoral committee.

I am particularly indebted to Daniel Reidenbach for his mentoring and his support that had already begun during my student time. I have learned much from him about pattern languages and the ambiguity of morphisms as well as, in general, about scientific working and the presentation of mathematical results in English. He has always had an open mind for my ideas and dedicated a lot of time to me despite his own pressure of work. His advice and encouragement have substantially promoted my research and, thus, this thesis as well.

Last, but not least, I am very grateful to my family – to my parents for acknowledging and always supporting my interests, to my brother Benjamin for comprehensive proof-reading, to my wife Astrid who has always been curious about my work, even though its content is not easy to communicate. I am especially thankful to her for granting me all the time I needed to write down this thesis since, during this time, our only a few months old daughter was demanding a lot of her energy. Finally, I thank my daughter Marlene. Nothing is as encouraging as her smile.

Contents

Chapter 1

Introduction

Ἐν ἀρχῇ ἦν ὁ λόγος.

In the beginning was the Word.

(John 1.1)

Words are the basis of human communication. As such, also in Mathematics, words are needed to express formal findings and to prove their correctness. However, in various classical disciplines of Mathematics like arithmetic and geometry, numbers play the leading part, certainly motivated from the fact that the first mathematical problems in the ancient world arose from the counting and measuring of estate and arable land, calculating of the statics of monuments, trading and exchanging of currencies etc. Nevertheless, those mathematical disciplines that purely deal with abstract properties of numbers are almost equally old and date back to ancient Greece where mathematicians like Euklid already did fundamental research on prime numbers. The property of a number being prime or composite is independent from the number representing a geometrical length or a certain amount of money, but has major impact on certain formal properties in number theory.

With all this in mind, it is evident to investigate abstract properties of words as well. For instance, a well-known property of this kind is the question if a word is a palindrome. Palindromes are "level", "madam", "racecar", "rotator", but also "abccba" and "xyyzyyx", showing that this property is independent of a word having a known semantics or belonging to a certain language. This field of research, which deals with abstract, combinatorial properties of words and operations on words, is called "Combinatorics on Words", which is attributed to the first text book with the same title [20], where many previous and new results on this topic have been collected by various experts in this area of research. These results date back to the beginning of the 20th century, when A. Thue studied regularities of infinite sequences of letters [38]. However, publications on Combinatorics on Words were rather sporadic and scattered until the sixties and later, when the appearance of computers made it possible to deal with a large amount of data and created new tasks and challenges such as string matching (finding a subword of a large word in a most efficient way) and string compression (finding a most compact representation of a word). Nevertheless, most of the classical problems in Combinatorics on Words are more abstract and not directly motivated by certain applications.

While it is very clear which operations can be applied on numbers (addition, multiplication, etc.), it is, at first sight, not obvious which analogous operations exist for words.

Probably the most simple ones are the concatenation of different words ("race", "car" $\to$ "racecar") and the reversal of words ("gateman" $\to$ "nametag"). Additionally, the substitution of letters with other letters or words, mapping the same letter always to the same letter or word, is a very simple and natural operation on words. These mappings, extended to words, are called *morphisms*. To give an example, the well-known Caesar cipher is the iteration of a morphism $h : \{\mathtt{A}, \mathtt{B}, \ldots, \mathtt{Z}\}^+ \to \{\mathtt{A}, \mathtt{B}, \ldots, \mathtt{Z}\}^+$, where $\{\mathtt{A}, \mathtt{B}, \ldots, \mathtt{Z}\}^+$ stands for arbitrary words over the alphabet $\{\mathtt{A}, \mathtt{B}, \ldots, \mathtt{Z}\}$ and h is defined by $h(\mathtt{A}) := \mathtt{B}$, $h(\mathtt{B}) := \mathtt{C}$, $\ldots$, $h(\mathtt{Y}) := \mathtt{Z}$ and $h(\mathtt{Z}) := \mathtt{A}$. A word w is encrypted by applying n times h to w, where n is the shift which is agreed on beforehand. With $n := 2$, the word CAESAR is encrypted to $h(h(\mathtt{CAESAR})) = h(\mathtt{DBFTBS}) = \mathtt{ECGUCT}$. For this application, one of the main features of h is its "reversibility", in mathematical terms called injectivity, which makes it possible to undo the effect of h to a word simply by selecting the respective previous letters in the alphabet $\{\mathtt{A}, \mathtt{B}, \ldots, \mathtt{Z}\}$. Of course, this is essential to decrypt the word. A morphism h, defined by $h(\mathtt{A}) := \mathtt{A}$, $h(\mathtt{B}) := \mathtt{A}$, $\ldots$, $h(\mathtt{Z}) := \mathtt{A}$ would hardly qualify for a cipher method.

Another example for a morphism that is well-known and well-studied in Combinatorics on Words is the *Fibonacci morphism* (see, e.g., de Luca [21], Karhumäki [17], Saari [33] and the references therein). This morphism $h : \{\mathtt{a}, \mathtt{b}\}^+ \to \{\mathtt{a}, \mathtt{b}\}^+$ is defined by $h(\mathtt{a}) := \mathtt{ab}$ and $h(\mathtt{b}) := \mathtt{a}$, having the property that the length of the words $\mathtt{a}$, $h(\mathtt{a}) = \mathtt{ab}$, $h(h(\mathtt{a})) = h(\mathtt{ab}) = \mathtt{aba}$, $h^3(\mathtt{a}) = \mathtt{abaab}$, $h^4(\mathtt{a}) = \mathtt{abaababa}$, etc. equals the Fibonacci number sequence 1, 2, 3, 5, 8, etc.

The expressive power of morphisms is enormous. Numerous models of formal languages are based upon morphisms, such as *pattern languages* (the set of *all* morphic images of a word, for an overview see Mateescu and Salomaa [22]) and *L systems* (iterative application of *one* morphism, an overview is given in Kari et al. [19]). In computational theory, one of the most famous *undecidable* problems – the Post Correspondence Problem (PCP for short, see Post [24]) – is usually formulated as a morphism problem: Given two arbitrary morphisms g, h, is there a nonempty word w on which the morphisms agree, i.e. $g(w) = h(w)$? Also many complexity questions as the well-known P-NP-Problem can be expressed using the PCP (cf. Mateescu et al. [23]).

This thesis is dedicated to a very basic phenomenon of morphisms that can occur every time when several (at least two) morphisms are applied to one word, which, for example, is the case for the above-mentioned pattern languages and also for the PCP. This phenomenon is called *ambiguity of morphisms*, meaning that *different* morphisms applied to one and the *same* word can generate the same image. If, for a given word and a morphism h, there exists another morphism that, applied to that word, generates the same image, we call this morphism h *ambiguous*; otherwise, if there is no such morphism, h is called *unambiguous*.

We shall introduce the definition of unambiguous morphisms a little more formally, i.e., aimed to the further usage in this thesis. For the sake of convenience, we use $\mathbb{N}$ as an infinite alphabet and consider words over $\mathbb{N}$ such as the word $2 \cdot 1 \cdot 2 \cdot 25 \cdot 17$, where $\cdot$ refers to the concatenation and is used to separate between different symbols in the word. Furthermore, for an arbitrary alphabet Σ, we consider morphisms $\sigma : \mathbb{N}^* \to \Sigma^*$ that map words over $\mathbb{N}$ to words over Σ. Since Σ^* stands for arbitrary words over the alphabet Σ including the *empty word* ε, these morphisms are allowed to "erase" symbols from the word, i.e., to map symbols to ε. Given an arbitrary alphabet Σ and a word $\alpha \in \mathbb{N}^+$, a morphism $\sigma : \mathbb{N}^* \to \Sigma^*$ is called *ambiguous* for α if and only if there exists *another* morphism $\tau : \mathbb{N}^* \to \Sigma^*$ (i.e., $\tau(i) \neq \sigma(i)$ for a symbol i occurring in α) such that $\tau(\alpha) = \sigma(\alpha)$. If such a morphism τ does not exist, σ is called *unambiguous* for α. For instance, the morphism $\sigma_1 : \mathbb{N}^* \to \{\mathtt{a}, \mathtt{b}\}^*$, $\sigma_1(i) := \mathtt{ab}^i$ for every $i \in \mathbb{N}$, is ambiguous with respect to $\alpha_1 := 1 \cdot 2 \cdot 2 \cdot 3 \cdot 1 \cdot 3$ since there exists another morphism $\tau : \mathbb{N}^* \to \{\mathtt{a}, \mathtt{b}\}^*$, given by $\tau(1) := \mathtt{a}$, $\tau(2) := \mathtt{bab}$, $\tau(3) := \mathtt{babbb}$, satisfying $\tau(\alpha_1) = \sigma_1(\alpha_1)$:

$$\sigma_1(\alpha_1) \;=\; \overbrace{\mathtt{a}\;\;\mathtt{b}}^{\sigma_1(1)}\,\overbrace{\mathtt{ab}\;\mathtt{b}}^{\sigma_1(2)}\,\overbrace{\mathtt{ab}\;\mathtt{b}}^{\sigma_1(2)}\,\overbrace{\mathtt{abbb}}^{\sigma_1(3)}\,\overbrace{\mathtt{a}\;\;\mathtt{b}}^{\sigma_1(1)}\,\overbrace{\mathtt{abbb}}^{\sigma_1(3)} = \underbrace{\mathtt{a}}_{\tau(1)}\,\underbrace{\mathtt{bab}}_{\tau(2)}\,\underbrace{\mathtt{bab}}_{\tau(2)}\,\underbrace{\mathtt{babbb}}_{\tau(3)}\,\underbrace{\mathtt{a}}_{\tau(1)}\,\underbrace{\mathtt{babbb}}_{\tau(3)} = \tau(\alpha_1).$$

In contrast to this, every morphism $\sigma : \mathbb{N}^* \to \Sigma^*$ is unambiguous with respect to, e. g., $\alpha_2 := 1 \cdot 1$.

We shall demonstrate the relevance of the concept of ambiguity of morphisms by giving some examples. First, let us consider equality sets as introduced by Salomaa [34] (an overview of this topic is given by Harju and Karhumäki [11]). Given morphisms g, h, $E(g, h) := \{w \mid g(w) = h(w)\}$ is the equality set of g and h. Ignoring the trivial case $g = h$, the existence of a word $w \in E(g, h)$ implies that g (and, thus, also h) is ambiguous for w. Equality sets are closely related to the Post Correspondence Problem since the PCP is the problem of deciding the emptiness of $E(g, h)$. Furthermore, Culik II and Karhumäki [3] investigate a problem which is dual to the PCP, namely the question if, for a given word w, there exist different morphisms g and h such that $w \in E(g, h)$. In other words, they ask if, for a given word, there exists an *ambiguous* morphism. Thus, this setting is exactly dual to one of our main questions: Does there exist an *unambiguous* morphism for a given word? In their work, Culik II and Karhumäki also characterise the set of all ambiguous morphisms with a binary target alphabet for the words ab, aba and aabb.

As another example, we consider pattern languages. For a word $\alpha \in \mathbb{N}^+$ (then called "pattern") and an alphabet Σ, the pattern language $L_\Sigma(\alpha)$ consists of all morphic images of morphisms $\sigma : \mathbb{N}^* \to \Sigma^*$ applied to α[†]. E. g., for $\alpha_2 := 1 \cdot 1 \cdot 2 \cdot 2$, it is $L_{\{\mathtt{a},\mathtt{b}\}}(\alpha_1) = \{uuww \mid u, w \in \{\mathtt{a}, \mathtt{b}\}^*\}$. Concerning pattern languages, we are massively confronted with ambiguity of morphisms since we apply *all* possible morphisms to a pattern and, thus, can receive the same word from different morphisms. In the above example, the word aaaa can be generated from α_2 by either replacing 1 and 2 both with a, by replacing 1 with aa and erasing 2 (mapping 2 to the empty word ε) or by erasing 1 and replacing 2 with aa. Thus, any of these three morphisms is ambiguous for α_2. Furthermore, for an arbitrary alphabet Σ, we consider any word w which is generated from the pattern $\alpha_2' := 1 \cdot 1 \cdot 2 \cdot 3 \cdot 2 \cdot 3$ by a morphism $\sigma : \mathbb{N}^* \to \Sigma^*$ that maps 3 to a nonempty word. We show that w can be generated from α_2' without the help of variable 3 in the pattern. To this purpose, let $\tau : \mathbb{N}^* \to \Sigma^*$ be a morphism, defined by $\tau(1) := \sigma(1)$, $\tau(2) := \sigma(2)\sigma(3)$ and $\tau(3) := \varepsilon$ (hence, 3 is erased). It is $\tau(\alpha_2') = \tau(1)\tau(1)\tau(2)\tau(3)\tau(2)\tau(3) = \sigma(1)\sigma(1)\sigma(2)\sigma(3)\sigma(2)\sigma(3) = \sigma(\alpha_2')$, but $\tau(2) \neq \sigma(2)$. Thus, σ is ambiguous for α_2. Since σ is chosen arbitrarily with $\sigma(3) \neq \varepsilon$, we can conclude that every morphism that maps 3 to a nonempty word is ambiguous and can be "replaced" by a morphism that erases 3. Thus, the variable 3 is not needed in α_2' to generate $L_\Sigma(\alpha_2')$. Indeed, it follows that $L_\Sigma(\alpha_2') = L_\Sigma(\alpha_2)$. Thus, in the field of pattern languages, ambiguity of morphisms can cause the phenomenon that there are patterns of different length that generate the same language.

[†]In the literature, this (restricted) type of pattern languages is usually called the *terminal-free erasing pattern language of* α.

As a final example, we consider learning theory, in particular inductive inference of formal languages. It has been an open problem for more than two decades to determine if pattern languages (as defined in the previous paragraph) can be learned in the limit (Gold-style learning, see Gold [10]). Recent results by Reidenbach [26, 28] show that the general answer is negative since the class of pattern languages over $\{\mathtt{a}, \mathtt{b}\}$ is not learnable. This result strongly relies on the phenomenon that certain morphisms $\sigma : \mathbb{N}^* \to \{\mathtt{a}, \mathtt{b}\}^*$ are ambiguous for the pattern $1 \cdot 1 \cdot 2 \cdot 2 \cdot 3 \cdot 3$, namely the morphisms with $\sigma(1), \sigma(2) \in \{\mathtt{a}\}^*$ or $\sigma(1), \sigma(2) \in \{\mathtt{b}\}^*$. On the other hand, the class of pattern languages[‡] over alphabets with at least three letters can be learned in the limit since, for every pattern, there exists a so-called "telltale" – a finite subset of the language generated by that pattern satisfying certain formal conditions. The existence of a telltale for every pattern implies the learnability of the respective class of pattern languages (see Angluin [2]). Reidenbach [28] shows that these telltales can be constructed by using certain words generated by morphisms with a *restricted ambiguity*. Thus, the learnability of terminal-free erasing pattern languages over alphabets with at least three letters is obtained by mastering the ambiguity of morphisms.

Further examples of the impact of ambiguity on properties of pattern languages include the equivalence and inclusion problem for pattern languages. For an overview, Reidenbach [25] is recommended.

All these examples show not only the relevance of ambiguity of morphisms but also their importance. Thus, it is self-evident to further investigate this topic in a more general manner. The systematic and explicit examination of the ambiguity of morphisms is initiated in Freydenberger, Reidenbach and Schneider [8] and continued in Freydenberger, Reidenbach [6] and Freydenberger et al. [5]. In [8], those words α are characterised for which there exists an unambiguous *nonerasing* morphism $\sigma : \mathbb{N}^* \to \Sigma^*$, i. e., $\sigma(i) \neq \varepsilon$ for every symbol i occurring in α. However, there are words for which every *nonerasing* morphism is ambiguous, but there exists an unambiguous *erasing* morphism, i. e., a morphism that maps certain symbols of the word to the empty word ε. For instance, consider $\alpha_3 := 1 \cdot 2 \cdot 2$. Every nonerasing morphism $\sigma_{\mathrm{NE}} : \mathbb{N}^* \to \Sigma^*$ is ambiguous since there exists another morphism $\tau : \mathbb{N}^* \to \Sigma^*$, defined by $\tau(1) := \sigma_{\mathrm{NE}}(1 \cdot 2 \cdot 2)$, $\tau(2) := \varepsilon$, satisfying $\sigma_{\mathrm{NE}}(\alpha_3) = \tau(\alpha_3)$. In contrast to this, every *erasing* morphism $\sigma_{\mathrm{E}} : \mathbb{N}^* \to \Sigma^*$ with $|\sigma_{\mathrm{E}}(1)| = 1$ and $\sigma_{\mathrm{E}}(2) = \varepsilon$ is unambiguous with respect to α_3. Finally, there also exist words for which every (erasing or nonerasing) morphism is ambiguous, provided that this morphism does not map *all* symbols in the pattern to the empty word. This is illustrated by, e. g., $\alpha_4 := 1 \cdot 2 \cdot 1 \cdot 2$. Let $\sigma : \mathbb{N}^* \to \Sigma^*$ be an arbitrary morphism. If $\sigma(1) \neq \varepsilon$, then the morphism $\tau(1) := \varepsilon$, $\tau(2) := \sigma(1 \cdot 2)$, satisfies $\tau(\alpha_4) = \sigma(\alpha_4)$ – the case $\sigma(2) \neq \varepsilon$ is analogous. Hence, no such morphism σ is unambiguous with respect to α_4.

In the present thesis, we shall examine the ambiguity of morphisms that are allowed to erase symbols. Our overall goal is to gain as much information and results as possible on words for which every morphism is ambiguous, on words for which there exists an unambiguous erasing morphism and on words for which at least a certain restricted ambiguity can be achieved.

In the next chapter, we give the basic formal definitions needed in this thesis as well as some preliminary results. In Chapter 3, we present the status quo concerning nonerasing morphisms. This does not only allow us to develop the theory of erasing morphisms in a certain analogy, but makes it also possible to discuss whether or not the methods used to

[‡]To be precise: the terminal-free erasing pattern languages.

study nonerasing morphisms are also suitable for erasing morphisms. Chapter 4 is dedicated to the examination of erasing morphisms. After some basic considerations concerning ambiguity of erasing morphisms, we first investigate a certain kind of strongly restricted ambiguity, so-called moderate ambiguity (Section 4.2). A characterisation of strings with a moderately ambiguous morphism is given. In the subsequent sections, it turns out that, in the case of erasing morphisms, their unambiguity strongly depends on the size of the target alphabet of the morphism. This is a novel and rather unexpected phenomenon, which makes an easy and simple characterisation of words with an unambiguous erasing morphism virtually impossible. At least, if the target alphabet size is infinite, such a simple characterisation is found (see Section 4.3). Section 4.4 and its subsections are dedicated to the case that the target alphabet is finite and describe different ambiguity phenomena. Concerning nonerasing morphisms, so-called "segmented morphisms" are one of the main tools to attain restricted ambiguity. In Section 4.5, their relevance for erasing morphisms is discussed. Finally, some notes on the complexity of the problems investigated so far are given in Section 4.6. The main result therein states that, unless P=NP, the problem of deciding whether or not, for a given word, there exists an unambiguous erasing morphism with an infinite target alphabet as well as the problem of deciding whether or not, for a given word and an arbitrary target alphabet, there exists a moderately ambiguous erasing morphism are both not in P (their complementary problems are NP-complete). Chapter 5 contains some topics which are closely related to the ambiguity of morphisms and presents some notes and results concerning the ambiguity of terminal-preserving morphisms, so-called substitutions, the connection to nonerasing multi-pattern languages and a different approach to the ambiguity of morphisms. All the main results are finally summarised in Chapter 6. A comparison between the results for nonerasing and erasing morphisms is given, and some open problems are discussed.

Many results of this work have been published by the author in [35] and its journal version [36] (mainly results concerning unambiguity) as well as in [30] and its journal version [31] (mainly results concerning moderate ambiguity).

Chapter 2

Basic definitions and preliminary results

In the present section, we give some basic definitions and results. This thesis is largely self-contained. If, nevertheless, a notion is not explained explicitly in this work, we refer the reader to Rozenberg and Salomaa [32].

2.1 Words, patterns and morphisms

Let $\mathbb{N} := \{1, 2, \ldots\}$ be the set of natural numbers. The *power set* of a set S is denoted by $\mathcal{P}(S)$. A *partition* of S is a tuple $(S_1, S_2, \ldots, S_n)$ for an $n \in \mathbb{N}$, satisfying $S_1 \cup S_2 \cup \ldots \cup S_n = S$ and $S_i \cap S_j = \emptyset$ for every $i, j \in \{1, 2, \ldots, n\}$ with $i \neq j$. An *alphabet* $\mathcal{A}$ is an enumerable set of symbols. A *word* w *(over* $\mathcal{A}$*)* is a finite sequence of symbols taken from $\mathcal{A}$. We denote by $\mathrm{symb}(w)$ the set of symbols occurring in w, hence $\mathrm{symb}(w) \subseteq \mathcal{A}$. By $|X|$ we denote the cardinality of a set X or the length of a word X. The *empty word* ε is the unique sequence of symbols of length 0. For the *concatenation* of words v, w, we write $v \cdot w$ (or vw for short). The word that results from the n-fold concatenation of a word w is denoted by w^n. The notation $\mathcal{A}^*$ refers to the set of all words over $\mathcal{A}$, i. e., more precisely, the *free monoid* generated by $\mathcal{A}$; furthermore, $\mathcal{A}^+ := \mathcal{A}^* \setminus \{\varepsilon\}$. The number of occurrences of a symbol $a \in \mathcal{A}$ in a word $w \in \mathcal{A}^*$ is written as $|w|_a$. With regard to arbitrary words $v, w \in \mathcal{A}^*$, we write $w = v \ldots$ if there exists a $u \in \mathcal{A}^*$ such that $w = vu$, we write $w = \ldots v$ if there exists a $u \in \mathcal{A}^*$ such that $w = uv$, and, finally, $w = \ldots v \ldots$ if there exist $u, u' \in \mathcal{A}^*$ such that $w = uvu'$. We call v a *prefix*, *suffix* and *factor* of w, respectively. In contrast to this notation, if we omit some parts of a canonically given word, then we henceforth use the symbol $[\ldots]$; e. g., $w = \ldots a\,b\,[\ldots]\,f$ means that w ends with the word $a\,b\,c\,d\,e\,f$. Moreover, we extend the operations *, $^+$ and the concatenation to sets of words in the usual manner; with regard to alphabets $\mathcal{A}$, $\mathcal{B}$, this means that, e. g., $(\mathcal{A}^*\mathcal{B})^+ = \{w \mid w = v_1{\cdot}b_1{\cdot}v_2{\cdot}b_2{\cdot}\ldots{\cdot}v_n{\cdot}b_n \text{ with } n \in \mathbb{N}, v_1, v_2, \ldots, v_n \in \mathcal{A}^*, b_1, b_2, \ldots, b_n \in \mathcal{B}\}$.

We often use $\mathbb{N}$ as an infinite alphabet of symbols. In order to distinguish between a word over $\mathbb{N}$ and a word over a (possibly finite) alphabet Σ, we call the former a *pattern*. Given a pattern $\alpha \in \mathbb{N}^*$, we call symbols occurring in α *variables* and denote the set of variables in α by $\mathrm{var}(\alpha)$. Hence, $\mathrm{var}(\alpha) \subseteq \mathbb{N}$. We use the symbol $\cdot$ to separate the variables in a pattern, so that, for instance, $1 \cdot 1 \cdot 2$ is not confused with $11 \cdot 2$.

Given arbitrary alphabets $\mathcal{A}, \mathcal{B}$, a *morphism* is a mapping $h : \mathcal{A}^* \to \mathcal{B}^*$ that is compatible with the concatenation, i. e., for all $v, w \in \mathcal{A}^*$, $h(vw) = h(v)h(w)$. Hence, h is fully defined for all $v \in \mathcal{A}^*$ as soon as it is defined for all symbols in $\mathcal{A}$. We call h *erasing* if and only if $h(a) = \varepsilon$ for an $a \in \mathcal{A}$; otherwise, h is called *nonerasing.* If we call a morphism h (non)erasing with a certain input word w in mind, we only demand h to be (non)erasing for the symbols occurring in w. A morphism $h : \mathcal{A}^* \to \mathcal{B}^*$ is said to be *injective* if, for any words $v, w \in \mathcal{A}^*$, the equality $h(v) = h(w)$ implies $v = w$. We want to note that h necessarily is nonerasing provided that it is injective. For the *composition* of two morphisms $g, h : \mathcal{A}^* \to \mathcal{A}^*$, we write $g \circ h$, i. e., for every $w \in \mathcal{A}^*$, $g \circ h(w) = g(h(w))$.

In this work, two kinds of morphisms are of major interest: morphisms $h : \mathbb{N}^* \to \mathbb{N}^*$ and $\sigma : \mathbb{N}^* \to \Sigma^*$. Morphisms $h : \mathbb{N}^* \to \mathbb{N}^*$ are also called *endomorphisms* since they map patterns to patterns again. Among these morphisms, fixed point morphisms play a special role. A pattern $\alpha \in \mathbb{N}^+$ is called a *fixed point (of a morphism h)* if $h(\alpha) = \alpha$. Obviously, every pattern is a fixed point of the identity morphism $\mathrm{id} : \mathbb{N}^* \to \mathbb{N}^*$, defined by $\mathrm{id}(x) := x$ for every $x \in \mathbb{N}$. However, there are nontrivial examples: Let $\alpha' := 1 \cdot 2 \cdot 1 \cdot 2$ and h' be defined by $h'(1) := 1 \cdot 2$ and $h'(2) := \varepsilon$. Then α' is a fixed point of h'. A morphism $h : \mathbb{N}^* \to \mathbb{N}^*$ is said to be *nontrivial* if $h(x) \neq x$ for an $x \in \mathbb{N}$. Thus, the previous example morphism h' is nontrivial and, hence, the example pattern α' is a fixed point of a nontrivial morphism. Let $V \subseteq \mathbb{N}$. We call $h : \mathbb{N}^* \to \mathbb{N}^*$ *nontrivial for V* if $h(x) \neq x$ for an $x \in V$. Additionally, another important endomorphism $\pi_V : \mathbb{N}^* \to \mathbb{N}^*$ is given by $\pi_V(x) := x$ if $x \in V$ and $\pi_V(x) := \varepsilon$ if $x \notin V$ and, therefore, called the *projection onto V* since it maps a pattern to its scattered subpattern consisting of variables in V only. Furthermore, a morphism $h : \mathbb{N}^* \to \mathbb{N}^*$ is said to be a *renaming* if and only if it is an injective letter to letter morphism, i.e., $|h(x)| = 1$ for every $x \in \mathbb{N}$ and $h(x) = h(y)$ implies $x = y$ for every $x, y \in \mathbb{N}$. Moreover, we call a pattern β a renaming of a pattern α if and only if there exists a renaming $h : \mathbb{N}^* \to \mathbb{N}^*$ with $h(\alpha) = \beta$.

The other important type of morphisms maps patterns to words over an alphabet Σ. For such morphisms $\sigma : \mathbb{N}^* \to \Sigma^*$, Σ is called *target alphabet of σ*. In this work, we are only interested in target alphabets that are at least binary. Unary target alphabets play a special role since the concatenation of words over a unary alphabet is commutative. For instance, it is $\mathtt{a}^2\,\mathtt{a}^3 = \mathtt{a}^3\,\mathtt{a}^2 = \mathtt{a}^5$. Nevertheless, all formal statements in this thesis where the size of Σ is not further specified also hold for unary alphabets.

In Chapter 5, we need yet another type of morphisms: For a given alphabet Σ, we call a morphism $\sigma : (\mathbb{N} \cup \Sigma)^* \to \Sigma^*$ a *substitution* if and only if it is terminal-preserving, i. e., $\sigma(a) = a$ for every $a \in \Sigma$. In this context, Σ is called *terminal alphabet.*

2.2 Pattern languages

Originally, patterns as introduced by Angluin [1] and Shinohara [37], consist of symbols in $\mathbb{N}$ (variables) and *terminal symbols* of a so-called *terminal alphabet* Σ. In this work, we call both $\alpha \in (\mathbb{N} \cup \Sigma)^+$ and $\alpha \in \mathbb{N}^+$ patterns, but, aside from Section 5.1, we deal with patterns $\alpha \in \mathbb{N}^+$ only. Since those patterns do not contain any terminal symbols from Σ, they are often referred to as *terminal-free* patterns in literature. For patterns $\alpha \in (\mathbb{N} \cup \Sigma)^+$, we denote by $\mathrm{var}(\alpha)$ the set of variables in α and by $\mathrm{term}(\alpha)$ the set of terminal symbols in α. Hence, $\mathrm{var}(\alpha) \subseteq \mathbb{N}$ and $\mathrm{term}(\alpha) \subseteq \Sigma$. If we consider, e. g., $\alpha := 1 \cdot \mathtt{aa} \cdot 2 \cdot 1 \cdot 1 \cdot \mathtt{ba} \cdot 3 \cdot \mathtt{b} \in (\mathbb{N}^* \cup \{\mathtt{a}, \mathtt{b}\})^*$, it is $\mathrm{var}(\alpha) = \{1, 2, 3\}$ and $\mathrm{term}(\alpha) = \{\mathtt{a}, \mathtt{b}\}$.

The language of a pattern $\alpha \in (\mathbb{N} \cup \Sigma)^+$ is the set of all images of α under substitutions $\sigma : (\mathbb{N} \cup \Sigma)^* \to \Sigma^*$ as formally expressed by the following definition.

Definition 2.1 (Pattern language). *Let* Σ *be an alphabet and let* $\alpha \in (\mathbb{N} \cup \Sigma)^+$. *We call*

$$L_{\mathrm{E},\Sigma}(\alpha) := \{\sigma(\alpha) \mid \sigma : (\mathbb{N} \cup \Sigma)^* \to \Sigma^* \textit{ is a substitution}\}$$

the erasing pattern language (generated by α) *and*

$$L_{\mathrm{NE},\Sigma}(\alpha) := \{\sigma(\alpha) \mid \sigma : (\mathbb{N} \cup \Sigma)^* \to \Sigma^* \textit{ is a nonerasing substitution}\}$$

the nonerasing pattern language (generated by α). *We use* E-pattern language *and* NE-pattern language *for short.*

The first type of pattern language $L_{\mathrm{E},\Sigma}(\alpha)$ is called *erasing* pattern language since the substitutions are allowed to *erase* variables in the pattern α. However, they do not need to erase variables. Thus, $L_{\mathrm{NE},\Sigma}(\alpha) \subset L_{\mathrm{E},\Sigma}(\alpha)$ for any pattern α and any alphabet Σ. For an overview over pattern languages, we recommend Mateescu and Salomaa [22]. More recent results can be found in Reidenbach [27], Freydenberger and Reidenbach [7] and Jain et. al [14].

From now on, we consider *terminal-free patterns* $\alpha \in \mathbb{N}^+$ only. In this case, we simply have $L_{\mathrm{E},\Sigma}(\alpha) := \{\sigma(\alpha) \mid \sigma : \mathbb{N}^* \to \Sigma^* \text{ is a morphism}\}$ and $L_{\mathrm{NE},\Sigma}(\alpha) := \{\sigma(\alpha) \mid \sigma : \mathbb{N}^* \to \Sigma^* \text{ is a nonerasing morphism}\}$. While for any $\alpha, \beta \in \mathbb{N}^+$, $L_{\mathrm{NE},\Sigma}(\alpha) = L_{\mathrm{NE},\Sigma}(\beta)$ implies $|\alpha| = |\beta|$ (see Angluin [1]), patterns of different length can generate the same *erasing* pattern language. Let Σ be an alphabet and consider, for example, $\alpha = 1$ and $\beta = 1 \cdot 2 \cdot 2$. It is $L_{\mathrm{E},\Sigma}(\alpha) = \Sigma^* = L_{\mathrm{E},\Sigma}(\beta)$. The first equality is trivial and the second easy to see since, for any $w \in \Sigma^*$, the morphism $\sigma : \mathbb{N}^* \to \Sigma^*$, defined by $\sigma(1) := w$, $\sigma(2) := \varepsilon$, satisfies $\sigma(\beta) = w$. Obviously, α is one of the shortest generators of the pattern language Σ^*. We name the shortest generators of erasing pattern languages in the following definition.

Definition 2.2 (Succinct/prolix). *Let* Σ *be an alphabet and let* $\alpha \in \mathbb{N}^+$. *We call* α succinct *if and only there is no pattern* β *with* $|\beta| < |\alpha|$ *and* $L_{\mathrm{E},\Sigma}(\beta) = L_{\mathrm{E},\Sigma}(\alpha)$. *We call* α prolix *if and only if it is not succinct.*

At first sight, it may not be easy to find out if a pattern is succinct or prolix. However, prolix patterns feature a specific structure, which is discussed in the following section.

2.3 Morphic primitivity

In Combinatorics on Words, a word w is called primitive if it cannot be written as the power of a shorter word v, i. e. $w \neq v^n$ for any v and any $n \geq 2$ (see, e. g., Lothaire [20]). Contrary to this classical notion of primitivity that involves the concatenation of words, *morphic primitivity* is based on a morphic relation between words. This concept has been introduced by Reidenbach [25] and is explicitly studied in Reidenbach and Schneider [29]. It leads to a partition of the set of all patterns subject to the following criterion:

Definition 2.3 (Morphically (im)primitive). *Let* $\alpha \in \mathbb{N}^*$. *We call* α morphically imprimitive *if and only if there exist a pattern* β *with* $|\beta| < |\alpha|$ *and morphisms* $g, h : \mathbb{N}^* \to \mathbb{N}^*$ *satisfying* $h(\alpha) = \beta$ *and* $g(\beta) = \alpha$. *If* α *is not morphically imprimitive, we call* α morphically primitive.

We give an example to illustrate this definition.

Example 2.4. Let $\alpha := 1 \cdot 2 \cdot 3 \cdot 3 \cdot 1 \cdot 2$. This pattern is morphically imprimitive since $\beta := 1 \cdot 3 \cdot 3 \cdot 1$, $h : \mathbb{N}^* \to \mathbb{N}^*$, given by $h(1) := 1$, $h(2) := \varepsilon$ and $h(3) := 3$, and $g : \mathbb{N}^* \to \mathbb{N}^*$, given by $g(1) := 1 \cdot 2$ and $g(3) := 3$, satisfy $|\beta| < |\alpha|$, $h(\alpha) = \beta$ and $g(\beta) = \alpha$. The pattern β is morphically primitive since every morphism h that maps β to a shorter pattern erases 1 or 3 (or both), resulting to $h(\beta) = 1 \cdot 1$, $h(\beta) = 3 \cdot 3$ or $h(\beta) = \varepsilon$, which all cannot be mapped to β again with the help of a morphism g. ◇

The concept of morphic primitivity is not only a very natural one, it is also important and relevant to other concepts, such as pattern languages and fixed points of morphisms. This fact is backed up by the following theorem.

Theorem 2.5. *Let $\alpha \in \mathbb{N}^+$. The following statements are equivalent:*

1. *α is not a fixed point of a nontrivial morphism $h : \mathbb{N}^* \to \mathbb{N}^*$.*
2. *α is morphically primitive.*
3. *α is succinct.*

Proof. From Head [12] and Reidenbach, Schneider [29]. □

At first sight, it can be hard to tell if a given pattern is morphically primitive or imprimitive. The following technical definition is helpful to facilitate this check.

Definition 2.6 (Imprimitivity factorisation). *Let $\alpha \in \mathbb{N}^+$. An* imprimitivity factorisation *(of α) is a mapping $f : \mathbb{N}^+ \to \mathbb{N}^n \times (\mathbb{N}^+)^n$, $n \in \mathbb{N}$, such that, for $f(\alpha) = (x_1, x_2, \ldots, x_n; \gamma_1, \gamma_2, \ldots, \gamma_n)$, there exist $\beta_0, \beta_1, \ldots, \beta_n \in \mathbb{N}^*$ satisfying $\alpha = \beta_0\, \gamma_1\, \beta_1\, \gamma_2\, \beta_2 \ldots \gamma_n\, \beta_n$ and*

(i) *for every $i \in \{1, 2, \ldots, n\}$, $|\gamma_i| \geq 2$,*

(ii) *for every $i \in \{0, 1, \ldots, n\}$ and for every $j \in \{1, 2, \ldots, n\}$, $\mathrm{var}(\beta_i) \cap \mathrm{var}(\gamma_j) = \emptyset$,*

(iii) *for every $i \in \{1, 2, \ldots, n\}$, $|\gamma_i|_{x_i} = 1$ and if $x_i \in \mathrm{var}(\gamma_{i'})$, $i' \in \{1, 2, \ldots, n\}$, then $\gamma_i = \gamma_{i'}$ and $x_i = x_{i'}$.*

As the name suggests, imprimitivity factorisations characterise morphically imprimitive patterns.

Corollary 2.7. *A pattern $\alpha \in \mathbb{N}^+$ is morphically primitive if and only if there exists no imprimitivity factorisation of α.*

Proof. Directly from Head [12] and Theorem 2.5. □

In Example 2.4, $f(\alpha) = (x_1, x_2; \gamma_1, \gamma_2) := (1, 1; 1 \cdot 2, 1 \cdot 2)$ is an imprimitivity factorisation of α since

$$\alpha = \underbrace{\varepsilon}_{\beta_0} \cdot \underbrace{1 \cdot 2}_{\gamma_1} \cdot \underbrace{3 \cdot 3}_{\beta_1} \cdot \underbrace{1 \cdot 2}_{\gamma_2} \cdot \underbrace{\varepsilon}_{\beta_2},$$

and points (i)–(iii) of Definition 2.6 are satisfied.

As we shall explain in the next section, the distinction of morphically primitive and imprimitive patterns is also crucial for the ambiguity of morphisms.

2.4 Ambiguity of morphisms

We begin this section with the central definition of this work.

Definition 2.8 (Ambiguity and unambiguity of morphisms). *Let Σ be an alphabet, $\alpha \in \mathbb{N}^+$ and let $\sigma : \mathbb{N}^* \to \Sigma^*$ be a morphism with $\sigma(\alpha) \neq \varepsilon$. We call σ* ambiguous *(for α) if and only if there is a morphism $\tau : \mathbb{N}^* \to \Sigma^*$ satisfying $\tau(\alpha) = \sigma(\alpha)$ and, for some $x \in \mathrm{var}(\alpha)$, $\tau(x) \neq \sigma(x)$. If σ is not ambiguous for α, it is called* unambiguous *(for α).*

First examples for ambiguous and unambiguous morphisms can be found in the Introduction of this thesis, and further examples are given in the following chapters.

One consequence of the morphic structure of morphically imprimitive patterns is formulated in the following theorem.

Theorem 2.9 (Freydenberger et al. [8]). *Let Σ be an alphabet and let $\alpha \in \mathbb{N}^+$. If α is morphically imprimitive, there is no* nonerasing *morphism $\sigma : \mathbb{N}^* \to \Sigma^*$ that is unambiguous for α.*

The proof makes use of the fact that certain variables in a morphically imprimitive pattern are redundant in the sense that they are not needed for the respective pattern language. This is reflected by the fact that morphically imprimitive patterns equal the prolix patterns (see Theorem 2.5). Hence, all words that are generated by a morphism which maps those variables to a nonempty word (such as any nonerasing morphism) can also be generated by another morphism erasing these variables. Similar observations can also be made for erasing morphisms that do not erase certain variables. For a detailed study, we refer to Section 4.1. Moreover, the partition of $\mathbb{N}^+$ into morphically primitive and imprimitive patterns even allows to formulate a stronger version of Theorem 2.9. We shall present this result (and the way of achieving it) in the next chapter.

Usually, we look for unambiguous morphisms with a fixed, small number of letters in the target alphabet Σ. However, if the size of Σ is unrestricted, we can find a simple unambiguous nonerasing morphism for every morphically primitive pattern.

Theorem 2.10. *Let $\alpha \in \mathbb{N}^+$ and $\Sigma \supseteq \mathrm{var}(\alpha)$. If α is morphically primitive, then any morphism $\sigma : \mathbb{N}^* \to \Sigma^*$ satisfying $\sigma(x) = x$ for every $x \in \mathrm{var}(\alpha)$ is unambiguous for α.*

Proof. Let α be morphically primitive. Assume to the contrary that σ is ambiguous and, hence, there exists a morphism $\tau : \mathbb{N}^* \to \Sigma^*$ with $\tau(\alpha) = \sigma(\alpha)$ and $\tau(x) \neq \sigma(x) = x$ for an $x \in \mathrm{var}(\alpha)$. Thus, τ is nontrivial and α is a fixed point of τ since $\tau(\alpha) = \sigma(\alpha) = \alpha$. Consequently, according to Theorem 2.5, α is morphically imprimitive, which is a contradiction. □

We conclude this section by noting that, for each finite target alphabet, there is no *single* morphism that is unambiguous for *every* morphically primitive pattern.

Proposition 2.11. *Let Σ be a finite alphabet. There is no morphism $\sigma : \mathbb{N}^* \to \Sigma^*$ that is unambiguous for every morphically primitive pattern.*

Proof. Freydenberger et al. [8] prove this result for nonerasing morphisms. If σ is erasing and $\sigma(x) = \varepsilon$ for every $x \in \mathbb{N}$, then σ is not unambiguous for any pattern by definition. If there exist variables $i, j \in \mathbb{N}$ with $\sigma(i) \neq \varepsilon = \sigma(j)$, then σ is ambiguous for the morphically primitive pattern $i \cdot i \cdot j \cdot j$ since the morphism $\tau : \mathbb{N}^* \to \Sigma^*$, defined by $\tau(i) := \varepsilon$ and $\tau(j) := \sigma(i)$, satisfies $\tau(\alpha) = \sigma(\alpha)$ and $\tau(i) \neq \sigma(i)$. □

Chapter 3

Nonerasing morphisms

The explicit research on the ambiguity of morphisms is initiated by Freydenberger et al. [8], where *nonerasing* morphisms are considered. This limitation is not only a very natural one, the use of nonerasing, especially injective morphisms also has some obvious advantages since images of those morphisms preserve much information on the preimage. For example, if we know that the word $w = \mathtt{ababbabbab}$ is created from a pattern α by a *nonerasing* morphism $\sigma : \mathbb{N}^* \rightarrow \{\mathtt{a}, \mathtt{b}\}^*$, we know that α has length 10 at most. Thus, there is only a finite number of patterns coming into consideration. If we know that the morphism is defined by $\sigma(i) = \mathtt{ab}^i$, $i \in \mathbb{N}$, and, thus, injective, we can even reconstruct α to be $1 \cdot 2 \cdot 2 \cdot 1$. Knowing that w is created from a pattern α by an *erasing* morphism $\sigma : \mathbb{N}^* \rightarrow \{\mathtt{a}, \mathtt{b}\}^*$ does not give us this kind of information on α since α can be of arbitrary length and structure, still generating w (e.g., $\alpha = 1 \cdot 2^{77}$, $\alpha = 1 \cdot 2^{10} \cdot 3 \cdot 3 \cdot 2^{10} \cdot 1$, where variable 2 is erased by the morphism). Information from the morphic image of a pattern on the length and the structure of the variables in the pattern is especially useful and needed in the field of inductive inference where a pattern is inferred after seeing finitely many words from the set of all its morphic images. Inductive inference of erasing pattern languages is one of the major applications of the theory of restricted ambiguity of nonerasing morphisms (cf. Reidenbach [25, 26, 28]).

In this chapter, we summarise some main results of the present knowledge on the ambiguity of nonerasing morphisms as presented by Freydenberger et al. [8] and Reidenbach [25]. We start with observations on a strongly restricted type of ambiguity, so-called moderate ambiguity. Aside from the intrinsic interest for moderately ambiguous nonerasing morphisms, this analysis can also be seen as an intermediate step in the search for maximally restricted, hence, unambiguous nonerasing morphisms and, thus, delivers a promising approach for erasing morphisms, too, which is discussed in Chapter 4.

3.1 Moderate ambiguity

By definition, if a morphism is ambiguous for a pattern, then there is another morphism which maps that pattern to the same image. However, the shape and structure of this other morphism is not restricted at all. Certain variables of the pattern can be mapped to completely different factors at different positions in the image.

Example 3.1. Let us consider $\alpha := 1 \cdot 2 \cdot 3$ and the morphism $\sigma : \mathbb{N}^* \rightarrow \{\mathtt{a}, \mathtt{b}\}^*$, defined by $\sigma(1) := \mathtt{a}$, $\sigma(2) := \mathtt{b}$ and $\sigma(3) := \mathtt{a}$, which is ambiguous for α since there is another morphism $\tau : \mathbb{N}^* \rightarrow \{\mathtt{a}, \mathtt{b}\}^*$, defined by $\tau(1) := \mathtt{ab}$, $\tau(2) := \mathtt{a}$ and $\tau(3) := \varepsilon$, which satisfies

$\tau(\alpha) = \mathtt{aba} = \sigma(\alpha)$. We can observe that the ambiguity of σ is largely unrestricted since variable 3 does not contribute anymore to generate the image $\sigma(\alpha)$ and variable 2 is mapped to a completely different word at another position in $\sigma(\alpha)$. ◇

However, there are ambiguous nonerasing morphisms that do not show this behaviour.

Example 3.2. Let $\alpha := 1\cdot 2\cdot 3\cdot 1\cdot 2\cdot 2\cdot 3$ and $\sigma : \mathbb{N}^* \to \{\mathtt{a},\mathtt{b},\mathtt{c},\mathtt{d}\}^*$ be a morphism, defined by $\sigma(1) := \mathtt{a}$, $\sigma(2) := \mathtt{bc}$ and $\sigma(3) := \mathtt{bd}$. We can easily verify that there is only one other morphism $\tau : \mathbb{N}^* \to \{\mathtt{a},\mathtt{b},\mathtt{c},\mathtt{d}\}^*$ that satisfies $\sigma(\alpha) = \tau(\alpha)$, namely the morphism defined by $\tau(1) := \mathtt{ab}$, $\tau(2) := \mathtt{cb}$ and $\tau(3) := \mathtt{d}$. Hence, the situation looks as follows:

$$\sigma(\alpha) = \overbrace{\mathtt{a}}^{\sigma(1)}\overbrace{\mathtt{b\,c}}^{\sigma(2)}\overbrace{\mathtt{b\,d}}^{\sigma(3)}\overbrace{\mathtt{a}}^{\sigma(1)}\overbrace{\mathtt{b\,c}}^{\sigma(2)}\overbrace{\mathtt{b\,c}}^{\sigma(2)}\overbrace{\mathtt{b\,d}}^{\sigma(3)} = \tau(\alpha).$$

$$\underbrace{\mathtt{a\,b}}_{\tau(1)}\underbrace{\mathtt{c\,b}}_{\tau(2)}\underbrace{\mathtt{d}}_{\tau(3)}\underbrace{\mathtt{a\,b}}_{\tau(1)}\underbrace{\mathtt{c\,b}}_{\tau(2)}\underbrace{\mathtt{c\,b}}_{\tau(2)}\underbrace{\mathtt{d}}_{\tau(3)}$$

Although σ is not unambiguous for α, one would certainly agree that its ambiguity on α is largely restricted since all morphisms that map α to $\sigma(\alpha)$ (which are only τ and σ itself) map variable 1 to a word containing a, variable 2 to a word containing c and variable 3 to a word containing d. We can even sharpen this statement since the first occurrence of variable 1 is always mapped to the first occurrence of a in $\sigma(\alpha)$, the second occurrence of variable 1 is always mapped to the second occurrence of a, the first occurrence of variable 2 is always mapped to the first occurrence of b and so on. ◇

We use the restricted ambiguity of σ on α in Example 3.2 as a starting point for the general notion of moderate ambiguity. Intuitively, it can be understood as follows: A nonerasing morphism $\sigma : \mathbb{N}^* \to \Sigma^*$ is called *moderately ambiguous* for a pattern α if, for every variable position j of a variable x in α, there exists a certain factor w_j of $\sigma(\alpha)$ at a certain position (between the l_jth and r_jth letter in $\sigma(\alpha)$) such that *every* morphism $\tau : \mathbb{N}^* \to \Sigma^*$ with $\tau(\alpha) = \sigma(\alpha)$ maps the variable x at position j to a word which covers at least the factor w_j at this particular position. We illustrate this more general notion with the help of Example 3.2.

Example 3.2 (continued). We write

$$\begin{array}{rcccccccccccccc} \alpha & = & 1 & \cdot & 2 & \cdot & 3 & \cdot & 1 & \cdot & 2 & \cdot & 2 & \cdot & 3 \\ & = & i_1 & \cdot & i_2 & \cdot & i_3 & \cdot & i_4 & \cdot & i_5 & \cdot & i_6 & \cdot & i_7 \end{array}$$

and

$$\begin{array}{rcccccccccccccc} \sigma(\alpha) & = & \mathtt{a} & \mathtt{b} & \mathtt{c} & \mathtt{b} & \mathtt{d} & \mathtt{a} & \mathtt{b} & \mathtt{c} & \mathtt{b} & \mathtt{c} & \mathtt{b} & \mathtt{d}. \\ \text{Position} & & 1 & 2 & 3 & 4 & 5 & 6 & 7 & 8 & 9 & 10 & 11 & 12 \end{array}$$

Now, we see that, under σ as well as under τ, variable $i_1 = 1$ at position $j = 1$ in α is mapped to a word covering at least $w_1 = \mathtt{a}$ between position $l_1 = 1$ and $r_1 = 1$ in $\sigma(\alpha)$. Similarly, variable $i_2 = 2$ at position $j = 2$ in α is mapped to a word covering at least $w_2 = \mathtt{c}$ between position $l_1 = 3$ and $r_1 = 3$ in $\sigma(\alpha)$. To pick a final example: Variable $i_5 = 2$ at position $j = 5$ in α is mapped to a word covering at least $w_5 = \mathtt{c}$ between position $l_1 = 8$ and $r_1 = 8$ in $\sigma(\alpha)$. ◇

We formalise this type of restricted ambiguity in the following definition.

Definition 3.3 (Moderate ambiguity of nonerasing morphisms†). *Let* Σ *be an alphabet. Let* $\alpha := i_1 \cdot i_2 \cdot [\ldots] \cdot i_n$, $n \in \mathbb{N}$, $i_k \in \mathbb{N}$, $1 \leq i_k \leq n$, *and* $\sigma : \mathbb{N}^* \to \Sigma^*$ *be a* nonerasing *morphism. Then* σ *is called* moderately ambiguous (for α) *provided that there exist* $l_2, l_3, \ldots, l_n \in \mathbb{N}$ *and* $r_1, r_2, \ldots, r_{n-1} \in \mathbb{N}$ *with*

$$1 \leq r_1 < l_2 \leq r_2 < l_3 \leq r_3 < l_4 \leq \ldots \leq r_{n-2} < l_{n-1} \leq r_{n-1} < l_n \leq |\sigma(\alpha)|$$

such that for every morphism $\tau : \mathbb{N}^* \to \Sigma^*$ *with* $\tau(\alpha) = \sigma(\alpha)$ *and for every* k, $1 \leq k \leq n-1$,

- $|\,\tau(i_1 \cdot i_2 \cdot [\ldots] \cdot i_k)\,| < l_{k+1}$ *and*
- $|\,\tau(i_1 \cdot i_2 \cdot [\ldots] \cdot i_k)\,| \geq r_k$.

The l_k, r_k are used to mark the left and right end, respectively, of a factor w_k which, for any morphism $\tau : \mathbb{N}^* \to \Sigma^*$ with $\tau(\alpha) = \sigma(\alpha)$, is contained in $\tau(i_k)$. For Example 3.2, Definition 3.3 is satisfied with $r_1 := 1$, $l_2 := r_2 := 3$, $l_3 := r_3 := 5$, $l_4 := r_4 := 6$, $l_5 := r_5 := 8$, $l_6 := r_6 := 10$ and $l_7 := 12$.

A major application of moderately ambiguous nonerasing morphisms can be found in the field of inductive inference of erasing pattern languages. In order to show the learnability of terminal-free pattern languages over an alphabet with three or more letters, a finite set called "telltale" is assigned to every pattern α. This set consists of several images of moderately ambiguous nonerasing morphisms applied to α. Such a telltale distinguishes the respective pattern language $L(\alpha)$ from all other pattern languages which are strictly included in $L(\alpha)$. For a deeper analysis, see Reidenbach [28].

As Example 3.2 shows, a detailed check if a pattern and a morphism meet the requirements of Definition 3.3 can be quite cumbersome. This holds even more if we want to show that a morphism is *not* moderately ambiguous. The following lemma states a sufficient condition for a nonerasing morphism being not moderately ambiguous and can therefore be used to cut short the check of Definition 3.3.

Lemma 3.4 (Reidenbach [25]). *Let* Σ *be an alphabet,* $\alpha \in \mathbb{N}^+$ *and* $\sigma : \mathbb{N}^* \to \Sigma^*$ *be a* nonerasing *morphism. If there exists a morphism* $\tau : \mathbb{N}^* \to \Sigma^*$ *such that* $\tau(\alpha) = \sigma(\alpha)$, *but* $\tau(x) = \varepsilon$ *for an* $x \in \mathrm{var}(\alpha)$, *then* σ *is not moderately ambiguous for* α.

This lemma makes it easy to verify that, in Example 3.1, σ is not moderately ambiguous for α since $\tau(3) = \varepsilon$. However, this does not imply that there is no moderately ambiguous morphism for α at all.

Consequently, the main question reads as follows: For which patterns do there exist moderately ambiguous morphisms? This question is answered in the following theorem.

Theorem 3.5 (Reidenbach [25]). *Let* Σ *be an alphabet,* $|\Sigma| \geq 2$ *and* $\alpha \in \mathbb{N}^+$. *There exists a moderately ambiguous nonerasing morphism* $\sigma : \mathbb{N}^* \to \Sigma^*$ *for* α *if and only if* α *is morphically primitive.*

†Note that this definition has been introduced by Reidenbach [25]. In the present thesis, it is slightly modified since we do not use the term "moderately ambiguous word". Furthermore, this definition refers to *nonerasing* morphisms only.

Consequently, there exists no moderately ambiguous nonerasing morphism for α from Example 3.1 since α is morphically imprimitive.

Not only does Theorem 3.5 support the importance of the partition of $\mathbb{N}^+$ into morphically primitive and imprimitive patterns, but its proof also uses a very interesting technique: Reidenbach [25] shows that every so-called "three-segmented morphism" is moderately ambiguous for morphically primitive patterns. In the following definition, we name one particular three-segmented-morphism:

Definition 3.6 ($\sigma_{\text{3-seg}}$). *Let Σ be an alphabet with $\Sigma \supseteq \{\mathtt{a}, \mathtt{b}\}$. The morphism $\sigma_{\text{3-seg}} : \mathbb{N}^* \to \Sigma^*$ is defined by*

$$\sigma_{\text{3-seg}}(i) := \mathtt{a}\,\mathtt{b}^{3i}\,\mathtt{a}\;\mathtt{a}\,\mathtt{b}^{3i+1}\,\mathtt{a}\;\mathtt{a}\,\mathtt{b}^{3i+2}\,\mathtt{a}$$

for every $i \in \mathbb{N}$.

Note that this morphism is nonerasing and even injective. We call the factors of the form $\mathtt{a}\mathtt{b}^+\mathtt{a}$ segments. Hence, $\sigma_{\text{3-seg}}$ maps every variable to three segments. The following theorem shows that $\sigma_{\text{3-seg}}$ is an essential tool to prove Theorem 3.5.

Theorem 3.7 (Reidenbach [25]). *Let Σ be an alphabet, $\Sigma \supseteq \{\mathtt{a}, \mathtt{b}\}$ and let $\alpha \in \mathbb{N}^+$. Then $\sigma_{\text{3-seg}}$ is moderately ambiguous for α if and only if α is morphically primitive.*

Segmented morphisms are not only of major importance for the ambiguity of nonerasing morphisms, they are also used to tackle basic decision problems for pattern languages such as inclusion and equivalence (cf. Jiang et al. [16]). E. g., for any $\alpha, \beta \in \mathbb{N}^+$, the inclusion of $L_{\text{E}}(\alpha)$ in $L_{\text{E}}(\beta)$ can be characterised by the question if a certain segmented morphism τ satisfies $\tau(\alpha) \in L_{\text{E}}(\beta)$. In Chapter 4, we shall study to which extent the principle of segmented morphisms is also useful when considering erasing morphisms. At first, however, we present the status quo concerning the unambiguity of nonerasing morphisms.

3.2 Unambiguity

We begin this section with a short lemma relating moderate ambiguity and unambiguity of nonerasing morphisms to each other:

Proposition 3.8 (Reidenbach [25]). *Let Σ be an alphabet, $\alpha \in \mathbb{N}^+$ and $\sigma : \mathbb{N}^* \to \Sigma^*$ be a* nonerasing *morphism. If σ is unambiguous for α, then σ is moderately ambiguous. In general, the converse of this statement does not hold true.*

The correctness of the second claim of Proposition 3.8 can be verified using Example 3.2.

In particular, there also exist morphically primitive example patterns for which $\sigma_{\text{3-seg}}$ is not unambiguous, although we know by Theorem 3.7 that it is moderately ambiguous for those patterns.

Example 3.9. Let $\alpha := 1 \cdot 2 \cdot 3 \cdot 1 \cdot 2 \cdot 2 \cdot 3$ (cf. Example 3.2) and let $\tau : \mathbb{N}^* \to \Sigma^*$ be defined by $\tau(1) = \mathtt{a}\,\mathtt{b}^3\,\mathtt{a}\;\mathtt{a}\,\mathtt{b}^4\,\mathtt{a}\;\mathtt{a}\,\mathtt{b}^5\mathtt{a}\;\mathtt{a}$, $\tau(2) = \mathtt{b}^6\,\mathtt{a}\;\mathtt{a}\,\mathtt{b}^7\,\mathtt{a}\;\mathtt{a}\,\mathtt{b}^8\mathtt{a}\;\mathtt{a}$, $\tau(3) = \mathtt{b}^9\,\mathtt{a}\;\mathtt{a}\,\mathtt{b}^{10}\,\mathtt{a}\;\mathtt{a}\,\mathtt{b}^{11}\mathtt{a}$. It can be verified straightforward that $\tau(\alpha) = \sigma_{\text{3-seg}}(\alpha)$ and, hence, $\sigma_{\text{3-seg}}$ is not unambiguous for α. However, since α is morphically primitive, $\sigma_{\text{3-seg}}$ is moderately ambiguous for α. ◇

If we take a closer look at the Examples 3.2 and 3.9, we note that the ambiguity generating principle is the same: Since the images of the variables 2 and 3 begin with the same letter, the alternate morphism τ can "steal" those letters and generate them with help of the variables 1 and 2. This can only happen because α has a special structure which can be generalised as follows:

Definition 3.10 (*SCRN*-factorisation). *We say a pattern $\alpha \in \mathbb{N}^+$ has an SCRN-factorisation if and only if $\alpha \in (N^*SC^*R)^+N^*$, where (S, C, R, N) is a partition of* $\mathrm{var}(\alpha)$.

In Example 3.9, $\alpha \in SCRSCCR$ for $S = \{1\}$, $C = \{2\}$ and $R = \{3\}$.

Freydenberger and Reidenbach [6] show that this structure is characteristic for $\sigma_{\text{3-seg}}$ being ambiguous.

Theorem 3.11 (Freydenberger, Reidenbach [6]). *Let $\alpha \in \mathbb{N}^+$. Then $\sigma_{\text{3-seg}}$ is ambiguous for α if and only if α is morphically imprimitive or α has an SCRN-factorisation.*

The proof of this theorem makes use of the special structure of $\sigma_{\text{3-seg}}$, in particular, its prefix and suffix homogeneity of the images of all variables which begin and end with the letter $\mathtt{a}$. It is, by the way, not very surprising that $\sigma_{\text{3-seg}}$ is not unambiguous for *every* morphically primitive pattern since there is no such single morphism (cf. Proposition 2.11). Nevertheless, the moderate ambiguity of $\sigma_{\text{3-seg}}$ for every morphically primitive pattern can be seen as a very important intermediate step towards an individual, tailor-made unambiguous morphism for a given morphically primitive pattern. The individual adaption of $\sigma_{\text{3-seg}}$, needed for an unambiguous morphism, is basically a change of the first and last (third) segment of $\sigma_{\text{3-seg}}$ for special variables. For instance, in Example 3.9, it is sufficient to "invert" the first and last segment of $\sigma_{\text{3-seg}}(2)$ in order to receive an unambiguous nonerasing morphism $\sigma : \mathbb{N}^* \to \{\mathtt{a}, \mathtt{b}\}^*$, thus, defined by $\sigma(1) := \sigma_{\text{3-seg}}(1)$, $\sigma(2) := \mathtt{b}\,\mathtt{a}^6\,\mathtt{b}\;\mathtt{a}\,\mathtt{b}^7\,\mathtt{a}\;\mathtt{b}\,\mathtt{a}^8\mathtt{b}$ and $\sigma(3) := \sigma_{\text{3-seg}}(3)$. This technique can indeed be used to receive an individual, unambiguous nonerasing morphism for *any* given morphically primitive pattern. However, a detailed analysis of variable neighbourhoods in the given pattern is necessary in order to determine which segments must be changed. This finally leads to the following result.

Theorem 3.12 (Freydenberger et al. [8]). *For every morphically primitive pattern, there exists an unambiguous nonerasing morphism $\sigma : \mathbb{N}^* \to \{\mathtt{a}, \mathtt{b}\}^*$.*

Together with Theorem 2.9, we can conclude the following:

Corollary 3.13 (Freydenberger et al. [8]). *Let Σ be an alphabet, $|\Sigma| \geq 2$, and let $\alpha \in \mathbb{N}^+$. There exists an unambiguous nonerasing morphism $\sigma : \mathbb{N}^* \to \Sigma^*$ for α if and only if α is morphically primitive.*

Consequently, aside from being a natural concept (cf. Theorem 2.5), the partition of $\mathbb{N}^+$ into morphically primitive and imprimitive patterns characterises not only the moderate ambiguity, but also the unambiguity of nonerasing morphisms. This situation is summarised in Figure 3.1 and in the following corollary.

Corollary 3.14. *Let Σ be an alphabet with $|\Sigma| \geq 2$ and let $\alpha \in \mathbb{N}^+$. The following statements are equivalent:*

1. *α is morphically primitive.*

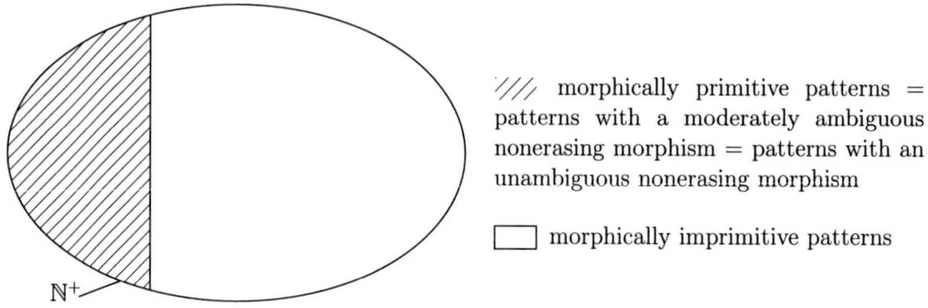

Figure 3.1: Ambiguity of nonerasing morphisms

2. *There is a moderately ambiguous nonerasing morphism* $\sigma : \mathbb{N}^* \to \Sigma^*$ *for* α.

3. *There is an unambiguous nonerasing morphism* $\sigma : \mathbb{N}^* \to \Sigma^*$ *for* α.

Proof. Directly from Theorem 3.5 and Corollary 3.13. □

In the next chapter, we examine the same questions concerning moderate ambiguity and unambiguity considered in the present chapter, but for *erasing* morphisms. In particular, we shall investigate, for erasing morphisms, to which extent moderate ambiguity is useful to achieve unambiguity, how useful segmented morphisms are and whether or not a comparatively simple partition of patterns can be found to characterise moderate ambiguity and unambiguity of erasing morphisms.

Chapter 4

Erasing Morphisms

In this chapter, we focus on the ambiguity of erasing morphisms. Since, concerning the overall question, for which patterns there exists an arbitrary morphism that is not ambiguous, the case of morphically primitive pattern is already answered by the results presented in Chapter 3, this chapter also constitutes a detailed study of morphically imprimitive patterns. If we omit the restriction of considering only nonerasing morphisms, we can yet find unambiguous morphisms for morphically imprimitive patterns. According to Theorem 2.9, these morphisms must then be erasing.

Example 4.1. Let Σ be an alphabet and let $\alpha := 1 \cdot 2 \cdot 1 \cdot 1$. Every nonerasing morphism $\sigma_{\mathrm{NE}} : \mathbb{N}^* \to \Sigma^*$ is ambiguous since there exists another morphism $\tau : \mathbb{N}^* \to \Sigma^*$, defined by $\tau(1) := \varepsilon$, $\tau(2) := \sigma_{\mathrm{NE}}(1 \cdot 2 \cdot 1 \cdot 1)$, satisfying $\sigma_{\mathrm{NE}}(\alpha) = \tau(\alpha)$ and $\tau(1) = \varepsilon \neq \sigma_{\mathrm{NE}}(1)$ (σ_{NE} is nonerasing). This is not surprising since α is morphically imprimitive (cf. Theorem 2.9).

In contrast to this, every *erasing* morphism $\sigma_{\mathrm{E}} : \mathbb{N}^* \to \Sigma^*$ with $\sigma_{\mathrm{E}}(1) = \varepsilon$ and $|\sigma_{\mathrm{E}}(2)| \leq 2$ is unambiguous for α since words of length 2 or less can be generated from α only by substituting variable 2. ◇

This example demonstrates that it is worth studying erasing morphisms since they can be unambiguous for patterns which do not have unambiguous nonerasing morphisms. Thus, the class of patterns with an arbitrary (possibly erasing) unambiguous morphism is strictly larger than the class of patterns with an unambiguous nonerasing morphism. This is illustrated in Figure 4.1.

Finally, we have to note that there are also patterns for which no (erasing or nonerasing) morphism is unambiguous at all.

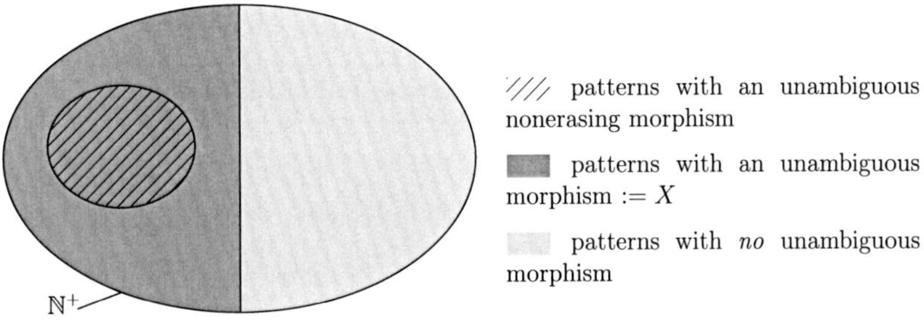

Figure 4.1: Unambiguity of morphisms

Example 4.2. Let Σ be an alphabet and let $\alpha := 1 \cdot 2 \cdot 1 \cdot 2 \cdot 1 \cdot 2$. Let $\sigma : \mathbb{N}^* \to \Sigma^*$ be an arbitrary morphism. If $\sigma(1) \neq \varepsilon$, then the morphism $\tau(1) := \varepsilon$, $\tau(2) := \sigma(1 \cdot 2)$, satisfies $\tau(\alpha) = \sigma(\alpha)$ – the case $\sigma(2) \neq \varepsilon$ is analogous. Hence, no such morphism σ is unambiguous for α. ◇

Thus, our research question of characterising set X in Figure 4.1 is not trivial since X neither equals the set of morphically primitive patterns (cf. Example 4.1) nor equals $\mathbb{N}^+$ (cf. Example 4.2).

This chapter is organised as follows: In the next section, we take a closer look at patterns similar to α from Example 4.2 and their ambiguity promoting structure. In the following sections, we show how this structure can be used to characterise moderate ambiguity of erasing morphisms and unambiguity of morphisms with an infinite target alphabet. The size of the target alphabet of the morphism under consideration plays an important role. We discuss this for morphisms with a finite target alphabet in Section 4.4. During our presentation, we shall also continuously compare the results and techniques for erasing morphisms with those obtained for nonerasing morphisms (cf. Chapter 3).

4.1 Ambiguity partitions

Since we have not defined moderate ambiguity for erasing morphisms, we first concentrate on ambiguity and unambiguity of erasing morphisms. Nevertheless, the techniques and results in this chapter are also highly relevant for the moderate ambiguity of erasing morphisms, which is then explained in Section 4.2.

We start our considerations with another example pattern.

Example 4.3. Let $\alpha := 1{\cdot}2{\cdot}1{\cdot}2{\cdot}3{\cdot}3{\cdot}4{\cdot}4{\cdot}4{\cdot}4{\cdot}5{\cdot}5{\cdot}5$. This pattern is morphically imprimitive since there exists a factorisation $\alpha = \beta_0\gamma_1\beta_1\gamma_2\beta_2$ with $\beta_0 := \beta_1 := \varepsilon$, $\gamma_1 := \gamma_2 := 1 \cdot 2$ and $\beta_2 := 3 \cdot 3 \cdot 4 \cdot 4 \cdot 4 \cdot 4 \cdot 5 \cdot 5 \cdot 5$, which satisfies the conditions of Definition 2.6. Hence, we can conclude from Theorem 2.9 that every morphism which is unambiguous for α must be erasing. Indeed, we can use the same argumentation as for the pattern α from Example 4.2 to show that a possible unambiguous morphism $\sigma : \mathbb{N}^* \to \Sigma^*$ must satisfy $\sigma(1) = \sigma(2) = \varepsilon$. Moreover, we show that σ must also map 3 to the empty word and argue by contradiction: Assume that $\sigma(3) \neq \varepsilon$. Then $\tau : \mathbb{N}^* \to \Sigma^*$, defined by $\tau(1) := \sigma(3)$, $\tau(2) := \tau(3) := \varepsilon$, $\tau(4) := \sigma(4)$, $\tau(5) := \sigma(5)$, satisfies $\tau(\alpha) = \sigma(\alpha)$, which contradicts σ being unambiguous. With an analogous argument, we can show that $\sigma(4) = \varepsilon$, too (with $\tau(1) := \sigma(4{\cdot}4)$). Thus, only variable 5 may be mapped to a nonempty word. In fact, every morphism $\sigma : \mathbb{N}^* \to \Sigma^*$ with $|\sigma(5)| = 1$ and $\sigma(x) = \varepsilon$, $x \neq 5$, is unambiguous for α. Informally speaking, regarding pattern α, the need to map 1 and 2 to the empty word provokes a type of "domino effect", which is carried forward to 3 and 4. ◇

To formalise this observation, we need the following definition:

Definition 4.4 (Ambiguity partition). *Let $\alpha \in \mathbb{N}^+$. We inductively define an* ambiguity partition *(for α):*

(i) *$(\emptyset, \mathrm{var}(\alpha))$ is an ambiguity partition for α.*

(ii) *If* (E, N) *is an ambiguity partition for* α *and there exists a morphism* $h : \mathbb{N}^* \to \mathbb{N}^*$ *that is nontrivial for* N *and satisfies* $h(\alpha) = \pi_N(\alpha)$*, then* (E', N') *is an ambiguity partition for* α *with*

$$\begin{aligned} E' &:= E \cup \{x \in N \mid h(x) = \varepsilon\}, \\ N' &:= \{x \in N \mid h(x) \neq \varepsilon\}. \end{aligned}$$

We want to note that E contains those variables for which it is certain that an unambiguous morphism $\sigma : \mathbb{N}^* \to \Sigma^*$ needs to map them to the empty word, whereas N consists of those variables that can either be mapped by σ to a nonempty word or for which this aspect is uncertain. This is formally shown below.

We now demonstrate how Definition 4.4 affects the example pattern α from Example 4.3. Let $E := \emptyset$, $N := \text{var}(\alpha)$. According to (i), (E, N) is an ambiguity partition of α. Let $h : \mathbb{N}^* \to \mathbb{N}^*$ be defined by $h(1) := \varepsilon$, $h(2) := 1 \cdot 2$ and $h(x) := x$ for all $x \neq 1, 2$. Then $h(\alpha) = \pi_N(\alpha) = \alpha$ and, thus, according to (ii), $(\{1\}, \{2, 3, 4, 5\})$ is an ambiguity partition for α. Furthermore, $h : \mathbb{N}^* \to \mathbb{N}^*$, defined by $h(1) := 2$, $h(2) := \varepsilon$ and $h(x) := x$ for all $x \neq 1, 2$, leads to the ambiguity partition $(\{1, 2\}, \{3, 4, 5\})$. In a similar manner, we can show that $(\{1, 2, 3\}, \{4, 5\})$ and $(\{1, 2, 3, 4\}, \{5\})$ are ambiguity partitions for α. In the latter ambiguity partition $(E, N) = (\{1, 2, 3, 4\}, \{5\})$, the set E is of maximal size.

Some simple observations on ambiguity partitions are made in the following proposition:

Proposition 4.5. *Let* $\alpha \in \mathbb{N}^+$.

1. *An ambiguity partition* (E, N) *for* α *is a partition of* $\text{var}(\alpha)$.
2. *If* (E', N') *is an ambiguity partition for* α *derived from an ambiguity partition* (E, N) *by the rules of condition (ii) of Definition 4.4, then* $|E'| > |E|$ *(and, thus,* $|N'| < |N|$*).*
3. α *is morphically imprimitive if and only if there exists an ambiguity partition* (E, N) *for* α *such that* $E \neq \emptyset$.

Proof. ad 1: Directly from Definition 4.4.

ad 2: Let $\alpha \in \mathbb{N}^+$, (E, N) be an ambiguity partition for α and $h : \mathbb{N}^* \to \mathbb{N}^*$ be a morphism that is nontrivial for N and satisfies $h(\alpha) = \pi_N(\alpha)$. We show that $\{x \in N \mid h(x) = \varepsilon\}$ is nonempty, which proves the statement. Assume to the contrary that, for every $x \in N$, $h(x) \neq \varepsilon$. Hence, $(\star)$ $|h(\pi_N(\alpha))| \geq |\pi_N(\alpha)|$. Furthermore, since $h(\alpha) = \pi_N(\alpha)$, it follows that $|h(\alpha)| = |\pi_N(\alpha)|$ and, thus, $|h(\pi_N(\alpha))| \leq |\pi_N(\alpha)|$. Consequently, with $(\star)$ we can conclude that $|h(\pi_N(\alpha))| = |\pi_N(\alpha)|$ and, hence, $h(e) = \varepsilon$ for every $e \in E$. Thus, $h(\pi_N(\alpha)) = \pi_N(\alpha)$. But then either h is nonerasing and, thus, trivial for N or there exists an $x \in N$ with $h(x) = \varepsilon$; both of these lead to a contradiction.

ad 3: We first show the *only if* direction. Hence, let α be morphically imprimitive. Furthermore, let $E = \emptyset$ and $N = \text{var}(\alpha)$. Then according to condition (i) of Definition 4.4, (E, N) is an ambiguity partition for α. Since α is morphically imprimitive, there exists a nontrivial morphism $h : \mathbb{N}^* \to \mathbb{N}^*$ satisfying $h(\alpha) = \alpha = \pi_N(\alpha)$. Consequently, (E', N'), where E', N' is defined as in condition (ii) of Definition 4.4, is an ambiguity partition of α, and, according to statement 2 of the proposition, $E' \neq \emptyset$.

We proceed with the *if* direction. Let (E, N) be an ambiguity partition for α and let $E \neq \emptyset$. Since $E \neq \emptyset$, the rule of condition (ii) of Definition 4.4 must be applied at least once to derive (E, N). Consequently, there must be an ambiguity partition (E', N') which is derived from the partition $(\emptyset, \text{var}(\alpha))$ by applying the rule of condition (ii). But this means that there exists a nontrivial morphism $h : \mathbb{N}^* \to \mathbb{N}^*$ satisfying $h(\alpha) = \pi_{\text{var}(\alpha)}(\alpha) = \alpha$. Hence, we can conclude from Theorem 2.5 that α is morphically imprimitive. □

Furthermore, we present the following lemma that is particularly useful to verify some of the ambiguity partitions in the examples of this thesis where certain variables always appear as "twins" next to each other:

Lemma 4.6. *Let $\alpha \in \mathbb{N}^+$. If there exist $i, j \in \text{var}(\alpha)$ with $i \neq j$, a $k \in \mathbb{N}$ and $\alpha_0, \alpha_1 \ldots \alpha_k \in (\mathbb{N} \setminus \{i, j\})^*$ such that $\alpha = \alpha_0 \cdot i \cdot j \cdot \alpha_1 \cdot i \cdot j \cdot [\ldots] \cdot \alpha_{k-1} \cdot i \cdot j \cdot \alpha_k$, then $(\{i, j\}, \text{var}(\alpha) \setminus \{i, j\})$ is an ambiguity partition for α.*

Proof. According to condition (i) of Definition 4.4, $(E, N) := (\emptyset, \text{var}(\alpha))$ is an ambiguity partition for α. We define a morphism $h : \mathbb{N}^* \to \mathbb{N}^*$ by $h(i) := i \cdot j$, $h(j) := \varepsilon$ and $h(x) := x$ for every $x \in \mathbb{N} \setminus \{i, j\}$. Thus, h is nontrivial for N and $h(\alpha) = \pi_N(\alpha)$ since j always appears as a direct right neighbour of i in α. Hence, according to condition (ii) of Definition 4.4, $(E', N') := (\{j\}, \text{var}(\alpha) \setminus \{j\})$ is an ambiguity partition for α, too. Let the morphism $h' : \mathbb{N}^* \to \mathbb{N}^*$ be defined by $h'(i) := \varepsilon$, $h'(j) := i$ and $h(x) := x$ for every $x \in \mathbb{N} \setminus \{i, j\}$. Thus, h' is nontrivial for N' and $h(\alpha) = \pi_{N'}(\alpha)$ since j always appears as a direct right neighbour of i in α. Hence, we can apply condition (ii) of Definition 4.4 again, which finally leads to the ambiguity partition $(\{i, j\}, \text{var}(\alpha) \setminus \{i, j\})$ for α. □

For instance, we can apply Lemma 4.6 to α from Example 4.3 with $i = 1$, $j = 2$, $k = 2$, $\alpha_0 = \alpha_1 = \varepsilon$ and $\alpha_2 = 3 \cdot 3 \cdot 4 \cdot 4 \cdot 4 \cdot 4 \cdot 5 \cdot 5 \cdot 5$ since $\alpha = \alpha_0 \cdot i \cdot j \cdot \alpha_1 \cdot i \cdot j \cdot \alpha_2$.

We now state our main result on ambiguity partitions, which substantiates the usefulness of Definition 4.4 regarding the (un)ambiguity of morphisms and shows that the term "ambiguity partition" is chosen in a reasonable way.

Theorem 4.7. *Let Σ be an alphabet. Let $\alpha \in \mathbb{N}^+$ and let (E, N) be an ambiguity partition for α. Then every morphism $\sigma : \mathbb{N}^* \to \Sigma^*$ satisfying $\sigma(x) \neq \varepsilon$ for an $x \in E$ is ambiguous for α.*

Proof. For $(E, N) = (\emptyset, \text{var}(\alpha))$, there is no such morphism since $E = \emptyset$. Thus, the statement is true.

Now, let (E', N') be an ambiguity partition derived from condition (ii) of Definition 4.4. Then there exist an ambiguity partition (E, N) and a nontrivial morphism $h : \mathbb{N}^* \to \mathbb{N}^*$ satisfying $(\star)\, h(\alpha) = \pi_N(\alpha)$. Furthermore, $E' = E \cup \{x \in N \mid h(x) = \varepsilon\}$ and $N' = \{x \in N \mid h(x) \neq \varepsilon\}$. We consider a morphism $\sigma : \mathbb{N}^* \to \Sigma^*$ satisfying $\sigma(x) \neq \varepsilon$ for an $x \in E'$. At first, we assume that $(\star\star)\, \sigma(x) = \varepsilon$ for all $x \in E$ and $\sigma(n) \neq \varepsilon$ for an $n \in N$ with $h(n) = \varepsilon$. Let $\tau : \mathbb{N}^* \to \Sigma^*$ be the morphism defined by $\tau(x) := \sigma(h(x))$ for all $x \in \text{var}(\alpha)$. Due to $(\star)$ and $(\star\star)$, $\tau(\alpha) = \sigma(h(\alpha)) = \sigma(\pi_N(\alpha)) = \sigma(\alpha)$, but $\tau(n) = \varepsilon \neq \sigma(n)$. Consequently, σ is ambiguous for α. If $\sigma(x) \neq \varepsilon$ for an $x \in E$, it follows by induction that σ is ambiguous. □

Hence, in order to find an unambiguous morphism for a pattern $\alpha \in \mathbb{N}^+$, we can initially investigate if α is morphically primitive. In this case, there exists an unambiguous morphism σ for α (cf. Theorem 3.12). If α is morphically imprimitive, according to Proposition 4.5, point (3), there exists an ambiguity partition (E, N) for α. Moreover, Theorem 4.7 states a necessary condition for unambiguous morphisms for α: Such a morphism must erase all variables in E. Consequently, we do not only know that σ must be erasing – which is already implied by Theorem 2.9 – but we even receive concrete evidence *which* variables at least must be mapped to ε. Of course, the more variables there are in E, the more information on α we get. In the following definition, we name those ambiguity partitions where E is of maximal size.

Definition 4.8 (Maximal ambiguity partition). *Let $\alpha \in \mathbb{N}^+$. An ambiguity partition (E, N) for α is called* maximal *if and only if every (other) ambiguity partition (E', N') for α satisfies $|E'| \leq |E|$ and $|N'| \geq |N|$.*

In Example 4.3, the ambiguity partition $(\{1, 2, 3, 4\}, \{5\})$ is maximal, whereas the ambiguity partition $(\{1, 2, 3\}, \{4, 5\})$ is not maximal.

From Definition 4.4, it is not obvious whether or not a maximal ambiguity partition for a pattern α is unique. In order to answer this question, the following technical lemma is useful:

Lemma 4.9. *Let $\alpha \in \mathbb{N}^+$ and (E_1, N_1), (E_2, N_2) be ambiguity partitions for α. Then $(E_1 \cup E_2, N_1 \cap N_2)$ is an ambiguity partition for α.*

Proof. To begin with, we note that, since (E_1, N_1) and (E_2, N_2) are partitions of $\mathrm{var}(\alpha)$, $N_1 \cap N_2 = \mathrm{var}(\alpha) \setminus (E_1 \cup E_2)$ and, thus, $(E_1 \cup E_2, N_1 \cap N_2)$ is a partition of $\mathrm{var}(\alpha)$, too.

If $(E_2, N_2) = (\emptyset, \mathrm{var}(\alpha))$, the statement is obviously true. Hence, let $(E_2, N_2) \neq (\emptyset, \mathrm{var}(\alpha))$. Then, according to condition (ii) of Definition 4.4, there exist ambiguity partitions $(E^{(0)}, N^{(0)}) := (\emptyset, \mathrm{var}(\alpha))$, $(E^{(1)}, N^{(1)})$, $(E^{(2)}, N^{(2)})$, ..., $(E^{(m)}, N^{(m)}) := (E_2, N_2)$, $m \in \mathbb{N}$ and, for every $k \in \{0, 1, \ldots, m\}$, a morphism $h^{(k)} : \mathbb{N}^* \to \mathbb{N}^*$ satisfying

(1) $h^{(k)}$ is nontrivial for $N^{(k)}$,

(2) $h^{(k)}(\alpha) = \pi_{N^{(k)}}(\alpha)$,

(3) $E^{(k+1)} = E^{(k)} \cup \{x \in N^{(k)} \mid h^{(k)}(x) = \varepsilon\}$, and

(4) $N^{(k+1)} = \{x \in N^{(k)} \mid h^{(k)}(x) \neq \varepsilon\}$.

We now give a procedure that, starting with (E_1, N_1), successively constructs ambiguity partitions (E', N') with growing sets $E' \supseteq E_1$ until $E' = E_1 \cup E_2$.

> $E' := E_1$, $N' := N_1$.
> `while` $(E' \neq E_1 \cup E_2)$ `do`
>   Let k be maximal with $E^{(k)} \subseteq E'$ and $E^{(k+1)} \not\subseteq E'$. $(\star)$
>   Let $h := \pi_{N'} \circ h^{(k)}$.
> $E'_{new} := E' \cup \{x \in N' \mid h(x) = \varepsilon\}$.
> $N'_{new} := \{x \in N' \mid h(x) \neq \varepsilon\}$.
> $E' := E'_{new}$, $N' := N'_{new}$.
> `od`

We show the following:

(a) Every (E', N') constructed by the algorithm is an ambiguity partition for α.

(b) The algorithm terminates.

ad (a). For $(E', N') = (E_1, N_1)$, the statement trivially holds. Hence, we show that, in every `while` loop, (E'_{new}, N'_{new}) is an ambiguity partition for α. Since $E^{(k)} \subseteq E'$ and $E^{(k+1)} \not\subseteq E'$, there is an $x \in E^{(k+1)} \setminus E'$ with $h^{(k)}(x) = \varepsilon$ (cf. point (3)). Furthermore, $x \notin E'$ implies $x \in N'$. Thus, h is nontrivial for N' since $h(x) = \pi_{N'}(h^{(k)}(x)) = \varepsilon \neq x$. Moreover, $h(\alpha) = \pi_{N'}(h^{(k)}(\alpha)) = \pi_{N'}(\pi_{N^{(k)}}(\alpha)) = \pi_{N'}(\alpha)$ since $h^{(k)}(\alpha) = \pi_{N^{(k)}}(\alpha)$ (cf. point (2)) and $N' \subseteq N^{(k)}$ (due to $E^{(k)} \subseteq E'$). Thus, (E'_{new}, N'_{new}) is an ambiguity partition for α according to condition (ii) of Definition 4.4.

ad (b). At first, we show that $\{x \in N' \mid h(x) = \varepsilon\} = E^{(k+1)} \setminus E'$. If $x \in N'$ and $h(x) = \pi_{N'}(h^{(k)}(x)) = \varepsilon$, then $h^{(k)}(x) = \varepsilon$. Due to $N' \subseteq N^{(k)}$, this implies $x \in E^{(k+1)}$ (cf. point (3)). Hence, $\{x \in N' \mid h(x) = \varepsilon\} \subseteq E^{(k+1)} \setminus E'$. Now let $x \in E^{(k+1)} \setminus E'$.

Since $E^{(k)} \subseteq E'$, it is $x \in E^{(k+1)} \setminus E^{(k)}$ and, thus, $h^{(k)}(x) = \varepsilon$ (cf. point (3)). Hence, $h(x) = \pi_{N'}(h^{(k)}(x)) = \varepsilon$. Furthermore, $x \notin E'$ directly implies $x \in N'$. This shows $\{x \in N' \mid h(x) = \varepsilon\} \supseteq E^{(k+1)} \setminus E'$, which proves the equality of both of the sets.

Consequently, E' is only extended by variables from some $E^{(k+1)} \subseteq E_2$, which implies $E' \subseteq E_1 \cup E_2$ for every E'. Moreover, $(\star)$ makes sure that all variables from $E_2 \setminus E_1$ are added to some E' such that, finally, $E' = E_1 \cup E_2$ and the `while` loop ends.

The statements (a) and (b) imply that there exists an algorithm that constructs the ambiguity partition $(E', N') = (E_1 \cup E_2, N_1 \cap N_2)$, which proves the lemma. □

From Lemma 4.9, we can conclude that, for any pattern, there is exactly one maximal ambiguity partition:

Theorem 4.10. *Let $\alpha \in \mathbb{N}^+$ and (E, N) be a maximal ambiguity partition for α. Then (E, N) is unique.*

Proof. Assume to the contrary that there exists a maximal ambiguity partition (E', N') for α such that $E' \neq E$. Then, according to Lemma 4.9, $(E \cup E', N \cap N')$ is an ambiguity partition for α, but $|E \cup E'| > |E|$. Consequently, (E, N) is not maximal, which contradicts the assumption. □

Evidently, the uniqueness of the maximal ambiguity partition (E, N) of a pattern α is a nontrivial property only if $E \neq \mathrm{var}(\alpha)$. On the other hand, if $(\mathrm{var}(\alpha), \emptyset)$ is the maximal ambiguity partition of α, then Theorem 4.7 directly implies that the following statement on the existence of unambiguous morphisms holds true:

Corollary 4.11. *Let Σ be an alphabet. Let $\alpha \in \mathbb{N}^+$. If $(\mathrm{var}(\alpha), \emptyset)$ is an ambiguity partition for α, no morphism $\sigma : \mathbb{N}^* \to \Sigma^*$ is unambiguous for α.*

Proof. Directly from Theorem 4.7. □

Thus, when investigating the existence of unambiguous erasing morphisms, the question of whether or not $(\mathrm{var}(\alpha), \emptyset)$ is an ambiguity partition for α leads to an important partition of $\mathbb{N}^+$. Therefore, we now introduce a new terminology reflecting this question.

Definition 4.12 (Morphically (un)erasable)**.** *Let $\alpha \in \mathbb{N}^+$. We call α* morphically erasable *if and only if $(\mathrm{var}(\alpha), \emptyset)$ is an ambiguity partition for α. Otherwise, α is called* morphically unerasable.

With this new terminology, we can rephrase Corollary 4.11 in the following manner.

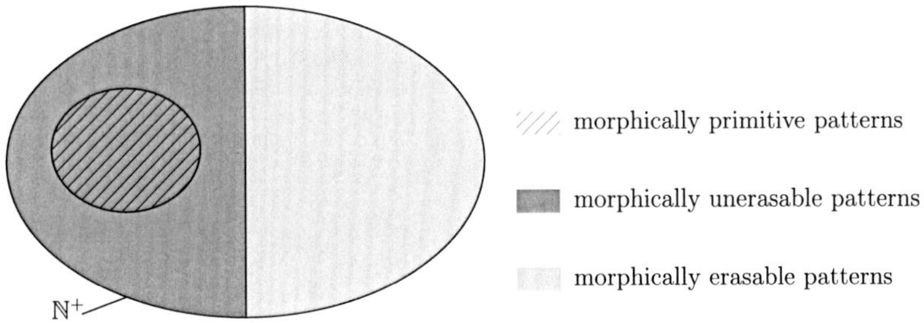

Figure 4.2: Partitions of $\mathbb{N}^+$

Corollary 4.13. *Let Σ be an alphabet. Let $\alpha \in \mathbb{N}^+$. If α is morphically erasable, no morphism $\sigma : \mathbb{N}^* \to \Sigma^*$ is unambiguous for α.*

Proof. Directly from Theorem 4.7 and Definition 4.12. □

The pattern α from Example 4.2 is morphically erasable, whereas α from Example 4.3 is morphically unerasable. The following proposition relates the property of a pattern being morphically unerasable to the property of being morphically primitive.

Proposition 4.14. *Let $\alpha \in \mathbb{N}^+$. If α is morphically primitive, it is morphically unerasable. In general, the converse of this statement does not hold true.*

Proof. We show the first statement by contraposition: Let α be morphically erasable. Thus, $(\mathrm{var}(\alpha), \emptyset)$ is an ambiguity partition for α. If follows from Proposition 4.5, point 3, that α is morphically imprimitive. The second claim can be verified with the help of the pattern α from Example 4.3 whose maximal ambiguity partition is $(E, N) = (\{1, 2, 3, 4\}, \{5\})$. Thus, this pattern is morphically unerasable ($N \neq \emptyset$), but not morphically primitive (see, again, Proposition 4.5, point 3). □

Consequently, the set of morphically primitive patterns is a proper subset of the set of morphically unerasable patterns. This is illustrated in Figure 4.2.

In the following sections, we shall investigate if the partition of $\mathbb{N}^+$ into morphically erasable and unerasable patterns is equally significant for the ambiguity of arbitrary (possibly erasing) morphisms as the partition of $\mathbb{N}^+$ into morphically primitive and imprimitive patterns is for the ambiguity of nonerasing morphisms (see Figure 3.1 on page 18). Since we already know from Corollary 4.13 that there are no unambiguous morphisms for morphically erasable patterns, we are particularly interested in the question for which morphically unerasable patterns there are unambiguous morphisms or, at least, morphisms with restricted ambiguity. As in Chapter 3, we begin with the examination of moderate ambiguity.

4.2 Moderate ambiguity

So far, we have defined moderate ambiguity for nonerasing morphisms only. However, we can define such a type of ambiguity as well for erasing morphism following the same concept as for nonerasing morphisms, but considering only those variables that are not erased by the morphism. We illustrate moderate ambiguity of erasing morphisms in the following example:

Example 4.15. Let $\Sigma := \{\mathtt{a}, \mathtt{b}\}$ and

$$\begin{array}{rcccccccccccccccccccc} \alpha & := & 1 & \cdot & 2 & \cdot & 1 & \cdot & 1 & \cdot & 2 & \cdot & 1 & \cdot & 1 & \cdot & 3 & \cdot & 1 & \cdot & 3 \\ & = & i_1 & \cdot & i_2 & \cdot & i_3 & \cdot & i_4 & \cdot & i_5 & \cdot & i_6 & \cdot & i_7 & \cdot & i_8 & \cdot & i_9 & \cdot & i_{10} \end{array}$$

Let $\sigma : \mathbb{N}^* \to \Sigma^*$ be a morphism defined by $\sigma(1) := \varepsilon$, $\sigma(2) := \mathtt{aba}$, $\sigma(3) := \mathtt{abb}$. The morphism σ is ambiguous for α since $\tau : \mathbb{N}^* \to \Sigma^*$, defined by $\tau(1) := \mathtt{a}$, $\tau(2) := \mathtt{b}$, $\tau(3) := \mathtt{bb}$, satisfies $\tau(\alpha) = \sigma(\alpha)$. Hence, the situation looks as follows:

$$\sigma(\alpha) = \overbrace{\underbrace{\mathtt{a}}_{\tau(1)}\underbrace{\mathtt{b}}_{\tau(2)}\underbrace{\mathtt{a}}_{\tau(1)}}^{\sigma(2)}\overbrace{\underbrace{\mathtt{a}}_{\tau(1)}\underbrace{\mathtt{b}}_{\tau(2)}\underbrace{\mathtt{a}}_{\tau(1)}}^{\sigma(2)}\overbrace{\underbrace{\mathtt{a}}_{\tau(1)}\underbrace{\mathtt{bb}}_{\tau(3)}}^{\sigma(3)}\overbrace{\underbrace{\mathtt{a}}_{\tau(1)}\underbrace{\mathtt{bb}}_{\tau(3)}}^{\sigma(3)} = \tau(\alpha).$$

We call σ moderately ambiguous since all morphisms τ' with $\tau'(\alpha) = \sigma(\alpha)$ map every variable i_k with $\sigma(i_k) \neq \varepsilon$ to a certain factor w_k of $\sigma(i_k)$ at a particular position. In this example, we have $w_2 = w_5 = \mathtt{b}$ and $w_8 = w_{10} = \mathtt{bb}$. We can verify that the only morphisms τ' with $\tau'(\alpha) = \sigma(\alpha)$ are σ itself and τ, and, as explained above, these two morphisms satisfy $\sigma(i_k) = \ldots w_k \ldots = \tau(i_k)$ for $k = 2, 5, 8, 10$. ◇

We proceed with the formal definition of moderate ambiguity for arbitrary (possibly erasing) morphisms. Again, our definition is quite involved, since we do not only postulate that, for a given pattern α and for every $x \in \text{var}(\alpha)$, there exists a word w_x such that, for every morphism τ with $\tau(\alpha) = \sigma(\alpha)$, $\tau(x)$ contains w_x as a factor (which could be called *factor-preserving* ambiguity), but we also demand that these factors are located at fixed positions for all τ. This means that we need to identify and mark the positions of the factors.

Definition 4.16 (Moderate and strong ambiguity of morphisms). *Let Σ be an alphabet, let $\alpha = i_1 \cdot i_2 \cdot [\ldots] \cdot i_n$ with $n, i_1, i_2, \ldots, i_n \in \mathbb{N}$, and let $\sigma : \mathbb{N}^* \to \Sigma^*$ be a morphism satisfying $\sigma(\alpha) \neq \varepsilon$. Then σ is called* moderately ambiguous (for α) *provided that there exist $l_2, l_3, \ldots, l_n, r_1, r_2, \ldots, r_{n-1} \in \mathbb{N} \cup \{0\}$ such that, for every morphism $\tau : \mathbb{N}^* \to \Sigma^*$ with $\tau(\alpha) = \sigma(\alpha)$,*

(i) *if $\sigma(i_1) \neq \varepsilon$ then $r_1 \geq 1$,*

(ii) *if $\sigma(i_n) \neq \varepsilon$ then $l_n \leq |\sigma(\alpha)|$,*

(iii) *for every $k \in \{2, 3, \ldots, n-1\}$ with $\sigma(i_k) \neq \varepsilon$, $l_k \leq r_k$,*

(iv) *for every k with $1 \leq k \leq n-1$, $|\tau(i_1 \cdot i_2 \cdot [\ldots] \cdot i_k)| < l_{k+1}$, and*

(v) *for every k with $1 \leq k \leq n-1$, $|\tau(i_1 \cdot i_2 \cdot [\ldots] \cdot i_k)| \geq r_k$.*

We call σ strongly ambiguous (for α) *if and only if it is not moderately ambiguous (for α).*

In the definition, for any pattern α and any moderately ambiguous morphism σ for α, a pair (l_k, r_k) for some $i_k \in \text{var}(\alpha)$ with $\sigma(i_k) \neq \varepsilon$ "marks" the factor w_k from position l_k to r_k in $\sigma(\alpha)$. This factor must be covered by the image of i_k under every morphism τ with $\tau(\alpha) = \sigma(\alpha)$ – this is guaranteed by the conditions (iv) and (v). Considering Example 4.15, we choose the following markers l_i, r_k: Let $r_1 := 0$, $(l_2, r_2) := (2, 2)$, $(l_5, r_5) := (5, 5)$, $(l_8, r_8) := (8, 9)$, $l_{10} := 11$ and finally $(l_k, r_k) := (|\sigma(\alpha)| + 1, 0)$ for $k \in \{1, 3, 4, 6, 7, 9\}$ since, for these k, $\sigma(i_k) = \varepsilon$, and, thus, no factor has to be marked. It can be verified that these values of l_j, $2 \leq j \leq n$, and r_k, $1 \leq k \leq n-1$ meet the requirements (i)–(v) of Definition 4.16. The main difference between Definition 4.16 and Definition 3.3 is caused by the fact that, if a variable is erased by the morphism, its image does not need to be marked by a pair $(l_k, r_k)^\dagger$. Thus, we have to replace the inequation chain in Definition 3.3 by the more involved conditions (i)–(iii) in Definition 4.16. However, (iv) and (v) remain unchanged.

The following lemma gives us the counterpart to Lemma 3.4 and, thus, is useful when studying moderate ambiguity of arbitrary morphisms since, in certain cases, it avoids a detailed check of Definition 4.16.

Lemma 4.17. *Let Σ be an alphabet, $\alpha \in \mathbb{N}^+$ and $\sigma : \mathbb{N}^* \to \Sigma^*$ be a morphism. If there exists a morphism $\tau : \mathbb{N}^* \to \Sigma^*$ such that $\tau(\alpha) = \sigma(\alpha)$, but $\tau(x) = \varepsilon \neq \sigma(x)$ for an $x \in \text{var}(\alpha)$, then σ is not moderately ambiguous for α.*

Proof. Let $\alpha = i_1 \cdot i_2 \cdot [\ldots] \cdot i_n$ with $n, i_1, i_2, \ldots, i_n \in \mathbb{N}$, and let k be minimal such that $x = i_k$. Assume to the contrary that σ is moderately ambiguous for α and let $l_2, l_3, \ldots, l_n, r_1, r_2, \ldots, r_{n-1} \in \mathbb{N}$ as defined in Definition 4.16.

Case 1: $k = 1$. Then $r_1 \geq 1$ since $\sigma(i_1) \neq \varepsilon$, but $|\tau(i_1)| = |\varepsilon| = 0 < r_1$. This contradicts condition (v) of Definition 4.16.

Case 2: $k = n$. Then $l_n \leq |\sigma(\alpha)|$ due to $\sigma(i_n) \neq \varepsilon$. But since $\tau(i_n) = \varepsilon$, $\tau(\alpha) = \tau(i_1 \cdot i_2 \cdot [\ldots] \cdot i_{n-1})$ and, thus, $|\tau(i_1 \cdot i_2 \cdot [\ldots] \cdot i_{n-1})| = |\tau(\alpha)| = |\sigma(\alpha)| \geq l_n$. This contradicts condition (iv) of Definition 4.16.

Case 3: $1 < k < n$. Thus, τ must satisfy $|\tau(i_1 \cdot i_2 \cdot [\ldots] \cdot i_{k-1})| < l_k$ and $|\tau(i_1 \cdot i_2 \cdot [\ldots] \cdot i_k)| \geq r_k$. However, since $\tau(i_1 \cdot i_2 \cdot [\ldots] \cdot i_{k-1}) = \tau(i_1 \cdot i_2 \cdot [\ldots] \cdot i_k)$, it follows that $l_k > r_k$, which contradicts σ being moderately ambiguous. □

With these new terms of ambiguity, we can give a stronger version of Theorem 4.7:

Theorem 4.18. *Let Σ be an alphabet. Let $\alpha \in \mathbb{N}^+$ and let (E, N) be an ambiguity partition for α. Then every morphism $\sigma : \mathbb{N}^* \to \Sigma^*$ satisfying $\sigma(x) \neq \varepsilon$ for an $x \in E$ is strongly ambiguous for α.*

Proof. We prove Theorem 4.18 by induction.

For $(E, N) = (\emptyset, \text{var}(\alpha))$, the statement is obviously true.

Now, let (E', N') be an ambiguity partition derived from an ambiguity partition (E, N) using condition (ii) of Definition 4.4. Then there exists a nontrivial morphism $h : \mathbb{N}^* \to \mathbb{N}^*$ satisfying $(\star)\, h(\alpha) = \pi_N(\alpha)$. Furthermore, $E' = E \cup \{x \in N \mid h(x) = \varepsilon\}$ and $N' = \{x \in N \mid h(x) \neq \varepsilon\}$. Consider a morphism $\sigma : \mathbb{N}^* \to \Sigma^*$ satisfying $\sigma(x) \neq \varepsilon$ for an $x \in E'$. If $x \in E$, it follows by induction that σ is strongly ambiguous. Now assume that $(\star\star)\, \sigma(x) = \varepsilon$ for all $x \in E$ and $\sigma(n) \neq \varepsilon$ for an $n \in N$ with $h(n) = \varepsilon$ and, thus, $n \in E'$.

† In fact, we can always use $(l_k, r_k) := (|\sigma(\alpha)| + 1, 0)$ for a variable x_k with $\sigma(x_k) = \varepsilon$.

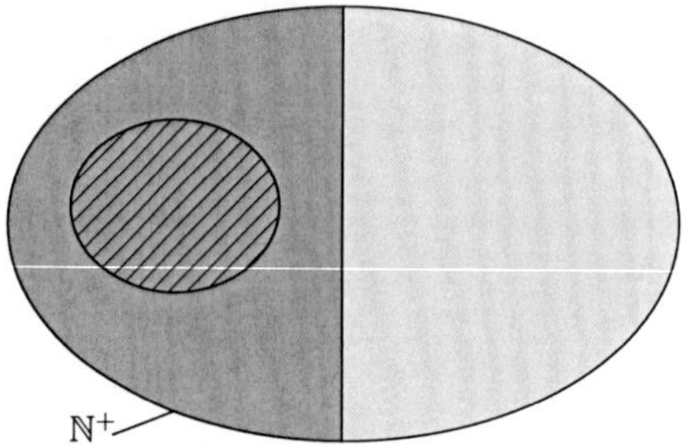

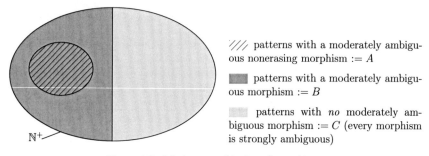

/// patterns with a moderately ambiguous nonerasing morphism := A

patterns with a moderately ambiguous morphism := B

patterns with *no* moderately ambiguous morphism := C (every morphism is strongly ambiguous)

Figure 4.3: Moderate ambiguity of morphisms

Let $\tau : \mathbb{N}^* \to \Sigma^*$ be the morphism defined by $\tau(x) = \sigma(h(x))$ for all $x \in \text{var}(\alpha)$. Due to $(\star)$ and $(\star\star)$, $\tau(\alpha) = \sigma(h(\alpha)) = \sigma(\pi_N(\alpha)) = \sigma(\alpha)$, but $\tau(n) = \varepsilon \neq \sigma(n)$. With help of Lemma 4.17, we can conclude that σ is strongly ambiguous for α. □

Thus, there is no moderately ambiguous morphism for morphically erasable patterns.

Corollary 4.19. *Let Σ be an alphabet and let $\alpha \in \mathbb{N}^+$. There is no moderately ambiguous morphism $\sigma : \mathbb{N}^* \to \Sigma^*$ for α if α is morphically erasable.*

Proof. We prove the statement by contraposition: Let α be morphically erasable. Hence, there is an ambiguity partition $(\text{var}(\alpha), \emptyset)$ for α. Then it follows from Theorem 4.18 that no morphism is moderately ambiguous for α. □

Concluding our insights so far, we know that there are patterns with a moderately ambiguous nonerasing morphism (cf. Example 3.2), patterns with a moderately ambiguous erasing morphism but no moderately ambiguous nonerasing morphism (cf. Example 4.15 and Theorem 3.5 since this example pattern is morphically imprimitive) and patterns with no moderately ambiguous morphism at all (cf. Example 4.2 and Corollary 4.19). Consequently, the sets A, B, C in Figure 4.3 are all non-empty and $A \subset B$ and $B \subset \mathbb{N}^+$ hold true.

The main result of this section now characterises those patterns that have a moderately ambiguous morphism. More precisely, it states that moderate ambiguity can be achieved if and only if the pattern is morphically unerasable:

Theorem 4.20. *Let Σ be an alphabet, $|\Sigma| \geq 2$, let $\alpha \in \mathbb{N}^+$. There exists a moderately ambiguous morphism $\sigma : \mathbb{N}^* \to \Sigma^*$ for α if and only if α is morphically unerasable.*

Proof. The *only if* is proved by Corollary 4.19.

We continue with the *if* direction. Let α be morphically unerasable. Hence, for the maximal ambiguity partition (E, N) for α, it is $N \neq \emptyset$. Furthermore, let $\alpha = i_1 \cdot i_2 \cdot [\ldots] \cdot i_n$ with $n, i_1, i_2, \ldots, i_n \in \mathbb{N}$, and let $\sigma : \mathbb{N}^* \to \{\mathtt{a}, \mathtt{b}\}^*$ be a morphism defined by

$$\sigma(i) := \begin{cases} \mathtt{a}\mathtt{b}^{(i-1)(2n+1)+1}\mathtt{a}\mathtt{a}\mathtt{b}^{(i-1)(2n+1)+2}\mathtt{a}[\ldots]\mathtt{a}\mathtt{b}^{i(2n+1)}\mathtt{a}, & \text{if } i \in N, \\ \varepsilon, & \text{else,} \end{cases}$$

for every $i \in \mathbb{N}$. Hence, every $\sigma(i)$, $i \in N$, consists of exactly $2n+1$ segments of the form $\mathtt{a}\mathtt{b}^+\mathtt{a}$. Note that, for variables in N, σ is similar to the morphism $\tau_{k,a,b}$ as introduced by Jiang et. al. [16].

The idea now is to show that, for all k with $i_k \in N$, the factor $\mathtt{a}\,\mathtt{a}\,\mathtt{b}^{(i_k-1)(2n+1)+n+1}\,\mathtt{a}\,\mathtt{a}$, which comprises the middle segment of $\sigma(i_k)$, is always contained in the image of i_k under any morphism τ with $\tau(\alpha) = \sigma(\alpha)$. Thus, we first give $l_2, l_3, \ldots, l_n$, $r_1, r_2, \ldots, r_{n-1} \in \mathbb{N} \cup \{0\}$ as required by Definition 4.16, according to the factors $\mathtt{a}\,\mathtt{a}\,\mathtt{b}^{(i_k-1)(2n+1)+n+1}\,\mathtt{a}\,\mathtt{a}$ in $\sigma(\alpha)$. To this end, for all $k \in \{1, 2, \ldots, n\}$ with $i_k \in N$, let $v_k, w_k \in \{\mathtt{a}, \mathtt{b}\}^*$ such that $\sigma(i_k) = v_k\,\mathtt{a}\,\mathtt{a}\,\mathtt{b}^{(i_k-1)(2n+1)+n+1}\,\mathtt{a}\,\mathtt{a}\,w_k$. We define, for every $k \in \{2, 3, \ldots, n\}$,

$$l_k := \begin{cases} |\sigma(i_1 \cdot i_2 \cdot [\ldots] \cdot i_{k-1})\, v_k\, \mathtt{a}|, & \text{if } i_k \in N \\ |\sigma(\alpha)| + 1, & \text{else,} \end{cases}$$

and, for every $m \in \{1, 2, \ldots, n-1\}$,

$$r_m := \begin{cases} |\sigma(i_1 \cdot i_2 \cdot [\ldots] \cdot i_{m-1})\, v_m\, \mathtt{a}\,\mathtt{a}\,\mathtt{b}^{(i_m-1)(2n+1)+n+1}\,\mathtt{a}\,\mathtt{a}|, & \text{if } i_m \in N \\ 0, & \text{else.} \end{cases}$$

It can be verified with little effort that the l_k, r_m satisfy points (i)–(iii) of Definition 4.16. In the following, we verify points (iv) and (v). To this purpose, we introduce a new notion and prove some claims.

Auxiliary Definition. Let $\tau : \mathbb{N}^* \to \{\mathtt{a}, \mathtt{b}\}^*$ be a morphism with $\tau(\alpha) = \sigma(\alpha)$. Then a segment $\mathtt{a}\mathtt{b}^x\mathtt{a}$, $x \in \mathbb{N}$, is called *preserved by τ at position j* if and only if, for $\tau(\alpha) = u_1\,\mathtt{a}\mathtt{b}^x\mathtt{a}\,u_2$ and $|u_1| = j-1$, there exists an l, $0 \le l \le n-1$, such that

- $|\tau(i_1 \cdot i_2 \cdot [\ldots] \cdot i_l)| \le |u_1|$ and
- $|\tau(i_1 \cdot i_2 \cdot [\ldots] \cdot i_l \cdot i_{l+1})| \ge |u_1\mathtt{a}\mathtt{b}^x\mathtt{a}|$;

otherwise, this segment is called *split by τ at position j*.
A segment $\mathtt{a}\mathtt{b}^x\mathtt{a}$ is called *preserved by τ* if and only if it is preserved by τ at all its positions in $\sigma(\alpha)$; otherwise, it is called *split by τ*.

Claim 1. For every morphism $\tau : \mathbb{N}^* \to \{\mathtt{a}, \mathtt{b}\}^*$ with $\tau(\alpha) = \sigma(\alpha)$ and every $k \in N$, there exist at least $n+2$ different segments $\mathtt{a}\mathtt{b}^x\mathtt{a}$, $x \in I := \{(i_k-1)(2n+1)+1, (i_k-1)(2n+1)+2, \ldots, i_k(2n+1)\}$, that are preserved by τ.

Proof (Claim 1). Let τ be a morphism with $\tau(\alpha) = \sigma(\alpha)$ and let $k \in \{1, 2, \ldots, n\}$. Let $l := |\alpha|_{i_k}$. Thus, there exist exactly $l(2n+1)$ positions $p_1, p_2, \ldots, p_{l(2n+1)} \in \mathbb{N}$ in $\sigma(\alpha)$ where segments of the form $\mathtt{a}\mathtt{b}^x\mathtt{a}$, $x \in I$, begin. Since there are n variables in α, such a segment $\mathtt{a}\mathtt{b}^x\mathtt{a}$ can be split by τ at most at $n-1$ positions. Thus, there are at least $l(2n+1)-(n-1)$ positions in α where a segment $\mathtt{a}\mathtt{b}^x\mathtt{a}$ with $x \in I$ is preserved by τ. It is a simple combinatorial insight that, if there are $l(2n+1)$ coloured balls of which exactly l balls have the same colour, one can choose at maximum $(l-1)(2n+1)$ balls without having all l balls of one colour. Every ball more than $(l-1)(2n+1)$ gives another complete set of equally coloured balls. We can transfer these considerations to our setting by identifying balls with positions of segments having the same colour if they mark the same segment. We have at least $l(2n+1)-(n-1)$ positions in $\sigma(\alpha)$ where a segment $\mathtt{a}\mathtt{b}^x\mathtt{a}$ with $x \in I$ is preserved by τ, and $l(2n+1)-(n-1) = (l-1)(2n+1)+(n+2)$. Consequently, there are $n+2$ segments $\mathtt{ab}^x\mathtt{a}$ with $x \in I$ that are preserved by τ since they are preserved at each of their l positions. *q.e.d.(Claim 1).*

Claim 2. If there exists a morphism $\tau : \mathbb{N}^* \to \{\mathtt{a},\mathtt{b}\}^*$ with $\tau(\alpha) = \sigma(\alpha)$ that does not satisfy (iv) or (v) of Definition 4.16, then there exist $j_1, j_2 \in \operatorname{var}(\alpha)$, $j_1 \neq j_2$, with $\tau(j_2) = \ldots\mathtt{ab}^{(j_1-1)(2n+1)+s}\mathtt{a}\ldots$ for an $s \in \{1,2,\ldots,2n+1\}$. Furthermore, the segment $\mathtt{ab}^{(j_1-1)(2n+1)+s}\mathtt{a}$ is preserved by τ.

Proof (Claim 2). If (iv) is not satisfied, then there exists a $k \in \{1,2,\ldots,n-1\}$ with $|\tau(i_1 \cdot i_2 \cdot [\ldots] \cdot i_k)| \geq l_{k+1}$. It follows from the definition of l_{k+1} that $i_{k+1} \in N$. Hence, $\tau(i_1 \cdot i_2 \cdot [\ldots] \cdot i_k) = \sigma(i_1 \cdot i_2 \cdot [\ldots] \cdot i_k)\, v_{k+1}\, \mathtt{a}\ldots$ with

$$v_{k+1} = \mathtt{ab}^{(i_{k+1}-1)(2n+1)+1}\mathtt{aab}^{(i_{k+1}-1)(2n+1)+2}\mathtt{a}[\ldots]\mathtt{ab}^{(i_{k+1}-1)(2n+1)+n}.$$

From Claim 1, we know that $n+2$ segments $\mathtt{ab}^x\mathtt{a}$ with $x \in \{(i_{k+1}-1)(2n+1)+1, (i_{k+1}-1)(2n+1)+2, \ldots, i_{k+1}(2n+1)\}$ are preserved by τ and, hence, also at least one segment $\mathtt{ab}^{(i_{k+1}-1)(2n+1)+s}\mathtt{a}\ldots$ for an $s \in \{1,2,\ldots,n\}$ is preserved by τ. Thus, there is a $j \in \{i_1, i_2, \ldots, i_k\}$ with $\tau(j) = \ldots\mathtt{ab}^{(i_{k+1}-1)(2n+1)+s}\mathtt{a}\ldots$. If we assume $j = i_{k+1}$, then

- $\tau(i_{k+1}) = \ldots\mathtt{ab}^{(i_{k+1}-1)(2n+1)+s}\mathtt{a}\ldots\mathtt{ab}^{(i_{k+1}-1)(2n+1)+s}\mathtt{a}\ldots$ or
- $\tau(i_{k+1}) = \ldots\mathtt{ab}^{(i_{k+1}-1)(2n+1)+s}\mathtt{a}\ldots$ and $\tau(j') = \ldots\mathtt{ab}^{(i_{k+1}-1)(2n+1)+s}\mathtt{a}\ldots$ for a $j' \neq i_{k+1}$,

because the number of occurrences of j in $i_1 \cdot i_2 \cdot [\ldots] \cdot i_k$ is strictly smaller than the number of occurrences of $\mathtt{ab}^{(i_{k+1}-1)(2n+1)+s}\mathtt{a}$ in $\tau(i_1 \cdot i_2 \cdot [\ldots] \cdot i_k)$. However, then the number of occurrences of $\mathtt{ab}^{(i_{k+1}-1)(2n+1)+s}\mathtt{a}$ in $\tau(\alpha)$ is greater than the number of occurrences of $\mathtt{ab}^{(i_{k+1}-1)(2n+1)+s}\mathtt{a}$ in $\sigma(\alpha)$, which contradicts $\tau(\alpha) = \sigma(\alpha)$. Thus, $j \neq i_{k+1}$.

If (v) is not satisfied, then there exists a $k \in \{1,2,\ldots,n-1\}$ with $|\tau(i_1 \cdot i_2 \cdot [\ldots] \cdot i_k)| < r_k$. It follows from the definition of r_k that $i_k \in N$. Hence, $\tau(i_{k+1} \cdot i_{k+2} \cdot [\ldots] \cdot i_n) = \ldots\mathtt{a}\, w_k\, \sigma(i_{k+1} \cdot i_{k+2} \cdot [\ldots] \cdot i_n)$ with

$$w_k = \mathtt{b}^{(i_k-1)(2n+1)+1}\mathtt{aab}^{(i_k-1)(2n+1)+2}\mathtt{a}[\ldots]\mathtt{ab}^{(i_k-1)(2n+1)+n}\mathtt{a}.$$

Using an analogous reasoning to the one given in the case of (iv) not being satisfied, we can conclude that there is a $j \in \{i_1, i_2, \ldots, i_k\}$ with $j \neq i_k$ and $\tau(j) = \ldots\mathtt{ab}^{(i_k-1)(2n+1)+s}\mathtt{a}\ldots$ for an $s \in \{n+2, n+3, \ldots, 2n+1\}$ and a segment $\mathtt{ab}^{(i_k-1)(2n+1)+s}\mathtt{a}$ which is preserved by τ. This proves the claim. *q.e.d.(Claim 2).*

Claim 3. If there exist a morphism $\tau : \mathbb{N}^* \to \{\mathtt{a},\mathtt{b}\}^*$ with $\tau(\alpha) = \sigma(\alpha)$ and $j_1, j_2 \in \operatorname{var}(\alpha)$, $j_1 \neq j_2$, with $\tau(j_2) = \ldots\mathtt{ab}^{(j_1-1)(2n+1)+s}\mathtt{a}\ldots$ for an $s \in \{1,2,\ldots,2n+1\}$ and a segment $\mathtt{ab}^{(j_1-1)(2n+1)+s}\mathtt{a}$ that is preserved by τ, then the ambiguity partition (E, N) is not maximal.

Proof (Claim 3). For $i = j_2$, let $x_i := (j_1-1)(2n+1)+s$, and for $i \in N \setminus \{j_2\}$, we choose an $x_i \in \{(i-1)(2n+1)+1, (i-1)(2n+1)+2, \ldots, i(2n+1)\}$ such that the segment $\mathtt{ab}^{x_i}\mathtt{a}$ is preserved by τ. These x_i exist due to Claim 1.

Moreover, we define a morphism $h : \mathbb{N}^* \to \mathbb{N}^*$ for every $y \in \operatorname{var}(\alpha)$ as follows:

$$h(y) := \begin{cases} t_1 \cdot t_2 \cdot \ldots t_k, & \text{if } \tau(y) = w_0\, \mathtt{ab}^{x_{t_1}}\mathtt{a}\, w_1\, \mathtt{ab}^{x_{t_2}}\mathtt{a}\, w_2 \ldots \mathtt{ab}^{x_{t_k}}\, w_k, k \in \mathbb{N}, \\ & \text{satisfying } w_i \in \{\mathtt{a},\mathtt{b}\}^* \text{ and } w_i \neq \ldots\mathtt{ab}^{x_j}\mathtt{a}\ldots \\ & \text{for all } i \in \{0,1,\ldots,k\} \text{ and all } j \in N, \\ \varepsilon, & \text{else.} \end{cases}$$

If there exists a j_2 with $\tau(j_2) = \ldots \mathtt{ab}^{(j_1-1)(2n+1)+s}\mathtt{a}\ldots$, then h, by definition, is nontrivial for N. Furthermore, $h(\alpha) = \pi_N(\alpha)$ since, for every $i \in N$, there exists exactly one corresponding x_i. However, according to condition (ii) of Definition 4.4, (E', N'), as defined when applying the above morphism h to (E, N), is an ambiguity partition satisfying $|E'| > |E|$ and $|N'| < |N|$. This contradicts the assumption of (E, N) being maximal (cf. Definition 4.8). *q.e.d.(Claim 3).*

Since Claims 2 and 3 imply that any violation of (iv) or (v) of Definition 4.16 would lead to a contradiction, σ is moderately ambiguous for α. □

Since every morphically primitive pattern is morphically unerasable (as a consequence of Proposition 4.5, point 3), Theorem 4.20 can also be applied to morphically primitive patterns. Moreover, for every morphically primitive pattern, the morphism σ from the proof of Theorem 4.20 is nonerasing. Thus, Theorem 4.20 delivers an alternate proof for Theorem 3.5. However, the morphism used in the proof of Theorem 4.20 is not optimal in regard to its substitution length of $|\mathrm{var}(\alpha)|$ segments $\mathtt{ab}^+\mathtt{a}$ per variable since for morphically primitive patterns, three segments per variable are sufficient (cf. Theorem 3.7).

With Theorem 4.20, we have found a simple characterisation for moderate ambiguity of arbitrary (possibly erasing) morphisms that is purely based on the morphic structure of the pattern under consideration, namely its property of being morphically erasable or unerasable. This situation is similar to the case of nonerasing morphisms where the property of a pattern being morphically primitive or imprimitive is characteristic for the existence of a moderately ambiguous morphisms (cf. Theorem 3.5). Looking at Figure 4.2 and Figure 4.3, we can conclude that the sets are identical. Hence, allowing the morphisms to erase variables in the pattern strictly enlarges the class of patterns for which there exist moderately ambiguous morphisms.

We conclude this section by relating moderate ambiguity and unambiguity to each other. As suggested by the definitions and further substantiated by Example 4.15, for any given morphism, the requirement of being moderately ambiguous is less strict than that of being unambiguous, which gives us the expected counterpart to Proposition 3.8 for arbitrary morphisms.

Proposition 4.21. *Let Σ be an alphabet, let $\sigma : \mathbb{N}^* \to \Sigma^*$ be a morphism, and let $\alpha \in \mathbb{N}^+$. If σ is unambiguous for α, then σ is moderately ambiguous for α. In general, the converse does not hold.*

Proof. We begin with the first statement in Proposition 4.21. Let $\alpha = i_1 \cdot i_2 \cdot [\ldots] \cdot i_n$ with $n, i_1, i_2, \ldots, i_n \in \mathbb{N}$, and let $\sigma : \mathbb{N}^* \to \Sigma^*$ be a morphism that is unambiguous for α. We define $r_k := |\sigma(i_1 \cdot i_2 \cdot [\ldots] \cdot i_k)|$ and $l_{k+1} := |\sigma(i_1 \cdot i_2 \cdot [\ldots] \cdot i_k)| + 1$ for every $1 \leq k \leq n-1$. Since σ is unambiguous and, thus, every morphism τ with $\tau(\alpha) = \sigma(\alpha)$ for every $x \in \mathrm{var}(\alpha)$ necessarily satisfies $\tau(x) = \sigma(x)$, the correctness of conditions (i)–(v) of Definition 4.16 can be verified easily.

Regarding the second statement in Proposition 4.21, Example 4.15 gives a morphism σ and a pattern α such that σ is moderately ambiguous, but not unambiguous for α. □

This directly implies that, if there exists no moderately ambiguous morphism for a pattern α, then there exists no unambiguous morphism for α and, thus, every morphism is strongly ambiguous for α. We shall now investigate for which patterns there are unambiguous morphisms.

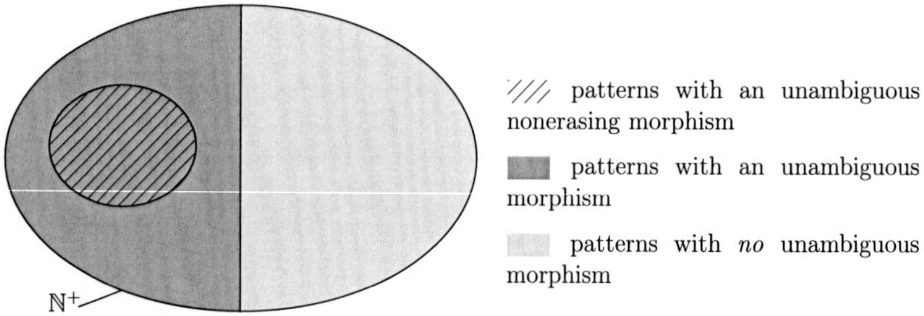

Figure 4.4: Unambiguity of morphisms with an *infinite* target alphabet

4.3 Unambiguity of morphisms with an infinite target alphabet

So far, we have not payed much attention to the size of the target alphabet of our morphisms. Concerning the ambiguity of nonerasing morphisms, this size does not play any role (as long as it is at least binary). The same holds true for the moderate ambiguity of erasing morphisms. However, as the following sections shall reveal, the size of Σ is essential in the case of erasing morphisms when we study unambiguity. We first start considering an infinite target alphabet because here, our theory can be developed in perfect analogy to the case of nonerasing morphisms since the condition of Corollary 4.13 becomes *characteristic*:

Theorem 4.22. *Let Σ_∞ be an infinite alphabet and let $\alpha \in \mathbb{N}^+$. There is an unambiguous morphism $\sigma : \mathbb{N}^* \to \Sigma_\infty^*$ for α if and only if α is morphically unerasable.*

Proof. We show the *only if* direction by contraposition: If $(\text{var}(\alpha), \emptyset)$ is an ambiguity partition for α, it follows from Corollary 4.11 that no morphism is unambiguous for α.

To show the *if* part, assume that $N \neq \emptyset$ for every ambiguity partition (E, N) for α. Let (E, N) be the maximal ambiguity partition for α. W.l.o.g. let $\Sigma_\infty := \mathbb{N}$. Furthermore, let the morphism $\sigma : \mathbb{N}^* \to \Sigma_\infty^*$ be defined by $\sigma := \pi_N$. We show by contradiction that σ is unambiguous for α. Assume that there exists a morphism $\tau : \mathbb{N}^* \to \Sigma_\infty^*$ satisfying $\tau(\alpha) = \sigma(\alpha)$ and $\tau(x) \neq \sigma(x)$ for an $x \in \text{var}(\alpha)$. Then, $\tau(\alpha) = \sigma(\alpha) = \pi_N(\alpha)$ and, additionally, τ is nontrivial for N. But, according to condition (ii) of Definition 4.4, with $h := \tau$, (E', N') as defined in this condition is an ambiguity partition, too, satisfying $|E'| > |E|$ and $|N'| < |N|$ (cf. Proposition 4.5, point 2). This contradicts (E, N) being maximal (cf. Definition 4.8). Thus, such a morphism τ cannot exist, and, hence, σ is unambiguous for α. □

Summarising our insights on the unambiguity of morphisms with an infinite target alphabet, we notice that the set of patterns with an arbitrary (possibly erasing) unambiguous morphism is strictly larger than the corresponding set for nonerasing morphisms. In the latter case, unambiguous morphisms exist for morphically primitive patterns only (cf. Corollary 3.13), while, concerning all (possibly erasing) morphisms, the set of patterns with an unambiguous morphism equals the set of morphically unerasable patterns, which strictly includes the set of morphically primitive patterns (cf. Proposition 4.14).

Moreover, due to Theorem 4.22, the sets in Figure 4.2, Figure 4.3 and Figure 4.4 are identical, and we can summarise our findings for infinite target alphabets in the following corollary, which is the analogous version of Corollary 3.14 for erasing morphisms.

Corollary 4.23. *Let $\alpha \in \mathbb{N}^+$. The following statements are equivalent:*

1. *α is morphically unerasable.*
2. *For any alphabet Σ with $|\Sigma| \geq 2$, there is a moderately ambiguous morphism $\sigma : \mathbb{N}^* \longrightarrow \Sigma^*$ for α.*
3. *For any infinite alphabet Σ_∞, there is an unambiguous morphism $\sigma : \mathbb{N}^* \longrightarrow \Sigma_\infty^*$ for α.*

Proof. Directly from Theorem 4.20 and Theorem 4.22. □

4.4 Unambiguity of morphisms with a finite target alphabet

Although the ambiguity of morphisms with an infinite target alphabet regarding morphically imprimitive patterns and, thus, erasing morphisms, offers a wider spectrum of results than regarding morphically primitive patterns for which the identity morphism is unambiguous (see Theorem 2.10 with $\Sigma = \mathbb{N}$), the more interesting question reads as follows: For which patterns α do there exist unambiguous morphisms mapping to words over a *finite* target alphabet Σ, especially if $|\Sigma| < |\text{var}(\alpha)|$, e. g. $|\Sigma| = 2$? Unfortunately, as to be shown below, Theorem 4.22 does not hold for finite alphabets. In order to find an explanation for this situation, we take a closer look at those *other* morphisms τ which exist if σ is ambiguous: If there is an ambiguity partition (E, N) for α and $\sigma(e) \neq \varepsilon$ for an $e \in E$, another morphism τ with $\tau(\alpha) = \sigma(\alpha)$ can generate the whole image of e under σ with another variable $e' \neq e$, i. e., $\tau(e') = \ldots\sigma(e)\ldots$ and $\tau(e) = \varepsilon$ (cf. Example 4.3). However, this is not the only type of ambiguity that can occur: Referring to example patterns from Example 3.1, Example 3.9 and Example 4.15, we observe that in this case τ only generates partial images of variables by σ. This phenomenon must be taken into account whenever we look for an unambiguous morphism $\sigma : \mathbb{N}^* \longrightarrow \Sigma^*$ for a pattern α, provided that Σ is finite and $|\Sigma| < |\text{var}(\alpha)|$, since then not every variable can be mapped to a different letter in Σ.

The following theorem states some fundamental insights into the ambiguity of morphisms with a finite target alphabet and, in particular, shows that Theorem 4.22 does not hold for finite alphabets:

Theorem 4.24. *Let $k \in \mathbb{N}$ and Σ_k, Σ_{k+1} be finite alphabets with k and $k+1$ letters, respectively. There exists a pattern $\alpha \in \mathbb{N}^+$ such that*

(i) *α is morphically unerasable,*

(ii) *no morphism $\sigma : \mathbb{N}^* \longrightarrow \Sigma_k^*$ is unambiguous for α, and*

(iii) *there exists an unambiguous morphism $\sigma' : \mathbb{N}^* \longrightarrow \Sigma_{k+1}^*$ for α.*

Proof. We give a pattern $\alpha_k \in \mathbb{N}^+$ that satisfies the conditions (i)–(iii). For every $i, i', j, j' \in \{1, 2, \ldots, k+1\}$, $i \neq j$, $i' \neq j'$, let $x_{\{i,j\}} \in \mathbb{N} \setminus \{1, 2, \ldots, k+1\}$ and $x_{\{i,j\}} \neq x_{\{i',j'\}}$ if and only if $\{i, j\} \neq \{i', j'\}$. We define α_k as follows:

$$\begin{aligned} \alpha_k &:= \beta_1 \, \beta_2 \, [\ldots] \, \beta_{k+1} \, \beta_{k+1} \, \beta_k \, [\ldots] \, \beta_1, \text{ with} \\ \beta_i &:= i \cdot \prod_{\substack{1 \le j \le k+1, \\ j \neq i}} x_{\{i,j\}}. \end{aligned}$$

For instance,

$$\begin{aligned} \alpha_2 = \; & 1 \cdot x_{\{1,2\}} \cdot x_{\{1,3\}} \cdot 2 \cdot x_{\{2,1\}} \cdot x_{\{2,3\}} \cdot 3 \cdot x_{\{3,1\}} \cdot x_{\{3,2\}} \cdot \\ & 3 \cdot x_{\{3,1\}} \cdot x_{\{3,2\}} \cdot 2 \cdot x_{\{2,1\}} \cdot x_{\{2,3\}} \cdot 1 \cdot x_{\{1,2\}} \cdot x_{\{1,3\}}. \end{aligned}$$

Note that, e. g., $x_{\{1,2\}} = x_{\{2,1\}}$ since $\{1, 2\} = \{2, 1\}$. Hence, $|\text{var}(\alpha_2)| = 6$. Thus, α_2 could equal $1 \cdot 4 \cdot 5 \cdot 2 \cdot 4 \cdot 6 \cdot 3 \cdot 5 \cdot 6 \cdot 3 \cdot 5 \cdot 6 \cdot 2 \cdot 4 \cdot 6 \cdot 1 \cdot 4 \cdot 5$. This pattern may be consulted for a better understanding of the proof although the subsequent argumentation deals with the general pattern α_k.

ad (i): Let $I := \{1, 2, \ldots, k+1\}$. We show that, for every ambiguity partition (E, N) for α_k and every $i \in I$, $i \notin E$. Assume to the contrary that there exists an ambiguity partition (E', A') for α_k such that $i \in E'$ for an $i \in I$. Then, there exist ambiguity partitions (E_1, N_1) and (E_2, N_2) such that

1. for every $i \in I$, $i \notin E_1$,
2. there exists a $j \in I$ with $j \in E_2$, and
3. there exists a morphism $h : \mathbb{N}^* \to \mathbb{N}^*$ that is nontrivial for N_1 and satisfies $h(\alpha_k) = \pi_{N_1}(\alpha_k)$ and $h(j) = \varepsilon$, according to condition (ii) of Definition 4.4.

Thus, following the inductive conception of Definition 4.4, the "step" from (E_1, N_1) to (E_2, N_2) is the first one where an $i \in I$ is included into the E-set of an ambiguity partition. Let $h' : \mathbb{N}^* \to \mathbb{N}^*$ be defined by $h' := \pi_I \circ h$. We can verify $h'(\pi_I(\alpha_k)) = \pi_I(\alpha_k)$ as follows: The above condition (1) implies $I \subseteq N_1$. Furthermore, since every $x_{\{l,m\}}$, $1 \le l, m \le k+1$, $l \neq m$, occurs four times in α_k while every $l \in I$ occurs only twice, every occurrence of an $l \in I$ in $h(\alpha_k)$ must be generated by h applied to an $m \in I$. Additionally, $h'(j) = \varepsilon$ and, thus, $\pi_I(\alpha_k)$ is a fixed point of the nontrivial morphism h'. Consequently, $\pi_I(\alpha_k)$ is morphically imprimitive (cf. Theorem 2.5), which is a contradiction since there exists no imprimitivity factorisation of $\pi_I(\alpha_k)$ (cf. Definition 2.6 and Corollary 2.7). Thus, for every ambiguity partition (E, N) for α_k and every $i \in I$, it is $i \notin E$ and, hence, $(\text{var}(\alpha_k), \emptyset)$ is not an ambiguity partition for α_k.

ad (ii): Assume to the contrary that there exists an unambiguous morphism $\sigma : \mathbb{N}^* \to \Sigma_k^*$ for α. Let $N := \{1, 2, \ldots, k+1\}$, $E := \text{var}(\alpha_k) \setminus N$. Since the morphism $h : \mathbb{N}^* \to \mathbb{N}^*$ defined by

$$h(i) := \begin{cases} \beta_i, & \text{if } 1 \le i \le k+1, \\ \varepsilon, & \text{else}, \end{cases}$$

is nontrivial for N and satisfies $h(\alpha_k) = \alpha_k$, (E, N) is an ambiguity partition for α (according to Definition 4.4). Thus, it follows from Theorem 4.7 that $\sigma(e) = \varepsilon$ for every $e \in E$. Hence, exactly one of the following cases must occur:

Case 1. $\sigma(n) = \varepsilon$ for an $n \in N$. If $n = 1$ then the morphism $\tau : \mathbb{N}^* \to \Sigma_k^*$, defined by $\tau(1) := \sigma(2)$, $\tau(2) := \varepsilon$, $\tau(x) := \sigma(x)$ for all $x \in N \setminus \{1, 2\}$, $\tau(y) = \varepsilon$ for all $y \in E$, satisfies $\tau(\alpha_k) = \sigma(\alpha_k)$ and, thus, contradicts σ being unambiguous for α_k. If $n > 1$ then the morphism $\tau : \mathbb{N}^* \to \Sigma_k^*$, defined by $\tau(n) = \sigma(n-1)$, $\tau(n-1) = \varepsilon$, $\tau(x) = \sigma(x)$ for all $x \in N \setminus \{n-1, n\}$, $\tau(y) = \varepsilon$ for all $y \in E$, satisfies $\tau(\alpha_k) = \sigma(\alpha_k)$ and, thus, contradicts σ being unambiguous for α_k.

Case 2. $\sigma(n) \neq \varepsilon$ for every $n \in N$. Since $|N| = k+1 > |\Sigma_k|$, the image of two variables under σ must end with the same letter, i. e. there exist $i, j \in N$, $w_i, w_j \in \Sigma_k^*$ and a letter $c \in \Sigma_k$ such that $\sigma(i) = w_i c$ and $\sigma(j) = w_j c$. We define a morphism $\tau : \mathbb{N}^* \to \Sigma_k^*$ as $\tau(i) := w_i$, $\tau(j) := w_j$, $\tau(x_{\{i,j\}}) := c$, $\tau(x) := \sigma(x)$ for all $x \in N \setminus \{i, j\}$, $\tau(y) := \varepsilon$ for all $y \in E \setminus \{x_{\{i,j\}}\}$. This morphism satisfies $\tau(\alpha_k) = \sigma(\alpha_k)$ and, thus, contradicts σ being unambiguous for α_k.

Consequently, there exists no unambiguous morphism $\sigma : \mathbb{N}^* \to \Sigma_k^*$ for α_k.

ad (iii). Let $\Sigma_{k+1} = N := \{1, 2, \ldots, k+1\}$ and $E := \mathrm{var}(\alpha_k) \setminus N$. We show that the morphism $\sigma' : \mathbb{N}^* \to \Sigma_{k+1}^*$, defined by $\sigma'(n) := n$ for every $n \in N$, $\sigma'(e) := \varepsilon$ for every $e \in E$, is unambiguous for α_k. Assume to the contrary that there exists a morphism $\tau : \mathbb{N}^* \to \Sigma_{k+1}^*$ satisfying $\tau(\alpha_k) = \sigma'(\alpha_k)$ and $\tau(i) \neq \sigma'(i)$ for an $i \in \mathrm{var}(\alpha_k)$. Since $|\sigma'(\alpha_k)|_n = 2$ for every $n \in N$ but $|\alpha_k|_e = 4$ for every $e \in E$, we get $\tau(e) = \varepsilon$ for every $e \in E$. Hence, $\tau(\pi_N(\alpha_k)) = \tau(\alpha_k) = \sigma'(\alpha_k) = \pi_N(\alpha_k)$ and, thus, $\pi_N(\alpha_k)$ is a fixed point of τ. Due to $\tau(i) \neq \sigma(i) = i$, τ is nontrivial. Consequently, $\pi_N(\alpha_k)$ is morphically imprimitive (cf. Theorem 2.5). But there exists no imprimitivity factorisation of $\pi_N(\alpha_k)$ (cf. Definition 2.6 and Corollary 2.7). Hence, $\pi_N(\alpha_k)$ is not morphically imprimitive, which contradicts the existence of τ. Thus, σ' is unambiguous for α_k. □

Theorem 4.24 allows us to compare the sets of patterns for which there exist no unambiguous morphisms when different target alphabets are chosen. To this purpose, we name these sets as following.

Definition 4.25 ($\mathrm{UNAMB}_\Sigma/\mathrm{AMB}_\Sigma$). *For any alphabet Σ, let UNAMB_Σ be the set of patterns for which there is an unambiguous morphism $\sigma : \mathbb{N}^* \to \Sigma^*$, and let $\mathrm{AMB}_\Sigma := \mathbb{N}^+ \setminus \mathrm{UNAMB}_\Sigma$.*

Now we can state the following:

Corollary 4.26. *Let Σ, Σ' be finite alphabets, $|\Sigma| < |\Sigma'|$. Then $\mathrm{AMB}_\Sigma \supset \mathrm{AMB}_{\Sigma'}$.*

Proof. Referring to the definition of AMB_Σ, we can verify $\mathrm{AMB}_\Sigma \supseteq \mathrm{AMB}_{\Sigma'}$. $\mathrm{AMB}_\Sigma \neq \mathrm{AMB}_{\Sigma'}$ follows from Theorem 4.24 (iii). □

This establishes a novel and rather unexpected aspect in the research on the ambiguity of morphisms. While, for a pattern α, there exists an unambiguous *nonerasing* morphism if and only if α is morphically primitive – no matter which Σ with $|\Sigma| \geq 2$ is chosen (cf. Corollary 3.13) – concerning arbitrary, possibly *erasing* morphisms, this question strongly depends on the size of Σ. In addition to this, the approach studied by previous literature of first defining Σ and then examining AMB_Σ could also be reversed as follows: Given an arbitrary pattern α, which is the minimal size of Σ such that there exists an unambiguous morphism $\sigma : \mathbb{N}^* \to \Sigma^*$ if such a morphism exists at all? The next corollary gives us an upper bound for the size of Σ.

Corollary 4.27. *Let $\alpha \in \mathbb{N}^+$ with $k := |\mathrm{var}(\alpha)| \geq 3$. There exist an alphabet Σ with $|\Sigma| \leq k-1$ and an unambiguous morphism $\sigma : \mathbb{N}^* \to \Sigma^*$ if and only if α is morphically unerasable.*

Proof. We first show the only-if part and argue by contraposition. If α is morphically erasable, it follows from Corollary 4.13 that no morphism is unambiguous for α.
To show the if part, we consider the following two cases:

If α is morphically primitive, then there exists an unambiguous (even nonerasing) morphism $\sigma : \mathbb{N}^* \to \Sigma^*$ with a binary alphabet Σ (cf. Theorem 3.12) which, thus, satisfies $|\Sigma| \leq k-1$ since $k \geq 3$.

If α is morphically imprimitive, then there exists an ambiguity partition (E, N) with respect to α such that $E \neq \emptyset$ (cf. Proposition 4.5). Hence, $|N| < k$. From the proof of Theorem 4.22, it follows that there exists an unambiguous morphism $\sigma : \mathbb{N}^* \to N^*$ for α. □

Thus, for every pattern with at least $k \geq 3$ variables, there exists an unambiguous morphism mapping to a target alphabet with at most $k-1$ letters if an unambiguous morphism exists at all. We want to note that unambiguous morphisms for patterns α with $|\mathrm{var}(\alpha)| = 2$ are characterised in Section 4.4.3.

As another consequence of Theorem 4.24, we observe that, for any finite, at least binary target alphabet, the set of patterns with an unambiguous morphism is strictly smaller than the set of patterns with a moderately ambiguous morphism:

Corollary 4.28. *Let Σ be an alphabet with $|\Sigma| \geq 2$. There exist an $\alpha \in \mathbb{N}^+$ and a morphism $\sigma : \mathbb{N}^* \to \Sigma^*$ such that σ is moderately ambiguous for α, but no morphism is unambiguous for α.*

Proof. Directly from Theorem 4.24 and Theorem 4.20 since the generic example pattern in the proof of Theorem 4.24 is morphically unerasable. □

This strongly contrasts with the results in Chapter 3 since, for every finite, at least binary target alphabet, there is an unambiguous nonerasing morphism for a pattern if and only if there is a moderately ambiguous nonerasing morphism (cf. Corollary 3.14).

In Figure 4.5, the present situation is summarised. All set inclusions are strict. This situation makes it difficult to find a characterisation of patterns with an arbitrary (possibly erasing) unambiguous morphism which is as simple as in the case of nonerasing morphisms where this property solely depends on the morphic structure of the pattern (cf. Corollary 3.13). In the general case, the size of Σ must be taken into account, which explains why ambiguity partitions that are independent from Σ are only of limited use concerning a characterisation of unambiguity. Additionally, it is not clear if a characterisation of patterns for which there exists an unambiguous morphism with, for example, a binary target alphabet would permit any conclusions on other target alphabet sizes. Nevertheless, such a characterisation would be highly appreciated.

In the following sections, we develop an understanding of which target alphabet dependent ambiguity phenomena can occur and how they can be avoided.

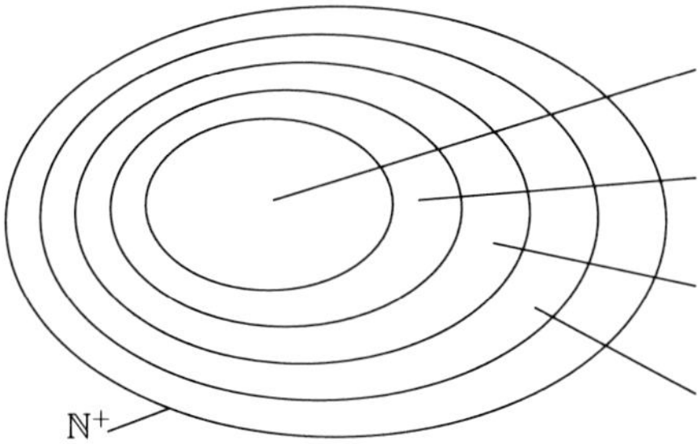

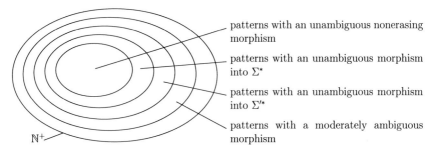

Figure 4.5: Ambiguity of morphisms, $\Sigma \subset \Sigma'$

4.4.1 Ambiguity through homogeneity

In this section, we study the pattern α_k from the proof of Theorem 4.24 in detail and generalise the ambiguity phenomenon which its structure promotes while applying morphisms with a target alphabet of size k. Thus, the construction of all patterns concerned in this section is based on the following, very simple observation: Let Σ be an alphabet with k letters. If a morphism $\sigma : \mathbb{N}^* \to \Sigma^*$ maps at least $k+1$ variables to nonempty words, the images of at least two variables $x, y \in \mathbb{N}$ begin (end) with the same letter. We then say that x, y are *left (right) homogeneous under σ*.

Example 4.29. Let us consider $\Sigma = \{\mathtt{a}, \mathtt{b}\}$ and the pattern

$$\begin{aligned} \alpha_2 \;=\; & 1 \cdot x_{\{1,2\}} \cdot x_{\{1,3\}} \cdot 2 \cdot x_{\{2,1\}} \cdot x_{\{2,3\}} \cdot 3 \cdot x_{\{3,1\}} \cdot x_{\{3,2\}} \cdot \\ & 3 \cdot x_{\{3,1\}} \cdot x_{\{3,2\}} \cdot 2 \cdot x_{\{2,1\}} \cdot x_{\{2,3\}} \cdot 1 \cdot x_{\{1,2\}} \cdot x_{\{1,3\}}. \end{aligned}$$

from the proof of Theorem 4.24. We note that all the $x_{\dots}$ are variables different from $\{1,2,3\}$, and $x_M = x_{M'}$ if and only if $M = M'$. Thus, e. g., $x_{\{1,2\}} = x_{\{2,1\}}$ since $\{1,2\} = \{2,1\}$. Hence, $|\mathrm{var}(\alpha_2)| = 6$. It can be easily verified that with $N := \{1,2,3\}$ and $E := \mathrm{var}(\alpha) \setminus N$, (E, N) is an ambiguity partition for α. By Theorem 4.18, all morphisms $\sigma : \mathbb{N}^* \to \{\mathtt{a}, \mathtt{b}\}^*$ with $\sigma(x) \neq \varepsilon$ for an $x \in E$ are strongly ambiguous for α_2. Furthermore, it can be shown that all morphisms that map at least one of the variables in N to the empty word are strongly ambiguous for α_2 as well. At this moment, we do not focus on strong ambiguity since this phenomenon is characterised with the help of ambiguity partitions (cf. Theorem 4.20). Therefore, we shall have a look at those morphisms σ that map only 1, 2 and 3 to nonempty words. Hence, we are finally in the situation where our initial observation becomes applicable: The target alphabet $\{\mathtt{a}, \mathtt{b}\}$ consists of $k = 2$ letters and σ maps $k+1 = 3$ letters to a nonempty word. Thus, $\sigma(1)$ and $\sigma(2)$, $\sigma(1)$ and $\sigma(3)$ or $\sigma(2)$ and $\sigma(3)$ must end with the same letter $c \in \{\mathtt{a}, \mathtt{b}\}$. Assume $\sigma(1) = w_1 c$ and $\sigma(2) = w_2 c$ with $w_1, w_2 \in \{\mathtt{a}, \mathtt{b}\}^*$ (the other cases are analogous), then τ, defined by $\tau(1) := w_1$, $\tau(2) = w_2$, $\tau(x_{\{1,2\}}) = c$, $\tau(3) = \sigma(3)$ and $\tau(y) = \varepsilon$ for all other variables y, satisfies $\tau(\alpha) = \sigma(\alpha)$ and, thus, contradicts σ being unambiguous. ◇

In this example, we see that the limited size of the target alphabet $\{\mathtt{a}, \mathtt{b}\}$ enforces at least two variables in N to be right homogeneous under every morphism σ with $\sigma(x) \neq \varepsilon$ for every $x \in \{1,2,3\}$. We can identify plenty of different other example patterns all having a similar structure, using both left and right homogeneity – even a mixed setting is possible. To this purpose, we introduce the following condition:

Condition 4.30. *Let $k \in \mathbb{N}$, $\alpha \in \mathbb{N}^+$ and (E,N) be the maximal ambiguity partition for α. We say that α* satisfies Condition 4.30 for k and N' *if and only if $N' \subseteq N$ with $|N'| = k\ell + s$ for some $\ell, s \in \mathbb{N}$, $1 \leq s \leq k$, and there exists a partition (N_l, N_r) of N' such that, for all $N'' \subseteq N'$ with $|N''| = \ell + 1$, there exists a morphism $h : \mathbb{N}^* \longrightarrow \mathbb{N}^*$ which satisfies $h(\alpha) = \gamma(\pi_N(\alpha))$ and $h(x) = x$ for an $x \in N''$, where, for $y = \max(\mathrm{var}(\alpha)) + 1$ and for every $x \in \mathbb{N}$, the morphism $\gamma : \mathbb{N}^* \longrightarrow \mathbb{N}^*$ is defined as follows*

$$\gamma(x) := \begin{cases} yx, & \text{if } x \in N'' \cap N_l, \\ xy, & \text{if } x \in N'' \cap N_r, \\ x, & \text{else.} \end{cases}$$

We demonstrate that the pattern α_2 from Example 4.29 satisfies Condition 4.30 for $k = 2$ and $N' := N$: It is $|N'| = 2\ell + s$ with $\ell := 1$ and $s := 1$. Furthermore, let $N_l := \emptyset$, $N_r := \{1,2,3\}$ and $y := \max(\mathrm{var}(\alpha_2)) + 1$. We now consider all subsets $N'' \subseteq N$ consisting of $\ell + 1 = 2$ elements. Let $N'' = \{1,2\}$. The morphism $h : \mathbb{N}^* \longrightarrow \mathbb{N}^*$, defined by $h(1) = 1$, $h(2) = 2$, $h(3) = 3$, $h(x_{\{1,2\}}) = y$ and $h(x) = \varepsilon$ for all other variables x, satisfies $h(\alpha) = 1 \cdot y \cdot 2 \cdot y \cdot 3 \cdot 3 \cdot 2 \cdot y \cdot 1 \cdot y = \gamma(\pi_N(\alpha))$ and $h(x) = x$ for $x = 1 \in N''$. Analogously, morphisms h can be found for $N'' = \{1,3\}$ and $N'' = \{2,3\}$.

The following theorem shows the use of Condition 4.30.

Theorem 4.31. *Let $\alpha \in \mathbb{N}^+$, let Σ be an alphabet with k letters. If α satisfies Condition 4.30 for k and N', then every morphism $\sigma : \mathbb{N}^* \longrightarrow \Sigma^*$ with $\sigma(n) \neq \varepsilon$ for every $n \in N'$ is ambiguous for α.*

Proof. Let (E,N) be the maximal ambiguity partition for α, let Condition 4.30 be satisfied for k and an $N' \subseteq N$ and let y, γ and h be the respective identifiers from Condition 4.30. Assume that there exists an unambiguous morphism $\sigma : \mathbb{N}^* \longrightarrow \Sigma^*$ with $\sigma(n) \neq \varepsilon$ for every $n \in N'$. From Theorem 4.18 we know that $\sigma(e) = \varepsilon$ for all $e \in E$.

First, for every $x \in N'$, let $c_x \in \Sigma$ and $w_x \in \Sigma^*$ such that $\sigma(x) = c_x w_x$ if $x \in N_l$ and $\sigma(x) = w_x c_x$ if $x \in N_r$.

Claim. If a list L contains $k\ell + s$, $1 \leq s \leq k$, elements from an alphabet Σ with $|\Sigma| = k$, then there is a letter $c \in \Sigma$ which occurs at least $\ell + 1$ times in L.

Proof. Assume that every letter $c \in \Sigma$ occurs m_c times in L with $m_c \leq \ell$ for every $c \in \Sigma$. Then, $|L| = \sum_{c \in \Sigma} m_c \leq k\ell < k\ell + s$ since $s \geq 1$, which contradicts $m_c \leq \ell$ for every $c \in \Sigma$.
q. e. d. Claim.

Let L be the list of all c_x, $x \in N'$. It follows from the Claim that there is a subset $N_\star \subseteq N'$ of size at least $\ell + 1$ and a $c \in \Sigma$ such that $c_x = c$ for all $x \in N_\star$. For $\ell = 1$ and $s = 1$, this exactly corresponds to the observation in Example 4.29: If a morphism $\sigma : \mathbb{N}^* \longrightarrow \Sigma^*$ maps at least $k + 1 = k + s$ variables to nonempty words, the images of at least $2 = \ell + 1$ variables $x, y \in \mathbb{N}$ begin (end) with the same letter.

Let $N'' \subseteq N_\star$ with $|N''| = \ell + 1$. For every $x \in \mathrm{var}(\alpha)$, we define the morphism $\tau : \mathbb{N}^* \to \Sigma^*$ as follows:

$$\tau(x) := \begin{cases} c & \text{if } x = y, \\ w_x & \text{if } x \in N'', \\ \sigma(x) & \text{else.} \end{cases}$$

Thus, $\tau(\gamma(x)) = \sigma(x)$ for every $x \in \mathrm{var}(\alpha)$ and, hence, $\tau(h(\alpha)) = \tau(\gamma(\pi_N(\alpha))) = \sigma(\pi_N(\alpha)) = \sigma(\alpha)$, but, for an $x \in N''$, $h(x) = x$ and, thus $\tau(h(x)) = \tau(x) = w_x \neq \sigma(x)$. Consequently, the morphism $\tau \circ h$ contradicts σ being unambiguous. □

Theorem 4.31 does not allow us to directly conclude that there is no unambiguous morphism for a pattern α. Nevertheless, if, for a pattern α, every morphism that maps a variable in N' to the empty word is ambiguous for α, Condition 4.30, satisfied for k and N', is sufficient for the non-existence of an unambiguous morphism $\sigma : \mathbb{N}^* \to \Sigma^*$ with $|\Sigma| = k$. For instance, we can observe this effect for α_2 from Example 4.29 where α_2 exactly shows this behaviour: Every morphism σ with $\sigma(1) = \varepsilon$, $\sigma(2) = \varepsilon$ or $\sigma(3) = \varepsilon$ is ambiguous for $\pi_N(\alpha_2)$ because of the shape of $\pi_N(\alpha_2)$. This structure is generalised in the following lemma.

Lemma 4.32. *Let Σ be an alphabet, $\alpha \in \mathbb{N}^+$ and (E, N) be an ambiguity partition for α such that $\pi_N(\alpha) = \beta_0\gamma_1\beta_1\gamma_2\beta_2 \cdots \gamma_n\beta_n$ for some $n \in \mathbb{N}$ and $\beta_0, \beta_1, \dots, \beta_n, \gamma_1, \gamma_2, \dots, \gamma_n \in \mathbb{N}^*$ such that there exist pairwise distinct variables $i_1, i_2, \dots, i_m \in N$, $m \geq 2$, with*

(i) *for every j, $0 \leq j \leq n$, $\beta_i \in (N \setminus \{i_1, i_2, \dots, i_m\})^*$,*

(ii) *for every j, $1 \leq j \leq n$, there exists an $\ell \in \mathbb{N}$ such that $\gamma_j = i_1^\ell \cdot i_2^\ell \cdot [\dots] \cdot i_m^\ell$ or $\gamma_j = i_m^\ell \cdot i_{m-1}^\ell \cdot [\dots] \cdot i_1^\ell$.*

Then every morphism $\sigma : \mathbb{N}^* \to \Sigma^*$ with $\sigma(i_k) = \varepsilon$ for a $k \in \{1, 2, \dots, m\}$ is strongly ambiguous for α.

Proof. If $\sigma(e) \neq \varepsilon$ for an $e \in E$, it follows from Theorem 4.18 that σ is strongly ambiguous. Hence, let $\sigma(e) = \varepsilon$ for every $e \in E$.

If $k = 1$, then the morphism $\tau : \mathbb{N}^* \to \Sigma_k^*$, defined by $\tau(i_1) = \sigma(i_2)$, $\tau(i_2) = \varepsilon$, $\tau(x) = \sigma(x)$ for all $x \in N \setminus \{i_1, i_2\}$, $\tau(y) = \varepsilon$ for all $y \in E$, satisfies $\tau(\alpha) = \sigma(\alpha)$ and, thus, contradicts σ being unambiguous for α. If $k > 1$ then the morphism $\tau : \mathbb{N}^* \to \Sigma_k^*$, defined by $\tau(i_k) = \sigma(i_{k-1})$, $\tau(i_{k-1}) = \varepsilon$, $\tau(x) = \sigma(x)$ for all $x \in N \setminus \{i_{n-1}, i_n\}$, $\tau(y) = \varepsilon$ for all $y \in E$, satisfies $\tau(\alpha) = \sigma(\alpha)$ and, thus, contradicts σ being unambiguous for α. Furthermore, by Lemma 4.17, σ is strongly ambiguous since $\tau(i_2) = \varepsilon \neq \sigma(i_2)$ or $\tau(i_{k-1}) = \varepsilon \neq \sigma(i_{k-1})$. □

For α_2 from Example 4.29, it is

$$\pi_N(\alpha_2) = \underbrace{\varepsilon}_{\beta_0} \cdot \underbrace{1 \cdot 2 \cdot 3}_{\gamma_1} \cdot \underbrace{\varepsilon}_{\beta_1} \cdot \underbrace{3 \cdot 2 \cdot 1}_{\gamma_2} \cdot \underbrace{\varepsilon}_{\beta_2},$$

and conditions (i) and (ii) of Lemma 4.32 are satisfied with $m = 3$ and $(i_1, i_2, i_3) = (1, 2, 3)$. For a more advanced example, consider a pattern $\alpha \in \mathbb{N}^+$ with

$$\pi_N(\alpha) = \underbrace{1^2}_{\beta_0} \cdot \underbrace{2^4 \cdot 3^4 \cdot 4^4 \cdot 5^4}_{\gamma_1} \cdot \underbrace{1 \cdot 6 \cdot 6}_{\beta_1} \cdot \underbrace{5^2 \cdot 4^2 \cdot 3^2 \cdot 2^2}_{\gamma_2} \cdot \underbrace{\varepsilon}_{\beta_2} \cdot \underbrace{2 \cdot 3 \cdot 4 \cdot 5}_{\gamma_3} \cdot \underbrace{6 \cdot 1}_{\beta_3}$$

which satisfies conditions (i) and (ii) of Lemma 4.32 with $m = 4$ and $(i_1, i_2, i_3, i_4) = (2, 3, 4, 5)$.

Although Condition 4.30 and, thus, Theorem 4.31 seem to be very restrictive, they apply to many example patterns of very different structures. We want to emphasise that it is only necessary to analyse morphically unerasable patterns with the help of Theorem 4.31 (and Lemma 4.32) since we already know from Corollary 4.13 that there is no unambiguous morphism for morphically erasable patterns. Hence, the following example patterns are all morphically unerasable. We give the maximal ambiguity partitions in the examples without the proof of maximality. However, in Section 4.6, an algorithm that, for any pattern α, computes the maximal ambiguity partition for α is given. This algorithm can be consulted to verify the ambiguity partitions in the examples if needed.

We start with an example that is similar to Example 4.29 from the beginning of this section.

Example 4.33. Let $|\Sigma| = k = 2$ and

$$\alpha := \mathbf{1} \cdot 4 \cdot 5 \cdot 4 \cdot 6 \cdot \mathbf{2} \cdot 5 \cdot 6 \cdot \mathbf{3} \cdot 5 \cdot 6 \cdot \mathbf{3} \cdot 4 \cdot 6 \cdot \mathbf{2} \cdot \mathbf{1} \cdot 4 \cdot 5.$$

Then $(E, N) := (\{4, 5, 6\}, \{1, 2, 3\})$ is the maximal ambiguity partition for α. Let $N' := N$, thus, $|N'| = k\ell + s$ with $\ell := 1$, $s := 1$. Let $N_l := \{2, 3\}$, $N_r := \{1\}$ and $y := 7$. We show that Condition 4.30 is satisfied for k and N':

- For $N'' = \{1, 2\}$, the morphism $h : \mathbb{N}^* \to \mathbb{N}^*$ defined by $h(1) := 1$, $h(2) := 2$, $h(3) := 3$, $h(4) := 7$, $h(5) := h(6) := \varepsilon$, satisfies $h(x) = x$ for an $x \in N''$ (e. g., $x = 1$) and $h(\alpha) = 1 \cdot 7 \cdot 7 \cdot 2 \cdot 3 \cdot 3 \cdot 7 \cdot 2 \cdot 1 \cdot 7 = \gamma(\pi_N(\alpha))$ with γ and y defined as in Condition 4.30. Informally speaking, this checks that, if the image of 1 ends with the same letter that the image of 2 begins with, then the variable 4 can "steal" this letter.

- For $N'' = \{1, 3\}$, we define the morphism $h : \mathbb{N}^* \to \mathbb{N}^*$ by $h(1) := 1$, $h(2) := 2$, $h(3) := 3$, $h(4) := \varepsilon$, $h(5) := 7$, $h(6) := \varepsilon$. Hence, $h(x) = x$ for an $x \in N''$ (e. g., $x = 1$) and $h(\alpha) = 1 \cdot 7 \cdot 2 \cdot 7 \cdot 3 \cdot 7 \cdot 3 \cdot 2 \cdot 1 \cdot 7 = \gamma(\pi_N(\alpha))$. Informally speaking, this represents the case that the image of 1 ends with the same letter that the image of 3 begins with. Then, the variable 5 can "steal" this letter.

- Finally, for $N'' = \{2, 3\}$, let $h : \mathbb{N}^* \to \mathbb{N}^*$ be the morphism defined by $h(1) := 1$, $h(2) := 2$, $h(3) := 3$, $h(4) := h(5) := \varepsilon$, $h(6) = 7$. Again, $h(x) = x$ for an $x \in N''$ (e. g., $x = 2$). Furthermore, $h(\alpha) = 1 \cdot 7 \cdot 2 \cdot 7 \cdot 3 \cdot 7 \cdot 3 \cdot 7 \cdot 2 \cdot 1 = \gamma(\pi_N(\alpha))$. Informally speaking, in this case, the images of 2 and 3 begin with the same letter. Thus, the variable 6 can "steal" this letter.

Consequently, the set N_l marks all variables such that other variables can "steal" the leftmost letter of their images and N_r marks all variables such that other variables can "steal" the rightmost letter of their images. Since this can happen for every pair of variables in N' and $|\Sigma| = 2$, no morphism $\sigma : \mathbb{N}^* \to \Sigma^*$ with $\sigma(n) \neq \varepsilon$ for every $n \in N'$ is unambiguous for α (cf. Theorem 4.31).

Furthermore, with $n = 2$, $\beta_0 = \beta_1 = \beta_2 = \varepsilon$, $\gamma_1 = 1 \cdot 2 \cdot 3$ and $\gamma_2 = 3 \cdot 2 \cdot 1$, α satisfies the preconditions of Lemma 4.32. Consequently, there is no unambiguous morphism for α. ◇

We continue showing more examples supporting the importance of the structure described by Condition 4.30. In the next example, we have $N' \neq N$.

Example 4.34. Let $|\Sigma| = k = 2$ and

$$\alpha := \mathbf{1} \cdot \mathbf{2} \cdot 7 \cdot 8 \cdot 9 \cdot 10 \cdot \mathbf{2} \cdot \mathbf{1} \cdot \mathbf{2} \cdot (13 \cdot 14)^2 \cdot \mathbf{3} \cdot \mathbf{4} \cdot 7 \cdot 8 \cdot 11 \cdot 12 \cdot \mathbf{4} \cdot \mathbf{3} \cdot \mathbf{4} \cdot (15 \cdot 16)^2 \cdot \mathbf{5} \cdot \mathbf{6} \cdot 9 \cdot 10 \cdot 11 \cdot 12 \cdot \mathbf{6} \cdot \mathbf{5} \cdot \mathbf{6}.$$

It follows from Lemma 4.6 and Lemma 4.9 that $(E, N) := (\{7, 8, \ldots, 16\}, \{1, 2, \ldots, 6\})$ is an ambiguity partition for α. Furthermore, (E, N) is maximal. Let $N' := \{2, 4, 6\}$, thus, $|N'| = k\ell + s$ with $\ell := 1$, $s := 1$. Let $N_l := N'$, $N_r := \emptyset$ and $y := 17$. We show that Condition 4.30 is satisfied for k and N'.

- For $N'' = \{2, 4\}$, the morphism $h : \mathbb{N}^* \to \mathbb{N}^*$, defined by $h(1) := 1 \cdot y$, $h(2) := 2$, $h(3) := 3 \cdot y$, $h(4) := 4$, $h(5) := 5$, $h(6) := 6$, $h(7) := y$ and $h(x) := \varepsilon$ for all other variables $x \in \mathbb{N}$, satisfies $h(x) = x$ for an $x \in N''$ (e.g., $x = 2$) and $h(\alpha) = 1 \cdot y \cdot 2 \cdot y \cdot 2 \cdot 1 \cdot y \cdot 2 \cdot 3 \cdot y \cdot 4 \cdot y \cdot 4 \cdot 3 \cdot y \cdot 4 \cdot 5 \cdot 6 \cdot 6 \cdot 5 \cdot 6 = \gamma(\pi_N(\alpha))$ with γ and y defined as in Condition 4.30.

- For $N'' = \{2, 6\}$, the morphism $h : \mathbb{N}^* \to \mathbb{N}^*$, defined by $h(1) := 1 \cdot y$, $h(2) := 2$, $h(3) := 3$, $h(4) := 4$, $h(5) := 5 \cdot y$, $h(6) := 6$, $h(9) := y$ and $h(x) := \varepsilon$ for all other variables $x \in \mathbb{N}$, satisfies $h(x) = x$ for an $x \in N''$ (e.g., $x = 2$) and $h(\alpha) = 1 \cdot y \cdot 2 \cdot y \cdot 2 \cdot 1 \cdot y \cdot 2 \cdot 3 \cdot 4 \cdot 4 \cdot 3 \cdot 4 \cdot 5 \cdot y \cdot 6 \cdot y \cdot 6 \cdot 5 \cdot y \cdot 6 = \gamma(\pi_N(\alpha))$.

- For $N'' = \{4, 6\}$, the morphism $h : \mathbb{N}^* \to \mathbb{N}^*$, defined by $h(1) := 1$, $h(2) := 2$, $h(3) := 3 \cdot y$, $h(4) := 4$, $h(5) := 5 \cdot y$, $h(6) := 6$, $h(11) := y$ and $h(x) := \varepsilon$ for all other variables $x \in \mathbb{N}$, satisfies $h(x) = x$ for an $x \in N''$ (e.g., $x = 4$) and $h(\alpha) = 1 \cdot 2 \cdot 2 \cdot 1 \cdot 2 \cdot 3 \cdot y \cdot 4 \cdot y \cdot 4 \cdot 3 \cdot y \cdot 4 \cdot 5 \cdot y \cdot 6 \cdot y \cdot 6 \cdot 5 \cdot y \cdot 6 = \gamma(\pi_N(\alpha))$.

In this example, the interesting point is that also variables from $\{1, 3, 5\} = N \setminus N'$ can be mapped to subpatterns containing y and, thus, "steal" letters from 2, 4, 6, respectively.

Hence, according to Theorem 4.31, no morphism $\sigma : \mathbb{N}^* \to \Sigma^*$ with $\sigma(x) \neq \varepsilon$ for every $x \in \{2, 4, 6\}$ is unambiguous for α. We show in the following that this even implies that no morphism is unambiguous for α. To this purpose, we assume to the contrary that there exists an unambiguous morphism $\sigma : \mathbb{N}^* \to \Sigma^*$ for α with $\sigma(x) = \varepsilon$ for an $x \in \{2, 4, 6\}$. Since (E, N) is an ambiguity partition for α, $\sigma(e) = \varepsilon$ for every $e \in E$ must be satisfied as well (cf. Theorem 4.18). Now, if $\sigma(2) = \varepsilon$, the morphism $\tau : \mathbb{N}^* \to \Sigma^*$, defined by $\tau(13) := \sigma(1)$, $\tau(x) := \sigma(x)$ for every $x \in \{3, 4, 5, 6\}$ and $\tau(x) := \varepsilon$ for every other variable x, satisfies $\tau(\alpha) = \sigma(\alpha)$ and, thus, contradicts σ being unambiguous. If $\sigma(4) = \varepsilon$, we consider the morphism $\tau : \mathbb{N}^* \to \Sigma^*$, defined by $\tau(13) := \sigma(3)$, $\tau(x) := \sigma(x)$ for every $x \in \{1, 2, 5, 6\}$ and $\tau(x) := \varepsilon$ for every other variable x. Again, $\tau(\alpha) = \sigma(\alpha)$ and, thus, σ is not unambiguous. Finally, if $\sigma(6) = \varepsilon$, let $\tau : \mathbb{N}^* \to \Sigma^*$ be the morphism defined by $\tau(15) := \sigma(5)$, $\tau(x) := \sigma(x)$ for every $x \in \{1, 2, 3, 4\}$ and $\tau(x) := \varepsilon$ for every other variable x. Hence, $\tau(\alpha) = \sigma(\alpha)$ and, thus, τ contradicts σ being unambiguous. Consequently, no morphism is unambiguous for α. ◇

The following example shows that variables in E can "steal" letters which are identical due to the homogeneity of the morphism from more than only two variables.

Example 4.35. Let $|\Sigma| = k = 2$ and

$$\begin{aligned}\beta_1 &:= \mathbf{1} \cdot 6 \cdot 7 \cdot 8 \cdot 9 \cdot 10 \cdot 11,\\ \beta_2 &:= \mathbf{2} \cdot 6 \cdot 7 \cdot 8 \cdot 12 \cdot 13 \cdot 14,\\ \beta_3 &:= \mathbf{3} \cdot 6 \cdot 9 \cdot 10 \cdot 12 \cdot 13 \cdot 15,\\ \beta_4 &:= \mathbf{4} \cdot 7 \cdot 9 \cdot 11 \cdot 12 \cdot 14 \cdot 15,\\ \beta_5 &:= \mathbf{5} \cdot 8 \cdot 10 \cdot 11 \cdot 13 \cdot 14 \cdot 15,\end{aligned}$$

and, finally,

$$\alpha := \beta_1 \cdot \beta_2 \cdot \beta_3 \cdot \beta_4 \cdot \beta_5 \cdot \beta_5 \cdot \beta_4 \cdot \beta_3 \cdot \beta_2 \cdot \beta_1.$$

Then $(E, N) := (\{6, 7, \ldots, 15\}, \{1, 2, \ldots, 5\})$ is the maximal ambiguity partition for α. Let $N' := N$, thus, $|N'| = k\ell + s$ with $\ell := 2$, $s := 1$. Let $N_l := \emptyset$, $N_r := N'$ and $y := 16$. We show that Condition 4.30 is satisfied for k and N' by exemplarily choosing $N'' = \{1, 2, 4\}$ (the other cases are analogous): In this case, the morphism $h : \mathbb{N}^* \to \mathbb{N}^*$, defined by $h(1) := 1$, $h(2) := 2$, $h(3) := 3$, $h(4) := 4$, $h(5) := 5$, $h(7) := y$ and $h(x) := \varepsilon$ for all other variables $x \in \mathbb{N}$, satisfies $h(x) = x$ for an $x \in N''$ (e. g., $x = 1$) and $h(\alpha) = 1 \cdot y \cdot 2 \cdot y \cdot 3 \cdot 4 \cdot y \cdot 5 \cdot 5 \cdot 4 \cdot y \cdot 3 \cdot 2 \cdot y \cdot 1 \cdot y = \gamma(\pi_N(\alpha))$. Thus, it follows from Theorem 4.31 that no morphism σ with $\sigma(x) \neq \varepsilon$ for every $x \in N' = N$ is unambiguous for α. Indeed, for every set $N'' \subseteq N'$ with $\ell + 1 = 3$ variables, there exists a variable which can "steal" the rightmost letter from the images of the variables in N''.

Furthermore, it is $\pi_N(\alpha) = \beta_0 \gamma_1 \beta_1 \gamma_2 \beta_2$ with $\gamma_1 = 1 \cdot 2 \cdot 3 \cdot 4 \cdot 5$, $\gamma_2 = 5 \cdot 4 \cdot 3 \cdot 2 \cdot 1$ and $\beta_0 := \beta_1 := \beta_2 := \varepsilon$, and this factorisation satisfies the conditions of Lemma 4.32. Consequently, no morphism is unambiguous for α. ◇

The next example follows the same principle as Example 4.35, but is a bit more involved.

Example 4.36. Let $|\Sigma| = k = 2$ and

$$\begin{aligned}\beta_1 := {} & \mathbf{1} \cdot x_{\{1,2,3,4\}} \cdot x_{\{1,2,3,5\}} \cdot x_{\{1,2,3,6\}} \cdot x_{\{1,2,3,7\}} \cdot x_{\{1,2,4,5\}} \cdot x_{\{1,2,4,6\}} \cdot x_{\{1,2,4,7\}} \cdot\\ & x_{\{1,2,5,6\}} \cdot x_{\{1,2,5,7\}} \cdot x_{\{1,2,6,7\}} \cdot x_{\{1,3,4,5\}} \cdot x_{\{1,3,4,6\}} \cdot x_{\{1,3,4,7\}} \cdot\\ & x_{\{1,3,5,6\}} \cdot x_{\{1,3,5,7\}} \cdot x_{\{1,3,6,7\}} \cdot x_{\{1,4,5,6\}} \cdot x_{\{1,4,5,7\}} \cdot x_{\{1,4,6,7\}} \cdot x_{\{1,5,6,7\}},\\ \beta_2 := {} & x_{\{1,2,3,5\}} \cdot x_{\{1,2,3,6\}} \cdot x_{\{1,2,3,7\}} \cdot x_{\{1,2,4,5\}} \cdot x_{\{1,2,4,6\}} \cdot x_{\{1,2,4,7\}}\\ & \cdot x_{\{1,2,5,6\}} \cdot x_{\{1,2,5,7\}} \cdot x_{\{1,2,6,7\}} \cdot x_{\{2,3,4,5\}} \cdot x_{\{2,3,4,6\}} \cdot x_{\{2,3,4,7\}} \cdot x_{\{2,3,5,6\}} \cdot\\ & x_{\{2,3,5,7\}} \cdot x_{\{2,3,6,7\}} \cdot x_{\{2,4,5,6\}} \cdot x_{\{2,4,5,7\}} \cdot x_{\{2,4,6,7\}} \cdot x_{\{2,5,6,7\}} \cdot \mathbf{2},\\ \beta_3 := {} & \mathbf{3} \cdot x_{\{1,2,3,4\}} \cdot x_{\{1,2,3,5\}} \cdot x_{\{1,2,3,6\}} \cdot x_{\{1,2,3,7\}} \cdot x_{\{1,3,4,5\}} \cdot x_{\{1,3,4,6\}} \cdot x_{\{1,3,4,7\}} \cdot\\ & x_{\{1,3,5,6\}} \cdot x_{\{1,3,5,7\}} \cdot x_{\{1,3,6,7\}} \cdot x_{\{2,3,4,5\}} \cdot x_{\{2,3,4,6\}} \cdot x_{\{2,3,4,7\}} \cdot x_{\{2,3,5,6\}} \cdot\\ & x_{\{2,3,5,7\}} \cdot x_{\{2,3,6,7\}} \cdot x_{\{3,4,5,6\}} \cdot x_{\{3,4,5,7\}} \cdot x_{\{3,4,6,7\}} \cdot x_{\{3,5,6,7\}},\\ \beta_4 := {} & x_{\{1,2,4,5\}} \cdot x_{\{1,2,4,6\}} \cdot x_{\{1,2,4,7\}} \cdot x_{\{1,3,4,5\}} \cdot x_{\{1,3,4,6\}} \cdot x_{\{1,3,4,7\}} \cdot\\ & x_{\{1,4,5,6\}} \cdot x_{\{1,4,5,7\}} \cdot x_{\{1,4,6,7\}} \cdot x_{\{2,3,4,5\}} \cdot x_{\{2,3,4,6\}} \cdot x_{\{2,3,4,7\}} \cdot x_{\{2,4,5,6\}} \cdot\\ & x_{\{2,4,5,7\}} \cdot x_{\{2,4,6,7\}} \cdot x_{\{3,4,5,6\}} \cdot x_{\{3,4,5,7\}} \cdot x_{\{3,4,6,7\}} \cdot x_{\{4,5,6,7\}} \cdot \mathbf{4},\\ \beta_5 := {} & \mathbf{5} \cdot x_{\{1,2,3,5\}} \cdot x_{\{1,2,4,5\}} \cdot x_{\{1,2,5,6\}} \cdot x_{\{1,2,5,7\}} \cdot x_{\{1,3,4,5\}} \cdot x_{\{1,3,5,6\}} \cdot x_{\{1,3,5,7\}} \cdot\\ & x_{\{1,4,5,6\}} \cdot x_{\{1,4,5,7\}} \cdot x_{\{1,5,6,7\}} \cdot x_{\{2,3,4,5\}} \cdot x_{\{2,3,5,6\}} \cdot x_{\{2,3,5,7\}} \cdot x_{\{2,4,5,6\}} \cdot\\ & x_{\{2,4,5,7\}} \cdot x_{\{2,5,6,7\}} \cdot x_{\{3,4,5,6\}} \cdot x_{\{3,4,5,7\}} \cdot x_{\{3,5,6,7\}} \cdot x_{\{4,5,6,7\}},\end{aligned}$$

$$\begin{aligned}\beta_6 &:= \mathbf{6} \cdot x_{\{1,2,3,6\}} \cdot x_{\{1,2,4,6\}} \cdot x_{\{1,2,5,6\}} \cdot x_{\{1,2,6,7\}} \cdot x_{\{1,3,4,6\}} \cdot x_{\{1,3,5,6\}} \cdot x_{\{1,3,6,7\}} \cdot \\ &\quad x_{\{1,4,5,6\}} \cdot x_{\{1,4,6,7\}} \cdot x_{\{1,5,6,7\}} \cdot x_{\{2,3,4,6\}} \cdot x_{\{2,3,5,6\}} \cdot x_{\{2,3,6,7\}} \cdot x_{\{2,4,5,6\}} \cdot \\ &\quad x_{\{2,4,6,7\}} \cdot x_{\{2,5,6,7\}} \cdot x_{\{3,4,5,6\}} \cdot x_{\{3,4,6,7\}} \cdot x_{\{3,5,6,7\}} \cdot x_{\{4,5,6,7\}}, \\ \beta_7 &:= \mathbf{7} \cdot x_{\{1,2,3,7\}} \cdot x_{\{1,2,4,7\}} \cdot x_{\{1,2,5,7\}} \cdot x_{\{1,2,6,7\}} \cdot x_{\{1,3,4,7\}} \cdot x_{\{1,3,5,7\}} \cdot x_{\{1,3,6,7\}} \cdot \\ &\quad x_{\{1,4,5,7\}} \cdot x_{\{1,4,6,7\}} \cdot x_{\{1,5,6,7\}} \cdot x_{\{2,3,4,7\}} \cdot x_{\{2,3,5,7\}} \cdot x_{\{2,3,6,7\}} \cdot x_{\{2,4,5,7\}} \cdot \\ &\quad x_{\{2,4,6,7\}} \cdot x_{\{2,5,6,7\}} \cdot x_{\{3,4,5,7\}} \cdot x_{\{3,4,6,7\}} \cdot x_{\{3,5,6,7\}} \cdot x_{\{4,5,6,7\}},\end{aligned}$$

and, finally,

$$\alpha := \beta_1 \cdot \beta_2 \cdot \beta_3 \cdot \beta_4 \cdot \beta_5 \cdot \beta_6 \cdot \beta_7 \cdot \beta_7 \cdot \beta_6 \cdot \beta_5 \cdot \beta_4 \cdot \beta_3 \cdot \beta_2 \cdot \beta_1,$$

where all $x_{\dots}$ and $y_{\dots}$ are pairwise distinct variables from $\mathbb{N} \setminus \{1, 2, \dots, 7\}$.

Then with $N := \{1, 2, \dots, 7\}$ and $E := \mathrm{var}(\alpha) \setminus N$, (E, N) is the maximal ambiguity partition for α. Let $N' := N$, thus, $|N'| = k\ell + s$ with $\ell := 3$, $s := 1$. Let $N_l := \{2, 4\}$, $N_r := N' \setminus N_l$ and $y := \max(\mathrm{var}(\alpha)) + 1$. This is mostly a standard example showing that, if a morphism σ maps $k\ell + s = 7$ variables to nonempty words over a binary alphabet then $l + 1 = 4$ variables begin/end with the same letter. Thus, it is not difficult to verify that Condition 4.30 is satisfied for k and N'. However, this example has one specific feature: While almost every $x_{\dots}$ occurs eight times in α, $x_{\{1,2,3,4\}}$ occurs only four times. Now, let us consider the case that $N'' = \{1, 2, 3, 4\}$. Then, the morphism $h : \mathbb{N}^* \to \mathbb{N}^*$, defined by $h(x_{\{1,2,3,4\}}) = y \cdot y$, $h(n) = n$ for every $n \in N$, $h(e) = \varepsilon$ for every $e \in E$, satisfies $h(1) = 1$ for $1 \in N''$ and $h(\alpha) = \gamma(\alpha)$. Thus, provided that $\sigma(1)$ and $\sigma(3)$ end with the same letter that $\sigma(2)$ and $\sigma(4)$ begin with, $x_{\{1,2,3,4\}}$ can "steal" both a beginning and an ending letter at the same time. Consequently, $x_{\{1,2,3,4\}}$ is only "needed" four times in total in α.

Thus, Theorem 4.31 can be applied and, hence, $\sigma(n) = \varepsilon$ for an $n \in N$. But since $\pi_N(\alpha) = \beta_0 \gamma_1 \beta_1 \gamma_2 \beta_2$ with $\gamma_1 := 1 \cdot 2 \cdot 3 \cdot 4 \cdot 5 \cdot 6 \cdot 7$, $\gamma_2 := 7 \cdot 6 \cdot 5 \cdot 4 \cdot 3 \cdot 2 \cdot 1$ and $\beta_0 := \beta_1 := \beta_2 := \varepsilon$, we can apply Lemma 4.32 and, thus, conclude that there is no unambiguous morphism for α. ◇

We continue with another example whose structure of the N-variables follows a well-known pattern (cf. Example 3.2).

Example 4.37. Let $|\Sigma| = k = 2$ and

$$\alpha := 4 \cdot 5 \cdot \mathbf{1} \cdot 4 \cdot \mathbf{2} \cdot 5 \cdot \mathbf{3} \cdot 4 \cdot 5 \cdot \mathbf{1} \cdot 4 \cdot \mathbf{2} \cdot 4 \cdot \mathbf{2} \cdot 5 \cdot \mathbf{3}.$$

Then $(E, N) := (\{4, 5\}, \{1, 2, 3\})$ is the maximal ambiguity partition for α. Let $N' := N$, thus, $|N'| = k\ell + s$ with $\ell := 1$, $s := 1$. Let $N_l := \{1, 2, 3\}$, $N_r := \emptyset$ and $y := 6$. We show that Condition 4.30 is satisfied for k and N':

- For $N'' = \{1, 2\}$, the morphism $h : \mathbb{N}^* \to \mathbb{N}^*$, defined by $h(1) := 1$, $h(2) := 2$, $h(3) := 3$, $h(4) := y$, $h(5) := \varepsilon$, satisfies $h(1) = 1$ for $1 \in N''$ and $h(\alpha) = y \cdot 1 \cdot y \cdot 2 \cdot 3 \cdot y \cdot 1 \cdot y \cdot 2 \cdot y \cdot 2 \cdot 3 = \gamma(\alpha)$.
- For $N'' = \{1, 3\}$, we define a morphism $h : \mathbb{N}^* \to \mathbb{N}^*$ by $h(1) := 1$, $h(2) := 2$, $h(3) := 3$, $h(4) := \varepsilon$, $h(5) := y$. Thus, $h(1) = 1$ for $1 \in N''$ and $h(\alpha) = y \cdot 1 \cdot 2 \cdot y \cdot 3 \cdot y \cdot 1 \cdot 2 \cdot 2 \cdot y \cdot 3 = \gamma(\alpha)$.

- For $N'' = \{2,3\}$, let the morphism $h : \mathbb{N}^* \to \mathbb{N}^*$ be defined by $h(1) := 1 \cdot y$, $h(2) := 2 \cdot y$, $h(3) := 3$, $h(4) := h(5) := \varepsilon$. Hence, $h(3) = 3$ for $3 \in N''$ and $h(\alpha) = 1 \cdot y \cdot 2 \cdot y \cdot 3 \cdot 1 \cdot y \cdot 2 \cdot y \cdot 2 \cdot y \cdot 3 = \gamma(\alpha)$. This case is particularly interesting since here even two variables of N' can "steal" a common letter from the beginning of $\sigma(2)$ and $\sigma(3)$. Note that $\pi_N(\alpha)$ has an SCRN-factorisation (cf. Definition 3.10) and, thus, has a structure which is well known and investigated in the research on the ambiguity of morphisms.

Consequently, due to Theorem 4.31, no morphism which maps 1, 2 and 3 to nonempty words is unambiguous for α. However, the morphism $\sigma : \mathbb{N}^* \to \Sigma^*$, defined by $\sigma(1) = \varepsilon$, $\sigma(2) = \mathtt{a}$ and $\sigma(3) = \mathtt{b}$ is unambiguous for α. ◇

An example which is similar to the previous one, but where $\pi_N(\alpha)$ has no SCRN-factorisation can be given as follows.

Example 4.38. Let $|\Sigma| = k = 2$ and

$$\alpha := 4 \cdot 5 \cdot \mathbf{1} \cdot 4 \cdot \mathbf{2} \cdot 6 \cdot 7 \cdot 4 \cdot \mathbf{2} \cdot 4 \cdot 5 \cdot \mathbf{1} \cdot 5 \cdot \mathbf{3} \cdot 6 \cdot 7 \cdot 5 \cdot \mathbf{3}.$$

Then $(E, N) := (\{4,5,6,7\}, \{1,2,3\})$ is the maximal ambiguity partition for α. Let $N' := N$, thus, $|N'| = k\ell + s$ with $\ell := 1$, $s := 1$. Let $N_l := \{1,2,3\}$, $N_r := \emptyset$ and $y := 8$. We show that Condition 4.30 is satisfied for k and N':

- For $N'' = \{1,2\}$, the morphism $h : \mathbb{N}^* \to \mathbb{N}^*$, defined by $h(1) := 1$, $h(2) := 2$, $h(3) := 3$, $h(4) := y$, $h(5) := h(6) := h(7) := \varepsilon$, satisfies $h(1) = 1$ for $1 \in N''$ and $h(\alpha) = y \cdot 1 \cdot y \cdot 2 \cdot y \cdot 2 \cdot y \cdot 1 \cdot 3 \cdot 3 = \gamma(\alpha)$.

- For $N'' = \{1,3\}$, the morphism $h : \mathbb{N}^* \to \mathbb{N}^*$, defined by $h(1) := 1$, $h(2) := 2$, $h(3) := 3$, $h(4) := \varepsilon$, $h(5) := y$, $h(6) := h(7) := \varepsilon$, satisfies $h(1) = 1$ for $1 \in N''$ and $h(\alpha) = y \cdot 1 \cdot 2 \cdot 2 \cdot y \cdot 1 \cdot y \cdot 3 \cdot y \cdot 3 = \gamma(\alpha)$.

- For $N'' = \{2,3\}$, the morphism $h : \mathbb{N}^* \to \mathbb{N}^*$, defined by $h(1) := 1 \cdot y$, $h(2) := 2$, $h(3) := 3$, $h(4) := h(5) := \varepsilon$, $h(6) := y$, $h(7) := \varepsilon$, satisfies $h(3) = 3$ for $3 \in N''$ and $h(\alpha) = 1 \cdot y \cdot 2 \cdot y \cdot 2 \cdot 1 \cdot y \cdot 3 \cdot y \cdot 3 = \gamma(\alpha)$. This third case again is a very interesting one since here even one variable of N' and another from E can "steal" a common letter from the beginning of $\sigma(2)$ and $\sigma(3)$.

Consequently, due to Theorem 4.31, no morphism which maps 1, 2 and 3 to nonempty words is unambiguous for α. However, the morphism $\sigma : \mathbb{N}^* \to \Sigma^*$, defined by $\sigma(1) = \mathtt{a}$, $\sigma(2) = \mathtt{b}$ and $\sigma(3) = \varepsilon$ is unambiguous for α. ◇

Finally, we present an example showing that the number of N-variables from which are "stolen" does not need to be the same for every set N'' in Condition 4.30.

Example 4.39. Let $|\Sigma| = k = 2$ and let

$$\alpha := \beta_1^2 \cdot \beta_2^2 \cdot \beta_3^2 \cdot \beta_4^2 \cdot \beta_5^2,$$

with

$$\begin{aligned}
\beta_1 &:= \mathbf{1} \cdot x_{\{1,2\}} \cdot x_{\{1,3,4\}} \cdot x_{\{1,3,5\}}, \\
\beta_2 &:= \mathbf{2} \cdot x_{\{1,2\}} \cdot x_{\{2,3,4\}} \cdot x_{\{2,3,5\}}, \\
\beta_3 &:= \mathbf{3} \cdot x_{\{1,3,4\}} \cdot x_{\{1,3,5\}} \cdot x_{\{2,3,4\}} \cdot x_{\{2,3,5\}} \cdot x_{\{3,4,5\}}, \\
\beta_4 &:= \mathbf{4} \cdot x_{\{1,3,4\}} \cdot x_{\{2,3,4\}} \cdot x_{\{3,4,5\}}, \\
\beta_5 &:= \mathbf{5} \cdot x_{\{1,3,5\}} \cdot x_{\{2,3,5\}} \cdot x_{\{3,4,5\}},
\end{aligned}$$

where all $x_{\dots}$ are pairwise distinct variables from $\mathbb{N} \setminus \{1,2,3,4,5\}$.

Then with $N := \{1,2,3,4,5\}$ and $E := \text{var}(\alpha) \setminus N$, (E, N) is the maximal ambiguity partition for α. Let $N' := N$, thus, $|N'| = k\ell + s$ with $\ell := 2$, $s := 1$. Let $N_l := \emptyset$, $N_r := N'$ and $y := \max(\text{var}(\alpha)) + 1$. We show that Condition 4.30 is satisfied for k and N'.

- For $N'' = \{1,2,z\}$, $z \in N' \setminus \{1,2\}$, the morphism $h : \mathbb{N}^* \to \mathbb{N}^*$, defined by $h(1) := 1$, $h(2) := 2$, $h(z) := z \cdot y$, $h(n) := n$, for every $n \in N' \setminus \{1,2,z\}$, $h(x_{\{1,2\}}) := y$ and $h(x) := \varepsilon$ for all other variables $x \in \mathbb{N}$, satisfies $h(x) = x$ for an $x \in N''$ (e. g., $x = 1$) and $h(\alpha) = \gamma(\pi_N(\alpha))$ with γ defined as in Condition 4.30. Here, only the y's behind 1 and 2 are generated by an E-variable, namely by $x_{\{1,2\}}$ which, thus, only "steals" from two variables. If, e. g., $z = 5$, we have $h(\alpha) = 1{\cdot}y{\cdot}2{\cdot}y{\cdot}3{\cdot}4{\cdot}5{\cdot}y{\cdot}5{\cdot}y{\cdot}4{\cdot}3{\cdot}2{\cdot}y{\cdot}1{\cdot}y = \gamma(\pi_N(\alpha))$.
- For $N'' \subseteq N'$ with $\{1,2\} \not\subseteq N''$, the morphism $h : \mathbb{N}^* \to \mathbb{N}^*$, defined by $h(n) := n$ for every $n \in N'$, $h(x_{N''}) := y$ and $h(x) := \varepsilon$ for all other variables $x \in \mathbb{N}$, satisfies $h(x) = x$ for all $x \in N''$ and $h(\alpha) = \gamma(\pi_N(\alpha))$. Here, all the y's behind the variables from N'' are generated by an E-variable, namely by $x_{N''}$ which, thus, "steals" from three variables.

Consequently, due to Theorem 4.31, no morphism which maps all the variables $1,2,3,4,5$ to nonempty words is unambiguous for α. But since $\pi_N(\alpha) = \gamma_1 := i_1^l \cdot i_2^l \cdot [\dots] \cdot i_m^l$ with $m = 5$, $\ell = 2$ and $\{i_1, i_2, \dots, i_m\} = \{1,2,3,4,5\}$, we can apply Lemma 4.32 and, thus, conclude that there is no unambiguous morphism for α.

A similar example pattern can be given by defining

$$\begin{aligned}
\beta_1 &:= \mathbf{1} \cdot x_{\{1,2\}} \cdot x_{\{1,3\}} \cdot x_{\{1,4\}} \cdot x_{\{1,5\}}, \\
\beta_2 &:= \mathbf{2} \cdot x_{\{1,2\}} \cdot x_{\{2,3,4\}} \cdot x_{\{2,3,5\}}, \\
\beta_3 &:= \mathbf{3} \cdot x_{\{1,3\}} \cdot x_{\{2,3,4\}} \cdot x_{\{2,3,5\}} \cdot x_{\{3,4,5\}}, \\
\beta_4 &:= \mathbf{4} \cdot x_{\{1,4\}} \cdot x_{\{2,3,4\}} \cdot x_{\{3,4,5\}}, \\
\beta_5 &:= \mathbf{5} \cdot x_{\{1,5\}} \cdot x_{\{2,3,5\}} \cdot x_{\{3,4,5\}},
\end{aligned}$$

where variables $x_{\{n_1,n_2\}}$ "steal" from two N-variables, while variables $x_{\{n_1,n_2,n_3\}}$ "steal" from three N-variables. ◇

All these examples show how different patterns can be for which we can apply Theorem 4.31. Although the underlying principle is the same – ambiguity is caused by homogeneous morphic images of some variables – the detailed interplay of different "stealing" E-variables (and sometimes also N-variables) strongly differs, which illustrates the combinatorial variety of the structure of patterns without an unambiguous erasing morphism.

We want to note that all examples can be adapted to a larger size of the target alphabet Σ.

It is an interesting question if the ambiguity phenomenon described in Condition 4.30 and Theorem 4.31 is the only one leading to target alphabet dependent ambiguity. We discuss this question in the next section where we concentrate on the number of unambiguous morphisms for a given pattern.

4.4.2 Finitely many unambiguous morphisms

In this section, we specify our overall question in the following manner: We do not only investigate whether or not, for a given pattern, there *exists* a morphism with a restricted ambiguity, we also want to know *how many* such morphisms there are. Concerning moderate ambiguity, the existence of one moderately ambiguous morphism for a given pattern immediately implies an infinite number of such morphisms:

Theorem 4.40. *Let $\alpha \in \mathbb{N}^+$ and let Σ be an alphabet with $|\Sigma| \geq 2$. If there exists a moderately ambiguous morphism $\sigma : \mathbb{N}^* \to \Sigma^*$ for α, there exist infinitely many morphisms $\tau_1, \tau_2, \tau_3, \ldots$ such that, for every $i \in \mathbb{N}$, τ_i is moderately ambiguous for α and, for every $i, j \in \mathbb{N}$ with $i \neq j$ and for every $x \in \text{var}(\alpha)$ with $\sigma(x) \neq \varepsilon$, $\tau_i(x) \neq \tau_j(x)$.*

Proof. The morphism σ in the proof of Theorem 4.20 can easily be generalised in the following way:

$$\sigma(i) := \begin{cases} \mathtt{ab}^{m((i-1)(2n+1)+1)}\mathtt{aab}^{m((i-1)(2n+1)+2)}\mathtt{a}[\ldots]\mathtt{ab}^{m(i(2n+1))}\mathtt{a}, & \text{if } i \in N, \\ \varepsilon, & \text{else,} \end{cases}$$

for every $i \in \mathbb{N}$ and an arbitrary $m \in \mathbb{N}$. For every m, this morphism σ is moderately ambiguous for α if there exists a moderately ambiguous morphism for α at all, which can be proved exactly like Theorem 4.20 since, in that proof, it is only important that $\sigma(i) = \ldots \mathtt{ab}^y\mathtt{a} \ldots = \sigma(j)$, $y \in \mathbb{N}$, implies $i = j$. Obviously, this is guaranteed by every σ for every $m \in \mathbb{N}$. □

We want to note that the existence of τ_1, τ_2, etc. is trivial if we omit the second requirement ($\tau_i(x) \neq \tau_j(x)$).

Concerning the *unambiguity* of erasing morphisms, the situation is much more interesting. Thus, we now study unambiguous morphisms. To this end, we introduce the following notation which addresses both erasing and nonerasing morphisms since we plan to compare the results for both types of morphisms.

Definition 4.41 ($\text{UNAMB}_\Sigma(\alpha)/\text{UNAMB}_{\text{NE},\Sigma}(\alpha)$)**.** *Let Σ be an alphabet and $\alpha \in \mathbb{N}^+$. Then $\text{UNAMB}_\Sigma(\alpha)$ is the set of all $\sigma(\alpha)$, where $\sigma : \mathbb{N}^* \to \Sigma^*$ is a morphism that is unambiguous for α, and $\text{UNAMB}_{\text{NE},\Sigma}(\alpha)$ is the set of all $\sigma(\alpha)$, where $\sigma : \mathbb{N}^* \to \Sigma^*$ is a morphism that is nonerasing and unambiguous for α.*

We wish to point out that the existence of one unambiguous morphism $\sigma : \mathbb{N}^* \to \Sigma^*$ for a pattern α trivially implies the existence infinitely many other morphisms $\tau_i : \mathbb{N}^* \to \Sigma^*$, $i \in \mathbb{N}$, by defining $\tau_i(x) := \sigma(x) \cdot c^i$ for a letter $c \in \Sigma$ and a variable $x \notin \text{var}(\alpha)$ and $\tau(y) := y$ for every $y \neq x$. Therefore, the sets $\text{UNAMB}_\Sigma(\alpha)$ and $\text{UNAMB}_{\text{NE},\Sigma}(\alpha)$ do not consist of morphisms, but of morphic images. This makes sure that all unambiguous morphisms indirectly collected by these sets necessarily differ on variables that are contained in $\mathrm{var}(\alpha)$.

We first consider the case of *nonerasing* morphisms.

Theorem 4.42. *Let $\alpha \in \mathbb{N}^+$. Either, for all alphabets Σ with $|\Sigma| \geq 2$, $\mathrm{UNAMB}_{\mathrm{NE},\Sigma}(\alpha)$ is empty or, for all alphabets Σ with $|\Sigma| \geq 2$, $\mathrm{UNAMB}_{\mathrm{NE},\Sigma}(\alpha)$ is infinite.*

Proof. Theorem 10 by Freydenberger et al. [8] states that $\mathrm{UNAMB}_{\mathrm{NE},\Sigma}(\alpha) = \emptyset$ for morphically imprimitive patterns α. For any morphically primitive pattern α, Definition 21 in [8] introduces a morphism $\sigma_\alpha^{\mathrm{su}} : \mathbb{N}^* \to \{\mathtt{a}, \mathtt{b}\}^*$ by, for every $k \in \mathbb{N}$,

$$\sigma_\alpha^{\mathrm{su}}(k) := \begin{cases} \mathtt{ab}^{3k}\mathtt{a}\ \mathtt{ab}^{3k+1}\mathtt{a}\ \mathtt{ab}^{3k+2}\mathtt{a}\,, & \forall\, i : k \neq \min L_i^\sim \,\wedge\, \forall\, i' : k \neq \min R_{i'}^\sim, \\ \mathtt{ba}^{3k}\mathtt{b}\ \mathtt{ab}^{3k+1}\mathtt{a}\ \mathtt{ab}^{3k+2}\mathtt{a}\,, & \forall\, i : k \neq \min L_i^\sim \,\wedge\, \exists\, i' : k = \min R_{i'}^\sim, \\ \mathtt{ab}^{3k}\mathtt{a}\ \mathtt{ab}^{3k+1}\mathtt{a}\ \mathtt{ba}^{3k+2}\mathtt{b}\,, & \exists\, i : k = \min L_i^\sim \,\wedge\, \forall\, i' : k \neq \min R_{i'}^\sim, \\ \mathtt{ba}^{3k}\mathtt{b}\ \mathtt{ab}^{3k+1}\mathtt{a}\ \mathtt{ba}^{3k+2}\mathtt{b}\,, & \exists\, i : k = \min L_i^\sim \,\wedge\, \exists\, i' : k = \min R_{i'}^\sim, \end{cases}$$

where the $L_i^\sim$ and $R_{i'}^\sim$ are equivalence classes over $\mathrm{var}(\alpha)$ and depend on the structure of α. This morphism is unambiguous for α (cf. Theorem 16 in [8]). However, the proof for Theorem 16 in [8] does not make use of the actual values $3k$, $3k+1$ and $3k+2$, but it is only required that, for every k, these three values are unique. Hence, we can use the same idea as in the proof of Theorem 4.40 and modify $\sigma_\alpha^{\mathrm{su}}$ in infinitely many ways by substituting $m3k$ for $3k$, $m(3k+1)$ for $3k+1$, $m(3k+2)$ for $3k+2$, where $m \in \mathbb{N}$ is arbitrarily chosen. The resulting morphism is then still unambiguous for α. □

If we study the equivalent question for the ambiguity of *erasing* morphisms, we can observe a novel phenomenon that establishes a further difference to the case of nonerasing morphisms. More precisely, for certain patterns α, the cardinality of $\mathrm{UNAMB}_\Sigma(\alpha)$ can be finite, and this essentially depends on the size of Σ:

Theorem 4.43. *Let $k \in \mathbb{N}$. Let $\Sigma_k, \Sigma_{k+1}, \Sigma_{k+2}$ be alphabets with $k, k+1, k+2$ letters, respectively. There exists an $\alpha_k \in \mathbb{N}^+$ such that*

(i) $\mathrm{UNAMB}_{\Sigma_k}(\alpha_k)$ *is empty,*

(ii) $\mathrm{UNAMB}_{\Sigma_{k+1}}(\alpha_k)$ *is a nonempty, finite set, and*

(iii) $\mathrm{UNAMB}_{\Sigma_{k+2}}(\alpha_k)$ *is an infinite set.*

Proof. We define α_k as follows:

$$\alpha_k := \beta_1\beta_2 \dots \beta_{k+1}\beta_{k+1}\beta_k \dots \beta_1$$

with

$$\beta_i := \prod_{\substack{(j,m)\in \\ \{1,2,\dots,k+1\}\times\{\mathrm{le},\mathrm{ri}\}\setminus\{(i,\mathrm{le})\}}} x_{\{(i,\mathrm{le}),(j,m)\}} \cdot i \cdot \prod_{\substack{(j,m)\in \\ \{1,2,\dots,k+1\}\times\{\mathrm{le},\mathrm{ri}\}\setminus\{(i,\mathrm{ri})\}}} x_{\{(i,\mathrm{ri}),(j,m)\}},$$

where, for all indices S, the x_S are distinct variables taken from $\mathbb{N} \setminus \{1, 2, \dots, k+1\}$[‡].

[‡]Note that the order of the pairs $(j, m) \in \{1, 2, \dots, k+1\} \times \{\mathrm{le}, \mathrm{ri}\} \setminus \{(i, \mathrm{le})\}$ can be arbitrarily chosen when composing β_i. The same holds for the order of the pairs $(j, m) \in \{1, 2, \dots, k+1\} \times \{\mathrm{le}, \mathrm{ri}\} \setminus \{(i, \mathrm{ri})\}$.

For instance,

$$\begin{aligned}\alpha_2 \;=\; & x_{\{(1,\text{le}),(1,\text{ri})\}} \cdot x_{\{(1,\text{le}),(2,\text{le})\}} \cdot x_{\{(1,\text{le}),(2,\text{ri})\}} \cdot x_{\{(1,\text{le}),(3,\text{le})\}} \cdot x_{\{(1,\text{le}),(3,\text{ri})\}} \cdot 1 \cdot \\ & x_{\{(1,\text{ri}),(1,\text{le})\}} \cdot x_{\{(1,\text{ri}),(2,\text{le})\}} \cdot x_{\{(1,\text{ri}),(2,\text{ri})\}} \cdot x_{\{(1,\text{ri}),(3,\text{le})\}} \cdot x_{\{(1,\text{ri}),(3,\text{ri})\}} \cdot \\ & x_{\{(2,\text{le}),(1,\text{le})\}} \cdot x_{\{(2,\text{le}),(1,\text{ri})\}} \cdot x_{\{(2,\text{le}),(2,\text{ri})\}} \cdot x_{\{(2,\text{le}),(3,\text{le})\}} \cdot x_{\{(2,\text{le}),(3,\text{ri})\}} \cdot 2 \cdot \\ & x_{\{(2,\text{ri}),(1,\text{le})\}} \cdot x_{\{(2,\text{ri}),(1,\text{ri})\}} \cdot x_{\{(2,\text{ri}),(2,\text{le})\}} \cdot x_{\{(2,\text{ri}),(3,\text{le})\}} \cdot x_{\{(2,\text{ri}),(3,\text{ri})\}} \cdot \\ & x_{\{(3,\text{le}),(1,\text{le})\}} \cdot x_{\{(3,\text{le}),(1,\text{ri})\}} \cdot x_{\{(3,\text{le}),(2,\text{le})\}} \cdot x_{\{(3,\text{le}),(2,\text{ri})\}} \cdot x_{\{(3,\text{le}),(3,\text{ri})\}} \cdot 3 \cdot \\ & x_{\{(3,\text{ri}),(1,\text{le})\}} \cdot x_{\{(3,\text{ri}),(1,\text{ri})\}} \cdot x_{\{(3,\text{ri}),(2,\text{le})\}} \cdot x_{\{(3,\text{ri}),(2,\text{ri})\}} \cdot x_{\{(3,\text{ri}),(3,\text{le})\}} \cdot \\ & x_{\{(3,\text{le}),(1,\text{le})\}} \cdot x_{\{(3,\text{le}),(1,\text{ri})\}} \cdot x_{\{(3,\text{le}),(2,\text{le})\}} \cdot x_{\{(3,\text{le}),(2,\text{ri})\}} \cdot x_{\{(3,\text{le}),(3,\text{ri})\}} \cdot 3 \cdot \\ & x_{\{(3,\text{ri}),(1,\text{le})\}} \cdot x_{\{(3,\text{ri}),(1,\text{ri})\}} \cdot x_{\{(3,\text{ri}),(2,\text{le})\}} \cdot x_{\{(3,\text{ri}),(2,\text{ri})\}} \cdot x_{\{(3,\text{ri}),(3,\text{le})\}} \cdot \\ & x_{\{(2,\text{le}),(1,\text{le})\}} \cdot x_{\{(2,\text{le}),(1,\text{ri})\}} \cdot x_{\{(2,\text{le}),(2,\text{ri})\}} \cdot x_{\{(2,\text{le}),(3,\text{le})\}} \cdot x_{\{(2,\text{le}),(3,\text{ri})\}} \cdot 2 \cdot \\ & x_{\{(2,\text{ri}),(1,\text{le})\}} \cdot x_{\{(2,\text{ri}),(1,\text{ri})\}} \cdot x_{\{(2,\text{ri}),(2,\text{le})\}} \cdot x_{\{(2,\text{ri}),(3,\text{le})\}} \cdot x_{\{(2,\text{ri}),(3,\text{ri})\}} \cdot \\ & x_{\{(1,\text{le}),(1,\text{ri})\}} \cdot x_{\{(1,\text{le}),(2,\text{le})\}} \cdot x_{\{(1,\text{le}),(2,\text{ri})\}} \cdot x_{\{(1,\text{le}),(3,\text{le})\}} \cdot x_{\{(1,\text{le}),(3,\text{ri})\}} \cdot 1 \cdot \\ & x_{\{(1,\text{ri}),(1,\text{le})\}} \cdot x_{\{(1,\text{ri}),(2,\text{le})\}} \cdot x_{\{(1,\text{ri}),(2,\text{ri})\}} \cdot x_{\{(1,\text{ri}),(3,\text{le})\}} \cdot x_{\{(1,\text{ri}),(3,\text{ri})\}} .\end{aligned}$$

Note that, e. g., $x_{\{(1,\text{le}),(2,\text{ri})\}} = x_{\{(2,\text{ri}),(1,\text{le})\}}$ since $\{(1,\text{le}),(2,\text{ri})\} = \{(2,\text{ri}),(1,\text{le})\}$. Hence, $|\text{var}(\alpha_2)| = 18$. With

$$\begin{aligned} x_{\{(1,\text{le}),(1,\text{ri})\}} &:= 4, & x_{\{(1,\text{le}),(2,\text{le})\}} &:= 5, & x_{\{(1,\text{le}),(2,\text{ri})\}} &:= 6, \\ x_{\{(1,\text{le}),(3,\text{le})\}} &:= 7, & x_{\{(1,\text{le}),(3,\text{ri})\}} &:= 8, & x_{\{(1,\text{ri}),(2,\text{le})\}} &:= 9, \\ x_{\{(1,\text{ri}),(2,\text{ri})\}} &:= 10, & x_{\{(1,\text{ri}),(3,\text{le})\}} &:= 11, & x_{\{(1,\text{ri}),(3,\text{ri})\}} &:= 12, \\ x_{\{(2,\text{le}),(2,\text{ri})\}} &:= 13, & x_{\{(2,\text{le}),(3,\text{le})\}} &:= 14, & x_{\{(2,\text{le}),(3,\text{ri})\}} &:= 15, \\ x_{\{(2,\text{ri}),(3,\text{le})\}} &:= 16, & x_{\{(2,\text{ri}),(3,\text{ri})\}} &:= 17, & x_{\{(3,\text{le}),(3,\text{ri})\}} &:= 18, \end{aligned}$$

α_2 looks as follows:

$$\begin{aligned}\alpha_2 \;=\; & 4 \cdot 5 \cdot 6 \cdot 7 \cdot 8 \cdot \mathbf{1} \cdot 4 \cdot 9 \cdot 10 \cdot 11 \cdot 12 \cdot 5 \cdot 9 \cdot 13 \cdot 14 \cdot 15 \cdot \mathbf{2} \cdot 6 \cdot 10 \cdot 13 \cdot 16 \cdot 17 \cdot \\ & (7 \cdot 11 \cdot 14 \cdot 16 \cdot 18 \cdot \mathbf{3} \cdot 8 \cdot 12 \cdot 15 \cdot 17 \cdot 18)^2 \cdot \\ & 5 \cdot 9 \cdot 13 \cdot 14 \cdot 15 \cdot \mathbf{2} \cdot 6 \cdot 10 \cdot 13 \cdot 16 \cdot 17 \cdot 4 \cdot 5 \cdot 6 \cdot 7 \cdot 8 \cdot \mathbf{1} \cdot 4 \cdot 9 \cdot 10 \cdot 11 \cdot 12.\end{aligned}$$

This example may be consulted for a better understanding of the proof although the subsequent argumentation deals with the general pattern α_k.

Now, let $N := \{1, 2, \ldots, k+1\}$ and $E := \text{var}(\alpha_k) \setminus N$. The morphism $h : \mathbb{N}^* \to \mathbb{N}^*$, defined by $h(i) := \beta_i$ for every $i \in N$ and $h(i) := \varepsilon$ for every $i \in E$, is nontrivial and satisfies $h(\alpha_k) = \alpha_k$. Thus, according to Definition 4.4, (E, N) is an ambiguity partition for α_k.

ad (i). W. l. o. g., let $\Sigma_k := \{1, 2, \ldots, k\}$. Assume to the contrary that there exists an unambiguous morphism $\sigma : \mathbb{N}^* \to \Sigma_k^*$ for α_k. Then, according to Theorem 4.18, $\sigma(e) = \varepsilon$ for every $e \in E$. Thus, one of the following cases must occur:

Case 1: For every $n \in N$, $\sigma(n) \neq \varepsilon$. Since N contains $k+1$ variables, but Σ_k consists of k letters only, there must be $i, j \in N$, $i \neq j$, and $y \in \Sigma_k$ such that $\sigma(i) = yw_i$ and $\sigma(j) = yw_j$ with $w_i, w_j \in \Sigma_k^*$. But then the morphism $\tau : \mathbb{N}^* \to \Sigma_k^*$, defined by $\tau(x_{\{(i,\text{le}),(j,\text{le})\}}) := y$, $\tau(i) := w_i$, $\tau(j) := w_j$, $\tau(n) := \sigma(n)$ for every $n \in N \setminus \{i, j\}$ and $\tau(e) := \varepsilon$ for every $e \in E \setminus \{x_{\{(i,\text{le}),(j,\text{le})\}}\}$, satisfies $\tau(\alpha_k) = \sigma(\alpha_k)$ and, thus, contradicts σ being unambiguous for α_k.

Case 2: There exists an $n \in N$ with $\sigma(n) = \varepsilon$. If $n = 1$, then the morphism $\tau : \mathbb{N}^* \to \Sigma_k^*$, defined by $\tau(1) = \sigma(2)$, $\tau(2) = \varepsilon$, $\tau(n') = \sigma(n')$ for all $n' \in N \setminus \{1, 2\}$, $\tau(e) := \varepsilon$ for all $e \in E$, satisfies $\tau(\alpha_k) = \sigma(\alpha_k)$ and, thus, contradicts σ being unambiguous for α_k. If $n > 1$, then the morphism $\tau : \mathbb{N}^* \to \Sigma_k^*$, defined by $\tau(n) := \sigma(n-1)$, $\tau(n-1) = \varepsilon$, $\tau(n') := \sigma(n')$ for all $n' \in N \setminus \{n-1, n\}$, $\tau(e) := \varepsilon$ for all $e \in E$, satisfies $\tau(\alpha_k) = \sigma(\alpha_k)$ and, thus, contradicts σ being unambiguous for α_k.

Thus, there is no unambiguous morphism $\sigma : \mathbb{N}^* \to \Sigma_k^*$ for α_k.

ad (ii). W.l.o.g., let $\Sigma_{k+1} := \{1, 2, \dots, k+1\}$. Then $\pi_N(\alpha_k) \in \mathrm{UNAMB}_{\Sigma_{k+1}}(\alpha_k)$, since every $e \in E$ occurs four times in α_k, whereas every $n \in N$ occurs only two times, and since $\pi_N(\alpha_k)$ is morphically primitive and, thus, the only morphism satisfying $h(\pi_N(\alpha_k)) = \pi_N(\alpha_k)$ is the trivial one (cf. Theorem 2.5). Now, let $\sigma : \mathbb{N}^* \to \Sigma_{k+1}^*$ be a morphism. If $\sigma(e) \neq \varepsilon$ for an $e \in E$, σ is ambiguous for α_k (cf. Theorem 4.18). Hence, let $\sigma(e) = \varepsilon$ for every $e \in E$. Assume that $|\sigma(n)| > 1$ for some $n \in N$. Then, for every $i \in N \setminus \{n\}$, there exist $a_i \in \Sigma_{k+1}$ and $w_i \in \Sigma_{k+1}^*$ such that $\sigma(i) = a_i w_i$, and there exist $a_{\mathrm{le}}, a_{\mathrm{ri}} \in \Sigma_{k+1}$, $w_n \in \Sigma_{k+1}^*$ such that $\sigma(n) = a_{\mathrm{le}} w_n a_{\mathrm{ri}}$. Since $a_{\mathrm{le}}, a_{\mathrm{ri}}$ and the a_i, $i \in N \setminus \{n\}$, stand for $k+2$ letters, but $|\Sigma_{k+1}| = k+1$, one of the following cases must occur:

Case 1: $a_{\mathrm{le}} = a_{\mathrm{ri}}$. Then, the morphism $\tau : \mathbb{N}^* \to \Sigma^*$, defined by $\tau(x_{\{(n,\mathrm{le}),(n,\mathrm{ri})\}}) := a_{\mathrm{le}}$, $\tau(n) := w_n$ and $\tau(i) := \sigma(i)$ for all $i \in \mathrm{var}(\alpha_k) \setminus \{n, x_{\{(n,\mathrm{le}),(n,\mathrm{ri})\}}\}$, contradicts σ being unambiguous for α_k, since $\tau(\alpha_k) = \sigma(\alpha_k)$, but $\tau(n) \neq \sigma(n)$.

Case 2: $a_{\mathrm{le}} = a_j$ for some $j \in N \setminus \{n\}$. Then, the morphism $\tau : \mathbb{N}^* \to \Sigma^*$, defined by $\tau(x_{\{(n,\mathrm{le}),(j,\mathrm{le})\}}) := a_{\mathrm{le}}$, $\tau(n) := w_n a_{\mathrm{ri}}$, $\tau(j) := w_j$ and $\tau(i) := \sigma(i)$ for all $i \in \mathrm{var}(\alpha_k) \setminus \{n, j, x_{\{(n,\mathrm{le}),(j,\mathrm{le})\}}\}$, contradicts σ being unambiguous for α_k, since $\tau(\alpha_k) = \sigma(\alpha_k)$, but $\tau(j) \neq \sigma(j)$.

Case 3: $a_{\mathrm{ri}} = a_j$ for some $j \in N \setminus \{n\}$. Then, the morphism $\tau : \mathbb{N}^* \to \Sigma^*$, defined by $\tau(x_{\{(n,\mathrm{ri}),(j,\mathrm{le})\}}) := a_{\mathrm{ri}}$, $\tau(n) := a_{\mathrm{le}} w_n$, $\tau(j) := w_j$ and $\tau(i) := \sigma(i)$ for all $i \in \mathrm{var}(\alpha_k) \setminus \{n, j, x_{\{(n,\mathrm{ri}),(j,\mathrm{le})\}}\}$, contradicts σ being unambiguous for α_k, since $\tau(\alpha_k) = \sigma(\alpha_k)$, but $\tau(j) \neq \sigma(j)$.

Case 4: $a_j = a_m$ for some $j, m \in N \setminus \{n\}$, $j \neq m$. Then, the morphism $\tau : \mathbb{N}^* \to \Sigma^*$, defined by $\tau(x_{\{(j,\mathrm{le}),(m,\mathrm{le})\}}) := a_j$, $\tau(j) := w_j$, $\tau(m) := w_m$ and $\tau(i) := \sigma(i)$ for all $i \in \mathrm{var}(\alpha_k) \setminus \{j, m, x_{\{(j,\mathrm{le}),(m,\mathrm{le})\}}\}$, contradicts σ being unambiguous for α_k, since $\tau(\alpha_k) = \sigma(\alpha_k)$, but $\tau(j) \neq \sigma(j)$.

Consequently, only morphisms $\sigma : \mathbb{N}^* \to \Sigma_{k+1}^*$ with $\sigma(e) = \varepsilon$ for every $e \in E$ and $\sigma(n) \in \Sigma_{k+1}$ for every $n \in N$ can be unambiguous for α_k. Since there are only finitely many $\sigma(\alpha)$ for such morphisms σ and since $\pi_N(\alpha_k) \in \mathrm{UNAMB}_{\Sigma_{k+1}}(\alpha_k)$, (ii) follows.

ad (iii): W.l.o.g., let $\Sigma_{k+2} := \{1, 2, \dots, k+2\}$. For every n, let $\sigma_n : \mathbb{N}^* \to \Sigma_{k+2}^*$ be a morphism defined by $\sigma_n(i) := i$, $1 \leq i \leq k$, and $\sigma_n(k+1) := (k+1) \cdot k^n \cdot (k+2)$. For instance, $\sigma_3(\alpha_2) = 1 \cdot 2 \cdot 3 \cdot 2 \cdot 2 \cdot 2 \cdot 4 \cdot 3 \cdot 2 \cdot 2 \cdot 2 \cdot 4 \cdot 2 \cdot 1$.

We show that, for every $n \in \mathbb{N}$, $\sigma_n(\alpha_k) \in \mathrm{UNAMB}_{\Sigma_{k+2}}(\alpha_k)$. This implies (iii). Let $n \in \mathbb{N}$. Assume to the contrary that there exists a morphism $\tau : \mathbb{N}^* \to \Sigma_{k+2}^*$ with $\tau(\alpha_k) = \sigma_n(\alpha_k)$ and $\tau(j) \neq \sigma_n(j)$ for a $j \in \mathrm{var}(\alpha_k)$.

Claim 1. For every $i \in \{1, 2, \dots, k-1\}$, $\tau(i) = \sigma_n(i)$. (Since $\alpha_k = 1 \dots 2 \dots [\dots] k-1 \dots k-1 \dots k-2 \dots [\dots] 1$.)

Claim 2. For every $e \in E$ and $n \in N \setminus \{k\}$, $\tau(e) \neq \dots n \dots$. (Since every $e \in E$ occurs four times in α_k, but n occurs only two times in $\sigma_n(\alpha_k)$.)

Due to Claim 1, $\tau(\beta_k\beta_{k+1}\beta_{k+1}\beta_k) = \sigma_n(\beta_k\beta_{k+1}\beta_{k+1}\beta_k) = k \cdot (k+1) \cdot k^n \cdot (k+2) \cdot (k+1) \cdot k^n \cdot (k+2) \cdot k$ must be satisfied. Because of Claim 2, for every $e \in E$ and $m \in \{k+1, k+2\}$, $\tau(e) \neq \ldots m \ldots$. Therefore, it can be verified by straightforward considerations on the structure of α that $\tau(k)$ or $\tau(k+1)$ must equal $\sigma_n(k+1)$. In both cases, all occurrences of k except for two are covered by $\tau(\pi_{\{1,2,\ldots,k\}}(\alpha))$ or $\tau(\pi_{\{1,2,\ldots,k-1,k+1\}}(\alpha))$. Thus, only $\tau(k) = \sigma_n(k)$ and $\tau(k+1) = \sigma_n(k+1)$ is possible, since every $e \in E$ occurs four times in α_k, which implies $\tau(e) \neq k$. This contradicts σ_n being ambiguous for α_k, and therefore $\sigma_n(\alpha_k) \in \mathrm{UNAMB}_{\Sigma_{k+2}}(\alpha_k)$. □

The proof of Theorem 4.43 gives, for every target alphabet Σ with size at least 2, a generic example pattern α such that $\mathrm{UNAMB}_\Sigma(\alpha)$ is finite. More precisely, every unambiguous morphism for α maps every variable to a word of length at most 1. In the following example, we introduce a pattern for which every unambiguous morphism maps every variable to a word of length 2 or less.

Example 4.44. Let $\Sigma := \{\mathtt{a}, \mathtt{b}\}$ and $\beta := 2 \cdot 2 \cdot 4 \cdot \mathbf{1} \cdot 3 \cdot 3 \cdot 4$. We first note that, for every $w \in \Sigma^*$, the morphism $\sigma_w : \mathbb{N}^* \to \Sigma^*$, defined by $\sigma_w(1) := w$, $\sigma_w(x) = \varepsilon$, $x \neq 1$, satisfies $\sigma_w(\beta) = w$. Let us first consider words $w \in \Sigma^*$ of length at least 3:

Case 1: $w = aaw'a$ for some $a \in \Sigma$ and $w' \in \Sigma^*$. Then, the morphism $\tau : \mathbb{N}^* \to \Sigma^*$, defined by $\tau(1) := aw'$, $\tau(4) := a$ and $\tau(x) := \varepsilon$ for all other variables x, satisfies $\tau(\beta) = \sigma_w(\beta)$, but $\tau(1) \neq \sigma_w(1)$. Consequently, $w \notin \mathrm{UNAMB}_\Sigma(\beta)$.

Case 2: $w = aaw'b$ for $\{a, b\} = \Sigma$ and some $w' \in \Sigma^*$. Here, we define a morphism $\tau : \mathbb{N}^* \to \Sigma^*$ by $\tau(1) := w'b$, $\tau(2) := a$ and $\tau(x) := \varepsilon$ for all other variables x. Thus, $\tau(\beta) = \sigma_w(\beta)$, but $\tau(1) \neq \sigma_w(1)$. Consequently, $w \notin \mathrm{UNAMB}_\Sigma(\beta)$.

Case 3: $w = abw'a$ for $\{a, b\} = \Sigma$ and some $w' \in \Sigma^*$. We consider the morphism $\tau : \mathbb{N}^* \to \Sigma^*$, defined by $\tau(1) := bw'$, $\tau(4) := a$ and $\tau(x) := \varepsilon$ for all other variables x, which satisfies $\tau(\beta) = \sigma_w(\beta)$, but $\tau(1) \neq \sigma_w(1)$. Thus, $w \notin \mathrm{UNAMB}_\Sigma(\beta)$.

Case 4: $w = abw'b$ for $\{a, b\} = \Sigma$ and some $w' \in \Sigma^*$. We distinguish between three subcases:

Case 4.1: $w = abb$ for $\{a, b\} = \Sigma$. Let $\tau : \mathbb{N}^* \to \Sigma^*$ be the morphism, defined by $\tau(1) := a$, $\tau(3) := b$ and $\tau(x) := \varepsilon$ for all other variables x. It is $\tau(\beta) = \sigma_w(\beta)$, but $\tau(1) \neq \sigma_w(1)$. Hence, $w \notin \mathrm{UNAMB}_\Sigma(\beta)$.

Case 4.2: $w = abw''ab$ for $\{a, b\} = \Sigma$ and some $w'' \in \Sigma^*$. In this case, we define a morphism $\tau : \mathbb{N}^* \to \Sigma^*$ by $\tau(1) := w''$, $\tau(4) := ab$ and $\tau(x) := \varepsilon$ for all other variables x, satisfies $\tau(\beta) = \sigma_w(\beta)$, but $\tau(1) \neq \sigma_w(1)$. Consequently, $w \notin \mathrm{UNAMB}_\Sigma(\beta)$.

Case 4.3: $w = abw''bb$ for $\{a, b\} = \Sigma$ and some $w'' \in \Sigma^*$. We consider the morphism $\tau : \mathbb{N}^* \to \Sigma^*$, defined by $\tau(1) := abw''$, $\tau(3) := b$ and $\tau(x) := \varepsilon$ for all other variables x. Thus, $\tau(\beta) = \sigma_w(\beta)$, but $\tau(1) \neq \sigma_w(1)$. Hence, $w \notin \mathrm{UNAMB}_\Sigma(\beta)$.

Consequently, there is no $w \in \mathrm{UNAMB}_\Sigma(\beta)$ with $|w| > 2$. Furthermore, it can easily be seen that $\mathtt{a}, \mathtt{b}, \mathtt{ab}, \mathtt{ba} \in \mathrm{UNAMB}_\Sigma(\beta)$, but $\mathtt{aa}, \mathtt{bb} \notin \mathrm{UNAMB}_\Sigma(\beta)$. Consequently, it is $\mathrm{UNAMB}_\Sigma(\beta) = \{\mathtt{a}, \mathtt{b}, \mathtt{ab}, \mathtt{ba}\}$.

We note that this is a special example pattern β for $|\Sigma| = 2$ where $\mathrm{UNAMB}_\Sigma(\beta)$ is finite and there is an unambiguous morphism mapping a variable to a word of length 2. For $|\Sigma| > 2$, no such examples are known so far. This can be a first sign for special ambiguity phenomena occurring only in small target alphabets. Furthermore, it is an open question if there exist patterns α for which $\mathrm{UNAMB}_\Sigma(\alpha)$ is finite and every unambiguous morphism maps a variable to a word of length m for an arbitrary $m \in \mathbb{N} \setminus \{1, 2\}$.

Again, the example in the proof of Theorem 4.43 is based on the phenomenon as described in Section 4.4.1 since α_k from the proof of Theorem 4.24 is a renaming of the projection of α_k from the proof of Theorem 4.43 onto the variables $\{1, 2, \ldots, k+1\} \cup \{x_{\{(i,\mathrm{ri}),(j,\mathrm{ri})\}} \mid 1 \leq i < j \leq k+1\}$. This immediately provokes the question if the phenomenon of Theorem 4.31 is the only one leading to target alphabet specific ambiguity of morphisms and, thus, even characterises this type of ambiguity. We shall answer this question later in this section.

The following theorem reveals a procedure how to construct, for any given target alphabet Σ, a pattern α with no unambiguous morphisms from a pattern β with a finite $\mathrm{UNAMB}_\Sigma(\beta)$.

Theorem 4.45. *Let Σ be an alphabet. Let $\beta \in \mathbb{N}^+$ such that $|\mathrm{UNAMB}_\Sigma(\beta)| = m \in \mathbb{N}$. Let β_i, $1 \leq i \leq m+1$, be renamings of β such that $\mathrm{var}(\beta_i) \cap \mathrm{var}(\beta_j) = \emptyset$ for every $1 \leq i < j \leq m+1$. Let $n \in \mathbb{N}$ and $s_1, s_2, \ldots, s_n$ be all possible surjective mappings from $\{1, 2, \ldots, m+1\}$ onto $\{1, 2, \ldots, m\}$. Finally, let $x_i, x'_i, y_l^{(k)}, z_l^{(k)} \in \mathbb{N} \setminus \bigcup_{1 \leq j \leq m+1} \mathrm{var}(\beta_j)$ be pairwise distinct variables for every $1 \leq i \leq m$, $1 \leq j \leq n$, $1 \leq k \leq m+1$ and*

$$\alpha := \beta_1\beta_2\ldots\beta_{m+1}\beta_{m+1}\beta_m\ldots\beta_1\ x_1x'_1x_2x'_2\ldots x_mx'_mx_mx'_mx_{m-1}x'_{m-1}\ldots x_1x'_1\ \gamma_1\gamma_2\ldots\gamma_n$$

with

$$\gamma_i := y^{(i)}_{s_i(1)}z^{(i)}_{s_i(1)}y^{(i)}_{s_i(2)}z^{(i)}_{s_i(2)}\ldots y^{(i)}_{s_i(m+1)}z^{(i)}_{s_i(m+1)}y^{(i)}_{s_i(m+1)}z^{(i)}_{s_i(m+1)}y^{(i)}_{s_i(m)}z^{(i)}_{s_i(m)}\ldots y^{(i)}_{s_i(1)}z^{(i)}_{s_i(1)}.$$

Then

(i) *α is morphically unerasable and*

(ii) *no morphism $\sigma : \mathbb{N}^* \to \Sigma^*$ is unambiguous for α.*

Proof. ad (i). Let $B := \bigcup_{1 \leq j \leq m+1} \mathrm{var}(\beta_j)$. Since every x_i has x'_i as a direct neighbour, as well as $y_l^{(k)}$ has $z_l^{(k)}$, it follows from Lemma 4.6 and Lemma 4.9 that $(\mathrm{var}(\alpha) \setminus B, B)$ is an ambiguity partition for α. Additionally, every β_i, $1 \leq i \leq m+1$, is morphically unerasable since β_i is a renaming of β and $|\mathrm{UNAMB}_\Sigma(\beta)| > 0$ (cf. Corollary 4.13). The structure $\beta_1\beta_2\ldots\beta_{m+1}\beta_{m+1}\beta_m\ldots\beta_1$ furthermore ensures that also this factor of α is morphically unerasable.

Assume now, that $(\mathrm{var}(\alpha), \emptyset)$ is an ambiguity partition for α. Then, according to the previous considerations and Definition 4.4, there must exist a morphism $h : \mathbb{N}^* \to \mathbb{N}^*$, satisfying

$$h(x_1x'_1x_2x'_2\ldots x_mx'_mx_mx'_mx_{m-1}x'_{m-1}\ldots x_1x'_1\ \gamma_1\gamma_2\ldots\gamma_n) = \beta_1\beta_2\ldots\beta_{m+1}\beta_{m+1}\beta_m\ldots\beta_1.$$

However,

$$\beta_1\beta_2\ldots\beta_{m+1}\beta_{m+1}\beta_m\ldots\beta_1 = \ldots i_1\ldots i_2\ldots[\ldots]\ldots i_{m+1}\ldots i_{m+1}\ldots i_m\ldots[\ldots]\ldots i_1\ldots$$

with $m+1$ distinct variables i_k, but $x_1x'_1x_2x'_2\ldots x_mx'_mx_mx'_mx_{m-1}x'_{m-1}\ldots x_1x'_1\ \gamma_1\gamma_2\ldots\gamma_n$ only consists of two non-overlapping sequences of m distinct variables, respectively. Thus, such a morphism h cannot exist.

ad (ii). Assume that there exists an unambiguous morphism $\sigma : \mathbb{N}^* \to \Sigma^*$ for α. We can conclude from the proof of (i) and Theorem 4.7 that $\sigma(x_i) = \sigma(x'_i) = \sigma(y_l^{(k)}) = \sigma(z_l^{(k)}) = \varepsilon$ for every $1 \leq i \leq m$, $1 \leq j \leq n$, $1 \leq k \leq m+1$.

Case 1: $\sigma(\beta_i) \neq \varepsilon$ for every $1 \leq i \leq m+1$. If $\sigma(\beta_i) \notin \mathrm{UNAMB}_\Sigma(\beta)$ for an $1 \leq i \leq m+1$, it directly follows that σ is ambiguous. Hence, assume that $\sigma(\beta_i) \in \mathrm{UNAMB}_\Sigma(\beta)$ for every $1 \leq i \leq m+1$. Now, due to $|\mathrm{UNAMB}_\Sigma(\beta)| = m$, there are $i, j \in \{1, 2, \ldots, m+1\}$ with $i \neq j$ and $\sigma(\beta_i) = \sigma(\beta_j)$. We choose $k \in \{1, 2, \ldots, n\}$ with $s_k(i) = s_k(j)$. Then the morphism $\tau : \mathbb{N}^* \to \Sigma^*$, defined by $\tau(\beta_1\beta_2\ldots\beta_{m+1}) := \varepsilon$, $\tau(\gamma_k) := \sigma(\beta_1\beta_2\ldots\beta_{m+1}\beta_{m+1}\beta_m\ldots\beta_1)$, $\tau(z) = \varepsilon$ for all other variables z, contradicts σ being unambiguous for α.

Case 2: $\sigma(\beta_i) = \varepsilon$ for an i with $1 \leq i \leq m+1$. Then the morphism $\tau : \mathbb{N}^* \to \Sigma^*$, defined by

$$\begin{aligned} \tau(\beta_1\beta_2\ldots\beta_{m+1}) &:= \varepsilon, \\ \tau(x_1x'_1x_2x'_2\ldots x_mx'_mx_mx'_mx_{m-1}x'_{m-1}\ldots x_1x'_1) &:= \sigma(\beta_1\beta_2\ldots\beta_{m+1}\beta_{m+1}\beta_m\ldots\beta_1), \\ \tau(z) &:= \varepsilon \text{ for all other variables } z, \end{aligned}$$

contradicts σ being unambiguous for α. □

We demonstrate the effect of Theorem 4.45 with an example.

Example 4.46. Let $\Sigma := \{\mathtt{a}, \mathtt{b}\}$ and

$$\begin{aligned} \beta := \; & x_{\{(1,le),(1,ri)\}} \cdot x_{\{(1,le),(2,le)\}} \cdot x_{\{(1,le),(2,ri)\}} \cdot 1 \cdot x_{\{(1,le),(1,ri)\}} \cdot x_{\{(1,ri),(2,le)\}} \cdot x_{\{(1,ri),(2,ri)\}} \cdot \\ & x_{\{(1,le),(2,le)\}} \cdot x_{\{(1,ri),(2,le)\}} \cdot x_{\{(2,le),(2,ri)\}} \cdot 2 \cdot x_{\{(1,le),(2,ri)\}} \cdot x_{\{(1,ri),(2,ri)\}} \cdot x_{\{(2,le),(2,ri)\}} \cdot \\ & x_{\{(1,le),(2,le)\}} \cdot x_{\{(1,ri),(2,le)\}} \cdot x_{\{(2,le),(2,ri)\}} \cdot 2 \cdot x_{\{(1,le),(2,ri)\}} \cdot x_{\{(1,ri),(2,ri)\}} \cdot x_{\{(2,le),(2,ri)\}} \cdot \\ & x_{\{(1,le),(1,ri)\}} \cdot x_{\{(1,le),(2,le)\}} \cdot x_{\{(1,le),(2,ri)\}} \cdot 1 \cdot x_{\{(1,le),(1,ri)\}} \cdot x_{\{(1,ri),(2,le)\}} \cdot x_{\{(1,ri),(2,ri)\}}. \end{aligned}$$

Hence, $\beta = \alpha_1$ from the proof of Theorem 4.43 and, thus, $\mathrm{UNAMB}_\Sigma(\beta)$ is finite. It follows from the proof and straightforward considerations that $\mathrm{UNAMB}_\Sigma(\beta) = \{\mathtt{abba}, \mathtt{baab}\}$. Hence, $|\mathrm{UNAMB}_\Sigma(\beta)| = 2 =: m$.

We now define a pattern α as in Theorem 4.45. To this purpose, let

$$\begin{aligned} \beta_1 := \; & x^{(1)}_{\{(1,le),(1,ri)\}} \cdot x^{(1)}_{\{(1,le),(2,le)\}} \cdot x^{(1)}_{\{(1,le),(2,ri)\}} \cdot \mathbf{1} \cdot x^{(1)}_{\{(1,le),(1,ri)\}} \cdot x^{(1)}_{\{(1,ri),(2,le)\}} \cdot x^{(1)}_{\{(1,ri),(2,ri)\}} \cdot \\ & x^{(1)}_{\{(1,le),(2,le)\}} \cdot x^{(1)}_{\{(1,ri),(2,le)\}} \cdot x^{(1)}_{\{(2,le),(2,ri)\}} \cdot \mathbf{2} \cdot x^{(1)}_{\{(1,le),(2,ri)\}} \cdot x^{(1)}_{\{(1,ri),(2,ri)\}} \cdot x^{(1)}_{\{(2,le),(2,ri)\}} \cdot \\ & x^{(1)}_{\{(1,le),(2,le)\}} \cdot x^{(1)}_{\{(1,ri),(2,le)\}} \cdot x^{(1)}_{\{(2,le),(2,ri)\}} \cdot \mathbf{2} \cdot x^{(1)}_{\{(1,le),(2,ri)\}} \cdot x^{(1)}_{\{(1,ri),(2,ri)\}} \cdot x^{(1)}_{\{(2,le),(2,ri)\}} \cdot \\ & x^{(1)}_{\{(1,le),(1,ri)\}} \cdot x^{(1)}_{\{(1,le),(2,le)\}} \cdot x^{(1)}_{\{(1,le),(2,ri)\}} \cdot \mathbf{1} \cdot x^{(1)}_{\{(1,le),(1,ri)\}} \cdot x^{(1)}_{\{(1,ri),(2,le)\}} \cdot x^{(1)}_{\{(1,ri),(2,ri)\}}, \end{aligned}$$

$$\begin{aligned} \beta_2 := \; & x^{(2)}_{\{(1,le),(1,ri)\}} \cdot x^{(2)}_{\{(1,le),(2,le)\}} \cdot x^{(2)}_{\{(1,le),(2,ri)\}} \cdot \mathbf{3} \cdot x^{(2)}_{\{(1,le),(1,ri)\}} \cdot x^{(2)}_{\{(1,ri),(2,le)\}} \cdot x^{(2)}_{\{(1,ri),(2,ri)\}} \cdot \\ & x^{(2)}_{\{(1,le),(2,le)\}} \cdot x^{(2)}_{\{(1,ri),(2,le)\}} \cdot x^{(2)}_{\{(2,le),(2,ri)\}} \cdot \mathbf{4} \cdot x^{(2)}_{\{(1,le),(2,ri)\}} \cdot x^{(2)}_{\{(1,ri),(2,ri)\}} \cdot x^{(2)}_{\{(2,le),(2,ri)\}} \cdot \\ & x^{(2)}_{\{(1,le),(2,le)\}} \cdot x^{(2)}_{\{(1,ri),(2,le)\}} \cdot x^{(2)}_{\{(2,le),(2,ri)\}} \cdot \mathbf{4} \cdot x^{(2)}_{\{(1,le),(2,ri)\}} \cdot x^{(2)}_{\{(1,ri),(2,ri)\}} \cdot x^{(2)}_{\{(2,le),(2,ri)\}} \cdot \\ & x^{(2)}_{\{(1,le),(1,ri)\}} \cdot x^{(2)}_{\{(1,le),(2,le)\}} \cdot x^{(2)}_{\{(1,le),(2,ri)\}} \cdot \mathbf{3} \cdot x^{(2)}_{\{(1,le),(1,ri)\}} \cdot x^{(2)}_{\{(1,ri),(2,le)\}} \cdot x^{(2)}_{\{(1,ri),(2,ri)\}}, \end{aligned}$$

$$\begin{aligned}\beta_3 \;:=\;& x^{(3)}_{\{(1,\mathrm{le}),(1,\mathrm{ri})\}} \cdot x^{(3)}_{\{(1,\mathrm{le}),(2,\mathrm{le})\}} \cdot x^{(3)}_{\{(1,\mathrm{le}),(2,\mathrm{ri})\}} \cdot \mathbf{5} \cdot x^{(3)}_{\{(1,\mathrm{le}),(1,\mathrm{ri})\}} \cdot x^{(3)}_{\{(1,\mathrm{ri}),(2,\mathrm{le})\}} \cdot x^{(3)}_{\{(1,\mathrm{ri}),(2,\mathrm{ri})\}} \cdot \\ & x^{(3)}_{\{(1,\mathrm{le}),(2,\mathrm{le})\}} \cdot x^{(3)}_{\{(1,\mathrm{ri}),(2,\mathrm{le})\}} \cdot x^{(3)}_{\{(2,\mathrm{le}),(2,\mathrm{ri})\}} \cdot \mathbf{6} \cdot x^{(3)}_{\{(1,\mathrm{le}),(2,\mathrm{ri})\}} \cdot x^{(3)}_{\{(1,\mathrm{ri}),(2,\mathrm{ri})\}} \cdot x^{(3)}_{\{(2,\mathrm{le}),(2,\mathrm{ri})\}} \cdot \\ & x^{(3)}_{\{(1,\mathrm{le}),(2,\mathrm{le})\}} \cdot x^{(3)}_{\{(1,\mathrm{ri}),(2,\mathrm{le})\}} \cdot x^{(3)}_{\{(2,\mathrm{le}),(2,\mathrm{ri})\}} \cdot \mathbf{6} \cdot x^{(3)}_{\{(1,\mathrm{le}),(2,\mathrm{ri})\}} \cdot x^{(3)}_{\{(1,\mathrm{ri}),(2,\mathrm{ri})\}} \cdot x^{(3)}_{\{(2,\mathrm{le}),(2,\mathrm{ri})\}} \cdot \\ & x^{(3)}_{\{(1,\mathrm{le}),(1,\mathrm{ri})\}} \cdot x^{(3)}_{\{(1,\mathrm{le}),(2,\mathrm{le})\}} \cdot x^{(3)}_{\{(1,\mathrm{le}),(2,\mathrm{ri})\}} \cdot \mathbf{5} \cdot x^{(3)}_{\{(1,\mathrm{le}),(1,\mathrm{ri})\}} \cdot x^{(3)}_{\{(1,\mathrm{ri}),(2,\mathrm{le})\}} \cdot x^{(3)}_{\{(1,\mathrm{ri}),(2,\mathrm{ri})\}}.\end{aligned}$$

Furthermore, there are 6 possible surjections from $\{1,2,3\}$ onto $\{1,2\}$, namely

j	$s_j(1)$	$s_j(2)$	$s_j(3)$
1	1	1	2
2	1	2	1
3	2	1	1
4	1	2	2
5	2	1	2
6	2	2	1

Thus, we have

$$\begin{aligned}\gamma_1 &:= y_1^{(1)} z_1^{(1)} y_1^{(1)} z_1^{(1)} y_2^{(1)} z_2^{(1)} y_2^{(1)} z_2^{(1)} y_1^{(1)} z_1^{(1)} y_1^{(1)} z_1^{(1)},\\ \gamma_2 &:= y_1^{(2)} z_1^{(2)} y_2^{(2)} z_2^{(2)} y_1^{(2)} z_1^{(2)} y_1^{(2)} z_1^{(2)} y_2^{(2)} z_2^{(2)} y_1^{(2)} z_1^{(2)},\\ \gamma_3 &:= y_2^{(3)} z_2^{(3)} y_1^{(3)} z_1^{(3)} y_1^{(3)} z_1^{(3)} y_1^{(3)} z_1^{(3)} y_1^{(3)} z_1^{(3)} y_2^{(3)} z_2^{(3)},\\ \gamma_4 &:= y_1^{(4)} z_1^{(4)} y_2^{(4)} z_2^{(4)} y_2^{(4)} z_2^{(4)} y_2^{(4)} z_2^{(4)} y_2^{(4)} z_2^{(4)} y_1^{(4)} z_1^{(4)},\\ \gamma_5 &:= y_2^{(5)} z_2^{(5)} y_1^{(5)} z_1^{(5)} y_2^{(5)} z_2^{(5)} y_2^{(5)} z_2^{(5)} y_1^{(5)} z_1^{(5)} y_2^{(5)} z_2^{(5)},\\ \gamma_6 &:= y_2^{(6)} z_2^{(6)} y_2^{(6)} z_2^{(6)} y_1^{(6)} z_1^{(6)} y_1^{(6)} z_1^{(6)} y_2^{(6)} z_2^{(6)} y_2^{(6)} z_2^{(6)},\end{aligned}$$

and finally

$$\alpha := \beta_1\,\beta_2\,\beta_3\,\beta_3\,\beta_2\,\beta_1\; x_1x_1'x_2x_2'x_2x_2'x_1x_1'\; \gamma_1\,\gamma_2\,\gamma_3\,\gamma_4\,\gamma_5\,\gamma_6.$$

Note that all $x_{\dots}, x'_{\dots}, x^{(\dots)}_{\dots}, y^{(\dots)}_{\dots}, z^{(\dots)}_{\dots}$ are distinct variables from $\mathbb{N}\setminus\{1,2,3,4,5,6\}$. It follows from Lemma 4.6 and Lemma 4.9 that $(E,N) := (\mathrm{var}(\alpha)\setminus\{1,2,3,4,5,6\},\{1,2,3,4,5,6\})$ is an ambiguity partition for α. Hence, any morphism mapping at least one variable from E to a nonempty word is ambiguous (cf. Theorem 4.7). Furthermore, any morphism $\sigma : \mathbb{N}^* \to \Sigma^*$ that maps β_1, β_2 or β_3 to a word different from $\mathtt{abba}$ and $\mathtt{baab}$ is ambiguous. Thus, any possibly unambiguous morphism $\sigma : \mathbb{N}^* \to \Sigma^*$ must satisfy $\sigma(\beta_i) \in \{\mathtt{abba}, \mathtt{baab}\}$ for every $i \in \{1,2,3\}$. This results to $\sigma(\beta_i) = \sigma(\beta_j)$ for $i,j \in \{1,2,3\}$, $i \neq j$. Assume that $i = 1$ and $j = 2$ (the other cases are analogous). Then the morphism $\tau : \mathbb{N}^* \to \Sigma^*$, defined by $\tau(y_1^{(1)}) := \sigma(\beta_1)(= \sigma(\beta_2))$ and $\tau(y_2^{(1)}) := \beta_3$ and $\tau(x) = \varepsilon$ for all variables in $\mathbb{N}\setminus\{y_1^{(1)}, y_2^{(1)}\}$, satisfies $\tau(\alpha) = \sigma(\alpha)$ with $\tau(\gamma_1) = \sigma(\beta_1\,\beta_2\,\beta_3\,\beta_3\,\beta_2\,\beta_1)$. Consequently, there is no unambiguous morphism $\sigma : \mathbb{N}^* \to \Sigma^*$ for α.

We note two aspects: First, it is important that Σ consists of two letters only, otherwise there are unambiguous morphisms for α. This is not surprising since $\mathrm{UNAMB}_\Sigma(\alpha)$ depends on the size of Σ (cf. Theorem 4.43). Second, it is not necessary to consider *all* surjections since there is a lot of redundancy in the resulting γ patterns. In this example, γ_1, γ_2 and γ_4 would be sufficient. In general, only surjections s_j are needed such that $\delta := s_j(1)s_j(2)\dots s_j(m+1)$ is a pattern in *canonical form*, i. e., for every $\delta' \in \mathbb{N}^+$ with $\delta = \delta' \dots$, there exists a $k \in \mathbb{N}$ with $\mathrm{var}(\delta') = \{1, 2, \dots, k\}$. ◇

Example 4.46 reveals a new category of patterns with no unambiguous morphism, which is not covered by previous formal statements: α is not morphically erasable. Hence, we cannot apply Corollary 4.13. Additionally, α does not satisfy Condition 4.30 for target alphabet size $k = 2$ and N from the maximal ambiguity partition (E, N) for α (the check of this statement is straightforward, yet quite involved and, thus, omitted here). Consequently, we cannot apply Theorem 4.31 either. Therefore, the question if the phenomenon described by Theorem 4.31 is the only target alphabet specific one which can lead to the nonexistence of unambiguous morphisms can finally be answered in the negative.

On the one hand, this situation nicely illustrates the combinatorial richness of patterns without unambiguous erasing morphisms. On the other hand, it demonstrates how intricate those phenomena can be that cause target alphabet dependent ambiguity. The phenomenon discussed in Section 4.4.1 already requires major technical effort and, although it covers many example patterns, it does not lead to a characterisation of terminal alphabet dependent ambiguity since patterns like α from Example 4.46 must be taken into account as well. Thus, the considerations in Section 4.4.1 and Section 4.4.2 suggest that the approach of classifying all target alphabet specific ambiguity phenomena with the help of adequate example pattern classes is not very promising. Thus, we shall not pursue this concept further in this thesis. However, in Section 5.2, we present a different approach towards a characterisation of patterns with an unambiguous morphism.

In the next section, we restrict the class of patterns to be considered.

4.4.3 Natural subclasses of patterns

Due to the various ambiguity phenomena as described in previous sections, a characterisation of patterns with an unambiguous morphism is difficult even for one single given target alphabet. Thus, in this section, we consider proper subclasses of $\mathbb{N}^+$. The first subclass are patterns with a finite maximal number of variables.

Definition 4.47 (k-variable pattern). *Let $k \in \mathbb{N}$. We call a pattern $\alpha \in \mathbb{N}^+$ a* k-variable pattern *if and only if* $\mathrm{var}(\alpha) = \{1, 2, \dots, k\}$.

In the following statements, we characterise the unambiguity of morphisms with a finite target alphabet for k-variable patterns. We begin with 2-variable patterns.

Proposition 4.48. *Let $\alpha \in \{1, 2\}^+$. There exists an unambiguous morphism $\sigma : \mathbb{N}^* \to \{\mathtt{a}, \mathtt{b}\}^*$ for α if and only if α is morphically primitive or $|\alpha|_1 \neq |\alpha|_2$.*

Proof. If α is morphically primitive, there is an unambiguous morphism according to Theorem 3.12. If α is not morphically primitive and $|\alpha|_1 \neq |\alpha|_2$, then $\sigma : \mathbb{N}^* \to \{\mathtt{a}, \mathtt{b}\}^*$ defined by $\sigma(1) := \mathtt{a}$, $\sigma(2) =: \varepsilon$ if $|\alpha|_1 < |\alpha|_2$, or $\sigma(1) := \varepsilon$, $\sigma(2) := \mathtt{a}$ if $|\alpha|_1 > |\alpha|_2$, can be easily verified to be unambiguous for α. This proves the if part.

We prove the only-if part by contraposition. Hence, let α be morphically imprimitive and $|\alpha|_1 = |\alpha|_2$. Thus, $\alpha = (1 \cdot 2)^n$ for an $n \in \mathbb{N}$. However, this implies that α is morphically erasable (to verify this, we can, for instance, apply Lemma 4.6). Thus, according Corollary 4.13, there is no unambiguous morphism for α. □

If α consists of more than two different variables, the following corollary can be applied.

Corollary 4.49. *Let $k \geq 3$, and α be a k-variable pattern. Let Σ_{k-1} be an alphabet with $k-1$ letters. Then there exists an unambiguous morphism $\sigma : \mathbb{N}^* \to \Sigma_{k-1}^*$ if and only if α is morphically unerasable.*

Proof. Directly from Corollary 4.27. □

In the above result, we are allowed to chose an arbitrary finite alphabet. If we fix the size of the target alphabet, the situation is not clear: Let Σ_k be an alphabet with $k \geq 2$ different letters. According to Corollary 4.49, there exists an unambiguous morphism for all morphically unerasable patterns with at most $k+1$ variables. However, counting the number of variables of α_k from the proof of Theorem 4.24 implies that there exist morphically unerasable patterns with $(k^2+3k+2)/2$ variables for which no morphism with target alphabet Σ_k is unambiguous. It is an open question for which maximal n between $k+1$ and $(k^2+3k+2)/2$ the property of α being morphically unerasable is still characteristic for α having an unambiguous morphism.

We conclude this section with a class of patterns which is not restricted in the number of variables, but in the structure of the patterns.

Theorem 4.50. *Let Σ be an alphabet, $|\Sigma| \geq 2$. Let $\alpha \in \mathbb{N}^+$, let (E, N) be a maximal ambiguity partition for α and, for every $i \in N$, let $i\,i$ be a factor of α.*

There exists an unambiguous morphism $\sigma : \mathbb{N}^* \to \Sigma^*$ for α if and only if α is morphically unerasable.

Proof. Let $n := |\alpha|$.

We first prove the *only if* part by contraposition: If α is morphically erasable, then $(\mathrm{var}(\alpha), \emptyset)$ is an ambiguity partition for α and, thus, according to Corollary 4.11, there exists no unambiguous morphism for α.

To show the *if* part, let $N \neq \emptyset$. Furthermore, let $\sigma : \mathbb{N}^* \to \{\mathtt{a}, \mathtt{b}\}^*$ be a morphism defined by

$$\sigma(i) := \begin{cases} \mathtt{ab}^{ni+1}\mathtt{aab}^{ni+2}\mathtt{a}\ldots\mathtt{ab}^{n(i+1)}\mathtt{a}, & \text{if } i \in N, \\ \varepsilon, & \text{else.} \end{cases}$$

Note that, for variables in N, σ corresponds to the morphism $\tau_{k,a,b}$ as introduced by Jiang et. al. [16].

We now prove that σ is unambiguous for α: Assume to the contrary that there exists a morphism $\tau : \mathbb{N}^* \to \{\mathtt{a}, \mathtt{b}\}^*$ such that $(\star)$ $\tau(\alpha) = \sigma(\alpha)$ and $\tau(j) \neq \sigma(j)$ for a $j \in \mathrm{var}(\alpha)$.

Case 1. For all $i \in N$, there exists an $x_i \in \{ni+1, ni+2, \ldots, n(i+1)\}$ such that $\tau(i) = \ldots\mathtt{ab}^{x_i}\mathtt{a}\ldots$. Assume that $\tau(i) = \sigma(i)$ for all $i \in N$. Then either $\tau(\alpha) \neq \sigma(\alpha)$ or $\tau(j) = \sigma(j)$ for all $j \in \mathrm{var}(\alpha)$, which contradicts $(\star)$. Thus, $\tau(i) \neq \sigma(i)$ for an $i \in N$. Since $\alpha = \ldots i\,i \ldots$, $\tau(i\,i)$ is a factor of $\tau(\alpha)$. But – due to $\tau(i) \neq \sigma(i)$ – it can be verified that $\tau(i\,i)$ is not a factor of $\sigma(\alpha)$, which contradicts $\tau(\alpha) = \sigma(\alpha)$.

Case 2. There exists a $j \in N$ such that, for all $x_j \in \{nj+1, nj+2, \ldots, n(j+1)\}$, $\tau(j) \neq \ldots\mathtt{ab}^{x_j}\mathtt{a}\ldots$. The following reasoning is directly taken from Jiang et. al. [16]: Because, for every $i \in N$, $\sigma(i)$ contains $n = |\alpha|$ "segments" of the form $\mathtt{ab}^m\mathtt{a}$, $m \in \mathbb{N}$, it follows that, for all $i \in N$, there exist $x_i \in \{ni+1, ni+2, \ldots, n(i+1)\}$ and $y \in \mathrm{var}(\alpha)$ such that $\tau(y) = \ldots \mathtt{ab}^{x_i}\mathtt{a}\ldots$. For every $i \in N$, we choose such an x_i and define a morphism $h : \mathbb{N}^* \to \mathbb{N}^*$ for every $y \in \mathrm{var}(\alpha)$ as follows:

$$h(y) := \begin{cases} i_1 i_2 \ldots i_k, & \text{if } \tau(y) = w_0\,\mathtt{ab}^{x_{i_1}}\mathtt{a}\,w_1\,\mathtt{ab}^{x_{i_2}}\mathtt{a}\,w_2 \ldots \mathtt{ab}^{x_{i_k}}\,w_k, k \in \mathbb{N}, \\ & \text{satisfying } w_i \in \Sigma^* \text{ and } w_i \neq \ldots \mathtt{ab}^{x_j}\mathtt{a}\ldots \\ & \text{for all } i \in \{0, 1, \ldots, k\} \text{ and all } j \in N, \\ \varepsilon, & \text{else.} \end{cases}$$

h is nontrivial for N because h is nontrivial for $\{j\}$. Furthermore, $h(\alpha) = \pi_N(\alpha)$ since, for every $i \in N$, there exists exactly one corresponding x_i. But, according to condition (ii) of Definition 4.4, (E', N') as defined in this condition, is an ambiguity partition, too, satisfying $|E'| > |E|$ and $|N'| < |N|$ (cf. Proposition 4.5, point 2). This contradicts the assumption that (E, N) is maximal (cf. Definition 4.8).

Consequently, such a morphism τ cannot exist since exactly one of the two cases must occur. Thus, σ is unambiguous for α. □

We want to note that, with the proof technique of Theorem 4.50, conditions similar to $\alpha = \ldots i\,i \ldots$ for every $i \in N$ can certainly be found since it is sufficient for any such condition to let case 1 in the proof lead to a contradiction.

4.5 The power and limits of segmented morphisms

In this section, we shortly discuss the benefit and limitation of segmented morphisms as introduced in Section 3.1. From the standard usage of segmented morphisms in literature and in this work, we infer the following formal definition.

Definition 4.51 (Segmented morphism). *We call a morphism $\sigma : \mathbb{N}^* \to \{\mathtt{a}, \mathtt{b}\}^*$ a* segmented morphism *if and only if, for all $x, i, j \in \mathbb{N}$,*

1. $\sigma(x) \in (\mathtt{ab}^+\mathtt{a})^*$ *and,*

2. *if $\sigma(i) = \ldots \mathtt{ab}^k\mathtt{a} \ldots = \sigma(j)$, then $i = j$.*

In this context, a segment *is a factor of the form* $\mathtt{ab}^+\mathtt{a}$.

Thus, a segmented morphism $\sigma : \mathbb{N}^* \to \Sigma^*$ maps each variable to a catenation of several segments. If a segmented morphism is nonerasing, point 2 makes it an injective morphism. For an example, consider $\sigma_{3\text{-seg}}$ from Definition 3.6.

Concerning the ambiguity of nonerasing morphisms, segmented morphisms are *the* main tool for achieving moderate ambiguity (cf. Theorem 3.5) and unambiguity (cf. the explanation above Theorem 3.12). In both cases, "only" three segments per variable are necessary. Concerning the ambiguity of arbitrary (possibly erasing) morphisms, we can still benefit from segmented morphisms since they can establish moderate ambiguity (cf. Theorem 4.20) and even unambiguity in some special case (cf. Theorem 4.50). However, for both cases, the respective morphisms have an unbounded number of segments per variable since this number is dependent on the length of the pattern under consideration.

Unfortunately, segmented morphisms are not suitable as a general tool to accomplish unambiguity for arbitrary patterns (including morphically imprimitive ones).

Proposition 4.52. *Let* $\alpha := (1 \cdot 2 \cdot 3^2 \cdot 4^3 \cdot 2)^2 \cdot (5 \cdot 6 \cdot 7^2 \cdot 8^3 \cdot 6)^2$. *There exists an unambiguous morphism* $\sigma : \mathbb{N}^* \rightarrow \{\mathtt{a}, \mathtt{b}\}^*$ *for* α, *but no segmented morphism is unambiguous for* α.

Proof. It can be easily verified that the morphism which maps 1 to a, 5 to b and erases all other variables is unambiguous for α.

Now assume to the contrary that there is an unambiguous segmented morphism σ for α. Since the maximal ambiguity partition for α is $(E, N) := (\{2,3,4,6,7,8\}, \{1,5\})$, σ must erase all variables in E (cf. Theorem 4.7). If $\sigma(1) = \varepsilon$, the morphism $\tau : \mathbb{N}^* \rightarrow \{\mathtt{a}, \mathtt{b}\}^*$, defined by $\tau(1) := \sigma(5)$ and $\tau(x) := \varepsilon$ for every $x \in \mathbb{N} \setminus \{1\}$, satisfies $\tau(\alpha) = \sigma(\alpha)$ and, thus, contradicts σ being unambiguous. The case $\sigma(5) = \varepsilon$ is analogous. Hence, $\sigma(1) \neq \varepsilon \neq \sigma(5)$, and, thus, $\sigma(1)$ or $\sigma(5)$ end with a segment $\mathtt{ab}^k\mathtt{a}$ with $k \geq 2$ (due to point 2 of Definition 4.51, they cannot both end with aba). Assume that $\sigma(1) = w\,\mathtt{ab}^k\mathtt{a}$ with $w \in \{\mathtt{a}, \mathtt{b}\}^*$ and $k \geq 2$ (the case $\sigma(5) = w\,\mathtt{ab}^k\mathtt{a}$ with $w \in \{\mathtt{a}, \mathtt{b}\}^*$ and $k \geq 2$ is analogous). Then, the morphism $\tau : \mathbb{N}^* \rightarrow \{\mathtt{a}, \mathtt{b}\}^*$, defined by $\tau(1) := w$, $\tau(2 \cdot 3^2 \cdot 4^3 \cdot 2) := \mathtt{ab}^k\mathtt{a}$ and and $\tau(x) := \sigma(x)$ for every $x \in \mathbb{N} \setminus \{1,2,3,4\}$, satisfies $\tau(\alpha) = \sigma(\alpha)$ and, thus, contradicts σ being unambiguous. Consequently, there is no unambiguous segmented morphism for α. □

In the pattern α of Proposition 4.52, the structure of a segment is recreated with the help of the E-variables of the maximal ambiguity partition (E, N) of α. Not only segmented morphisms are affected, but the structure of every morphism can be recreated in this way. Thus, such general concepts as segmented morphisms are not suited for being a universal tool to accomplish unambiguity. Unambiguous morphisms must rather be customised according to the special structure of E-variables in the pattern under consideration. So far, no general strategy to attain this goal is known.

4.6 Decidability and complexity

In this section, we investigate some of the criteria and conditions of the previous theorems in this chapter regarding their decidability and complexity. We assume the reader to be familiar with basic techniques and results in complexity theory. For an overview over this topic, Garey and Johnson [9] can be consulted.

First, we define the following sets of patterns. Some of these sets have already been defined in Definition 4.25. For a greater clarity, we shall recollect them here.

Definition 4.53. *Let* PRIM (IMPRIM) *be the set of morphically primitive (imprimitive) patterns, and let* UNERAS (ERAS) *be the set of morphically unerasable (erasable) patterns.*

For any alphabet Σ, *let* UNAMB_Σ *be the set of patterns for which there is an unambiguous morphism* $\sigma : \mathbb{N}^* \rightarrow \Sigma^*$, *let* MODAMB_Σ *be the set of patterns for which there is an moderately ambiguous morphism* $\sigma : \mathbb{N}^* \rightarrow \Sigma^*$ *and let* $\mathrm{AMB}_\Sigma := \mathbb{N}^+ \setminus \mathrm{UNAMB}_\Sigma$, $\mathrm{SAMB}_\Sigma := \mathbb{N}^+ \setminus \mathrm{MODAMB}_\Sigma$.

For any alphabet Σ, *let* $\mathrm{UNAMB}_{\mathrm{NE},\Sigma}$ *be the set of patterns for which there is an unambiguous nonerasing morphism* $\sigma : \mathbb{N}^* \rightarrow \Sigma^*$, *let* $\mathrm{MODAMB}_{\mathrm{NE},\Sigma}$ *be the set of patterns for which there is a moderately ambiguous nonerasing morphism* $\sigma : \mathbb{N}^* \rightarrow \Sigma^*$ *and let* $\mathrm{AMB}_{\mathrm{NE},\Sigma} := \mathbb{N}^+ \setminus \mathrm{UNAMB}_{\mathrm{NE},\Sigma}$, $\mathrm{SAMB}_{\mathrm{NE},\Sigma} := \mathbb{N}^+ \setminus \mathrm{MODAMB}_{\mathrm{NE},\Sigma}$.

For patterns in AMB_Σ, every morphism is unambiguous, where, for patterns in SAMB_Σ, every morphism is strongly ambiguous. We ask the reader not to confuse UNAMB_Σ and

$\mathrm{UNAMB}_\Sigma(\alpha)$ (cf. Definition 4.41) since the former set consists of patterns, whereas the latter contains morphic images over Σ.

With the help of the formal statements in Chapter 3 and Chapter 4, we can summarise the relation of the sets to each other in the following corollary.

Corollary 4.54. *The following statements hold true:*

1. PRIM $\subset$ UNERAS *and* IMPRIM $\supset$ ERAS.
2. *For any alphabet* Σ *with* $|\Sigma| \geq 2$, $\mathrm{PRIM} = \mathrm{UNAMB}_{\mathrm{NE},\Sigma} = \mathrm{MODAMB}_{\mathrm{NE},\Sigma}$. *Hence,* $\mathrm{IMPRIM} = \mathrm{AMB}_{\mathrm{NE},\Sigma} = \mathrm{SAMB}_{\mathrm{NE},\Sigma}$.
3. *For any alphabet* Σ *with* $|\Sigma| \geq 2$, $\mathrm{UNERAS} = \mathrm{MODAMB}_\Sigma$ *and, hence,* $\mathrm{ERAS} = \mathrm{SAMB}_\Sigma$.
4. *For any infinite alphabet* Σ_∞, $\mathrm{UNERAS} = \mathrm{UNAMB}_{\Sigma_\infty}$. *Hence,* $\mathrm{ERAS} = \mathrm{AMB}_{\Sigma_\infty}$.

Proof. ad 1. Directly from Proposition 4.14 and the fact that $\mathrm{PRIM} = \mathbb{N}^+ \setminus \mathrm{IMPRIM}$ and $\mathrm{ERAS} = \mathbb{N}^+ \setminus \mathrm{UNERAS}$.

ad 2. Directly from Theorem 3.5 and Corollary 3.13.

ad 3. Directly from Theorem 4.20.

ad 4. Directly from Theorem 4.22. □

Thus, if we can decide the sets PRIM and ERAS, we gain several positive answers concerning the decidability of ambiguity questions. A very positive result covers the decidability of PRIM.

Theorem 4.55 (Holub [13]). PRIM *is decidable in polynomial time.*

Holub [13] describes an algorithm that decides PRIM in time $O((|\mathrm{var}(\alpha)| + \log|\alpha|)|\alpha|)$.

We now introduce a canonical algorithm that outputs the maximal ambiguity partition for a pattern α and, thus, decides ERAS.

Definition 4.56 (MaxAmb). *Let* $\alpha \in \mathbb{N}^+$. *The algorithm* MaxAmb *is defined as follows:*

```
E := ∅, N := var(α).
loop:
   Find an n ∈ N and a morphism h : ℕ* → ℕ* with h(π_{var(α)\{n}}(α)) = π_N(α).
   if such n and h exist:
      E := E ∪ {x ∈ N | h(x) = ε}.
      N := {x ∈ N | h(x) ≠ ε}.
      goto loop.
   else
      output (E, N).
```

We write $\mathrm{MaxAmb}(\alpha) = (E, N)$ *if* MaxAmb *outputs* (E, N) *on* α.

In the next theorem, we prove the correctness and complexity of MaxAmb which, unfortunately, is exponential in $|\mathrm{var}(\alpha)|$ (and, thus, in $|\alpha|$).

Theorem 4.57. *Let $\alpha \in \mathbb{N}^+$. The algorithm* MaxAmb *outputs the maximal ambiguity partition for α in time $O(|\text{var}(\alpha)|^2 \cdot (|\alpha| + 1)^{|\text{var}(\alpha)|-1})$.*

Proof. Let $(E_1, N_1) := \text{MaxAmb}(\alpha)$ and let (E_2, N_2) be the maximal ambiguity partition of α. We show the following:

1. (E_1, N_1) is an ambiguity partition for α.
2. $(E_1, N_1) = (E_2, N_2)$.
3. (E_1, N_1) is found by MaxAmb in time $O(|\text{var}(\alpha)|^2 \cdot (|\alpha| + 1)^{|\text{var}(\alpha)|-1})$.

ad 1. If MaxAmb outputs $(\emptyset, \text{var}(\alpha))$, this is an ambiguity partition according to point (i) of Definition 4.4. Let $n \in N$ and $h : \mathbb{N}^* \to \mathbb{N}^*$ be a morphism with $h(\pi_{\text{var}(\alpha)\setminus\{n\}}(\alpha)) = \pi_N(\alpha)$. Without loss of generality, let $h(n) := \varepsilon$. Hence, h is nontrivial for n and satisfies $h(\alpha) = \pi_N(\alpha)$ and, thus, point (ii) of Definition 4.4 is satisfied and the new sets (E, N) describe an ambiguity partition for α. This inductively proves that MaxAmb outputs an ambiguity partition for α.

ad 2. First, assume that $E_1 \not\subseteq E_2$. Then, according to Lemma 4.9, $(E_1 \cup E_2, N_1 \cap N_2)$ is an ambiguity partition for α with $|E_1 \cup E_2| > |E_2|$, which contradicts (E_2, N_2) being maximal. Now assume that $E_1 \subset E_2$. Then, according to condition (ii) of Definition 4.4, there exist ambiguity partitions $(E^{(0)}, N^{(0)}) := (\emptyset, \text{var}(\alpha))$, $(E^{(1)}, N^{(1)})$, $(E^{(2)}, N^{(2)})$, ..., $(E^{(m)}, N^{(m)}) := (E_2, N_2)$, $m \in \mathbb{N}$ and, for every $k \in \{0, 1, \ldots, m\}$, a morphism $h^{(k)} : \mathbb{N}^* \to \mathbb{N}^*$ satisfying

(1) $h^{(k)}$ is nontrivial for $N^{(k)}$,

(2) $h^{(k)}(\alpha) = \pi_{N^{(k)}}(\alpha)$,

(3) $E^{(k+1)} = E^{(k)} \cup \{x \in N^{(k)} \mid h^{(k)}(x) = \varepsilon\}$, and

(4) $N^{(k+1)} = \{x \in N^{(k)} \mid h^{(k)}(x) \neq \varepsilon\}$.

Let k be maximal with $E^{(k)} \subseteq E_1$ and $E^{(k+1)} \not\subseteq E_1$ and let $h' := \pi_{N_1} \circ h^{(k)}$. Since $E^{(k)} \subseteq E_1$ and $E^{(k+1)} \not\subseteq E_1$, there is an $x \in E^{(k+1)} \setminus E_1$ with $h^{(k)}(x) = \varepsilon$ (cf. point (3)). Furthermore, $x \notin E_1$ implies $x \in N_1$. Consequently, $h'(\pi_{\text{var}(\alpha)\setminus\{x\}}(\alpha)) = h'(\alpha) = \pi_{N_1}(h^{(k)}(\alpha)) = \pi_{N_1}(\pi_{N^{(k)}}(\alpha)) = \pi_{N_1}(\alpha)$ since $h^{(k)}(\alpha) = \pi_{N^{(k)}}(\alpha)$ (cf. point (2)) and $N_1 \subseteq N^{(k)}$ (due to $E^{(k)} \subseteq E_1$). Thus, while $N = N_1$, MaxAmb finds suitable n, h (e. g., $n = x$ and $h = h'$) with $h(\pi_{\text{var}(\alpha)\setminus\{n\}}(\alpha)) = \pi_N(\alpha)$ and, thus, continues increasing E such that (E_1, N_1) can not be the final output of MaxAmb(α). This contradicts the assumption that $E_1 \subset E_2$. Thus, $E_1 = E_2$ and, hence, $(E_1, N_1) = (E_2, N_2)$.

ad 3. We first argue that, given E, N, n, a morphism h with $h(\pi_{\text{var}(\alpha)\setminus\{n\}}(\alpha)) = \pi_N(\alpha)$ can be found in $O((|\alpha| + 1)^{|\text{var}(\alpha)|-1})$: W.l.o.g., let $\text{var}(\pi_{\text{var}(\alpha)\setminus\{n\}}(\alpha)) = \{1, 2, \ldots, k\}$ for a $k \in \mathbb{N}$. Furthermore, let $m_i := |\alpha|_i$, $1 \leq i \leq k$, and $\pi_N(\alpha) = x_1 \cdot x_2 \cdot [\ldots] \cdot x_n$, $n \in \mathbb{N}$, $x_i \in \mathbb{N}$, $1 \leq i \leq n$. We now enumerate all tuples $(n_1, n_2, \ldots, n_k) \in \{0, 1, \ldots, n\}^k$ with $m_1 n_1 + m_2 n_2 + \ldots + m_k n_k = n$ and, for every such tuple, let $\pi_N(\alpha) = w_1 w_2 \ldots w_n$ with $|w_i| = n_j$ if and only if $x_i = j$. If $w_i = w_j$ for every i, j with $x_i = x_j$, then a corresponding morphism satisfying $h(\pi_{\text{var}(\alpha)\setminus\{n\}}(\alpha)) = \pi_N(\alpha)$ is found. Since $n \leq |\alpha|$, $k \leq |\text{var}(\alpha)| - 1$, and we have to check at most $(n+1)^k$ tuples, h can be found in $O((|\alpha| + 1)^{|\text{var}(\alpha)|-1})$.

Due to Proposition 4.5, point 2, every time, the `goto loop` is executed, $|N|$ decreases by at least one. Thus, the outer loop can be executed at most $|\text{var}(\alpha)|$ times. Furthermore, there are at most $|\text{var}(\alpha)|$ possibilities for n. Thus, the overall complexity sums up to $O(|\text{var}(\alpha)|^2 \cdot (|\alpha|+1)^{|\text{var}(\alpha)|-1})$. □

Thus, we can decide whether or not a pattern α is morphically erasable.

Corollary 4.58. ERAS *is decidable.*

Proof. We can use MaxAmb to decide ERAS since, for any $\alpha \in \mathbb{N}^+$, $\text{MaxAmb}(\alpha) = (\text{var}(\alpha), \emptyset)$ if and only if α is morphically erasable. □

Unfortunately, unless P=NP, there is no hope for a subexponential decision algorithm since a very related decision problem is NP-complete:

Theorem 4.59. *Let Σ_∞ be an infinite alphabet. The problem of deciding* $\text{AMB}_{\Sigma_\infty}$ *is NP-complete.*

Proof. We first show that $\text{AMB}_{\Sigma_\infty}$ is in NP. For this purpose, we describe a nondeterministic Turing machine M that accepts $\text{AMB}_{\Sigma_\infty}$: First, M writes nondeterministically a sequence $S := (E_1, N_1, h_1), (E_2, N_2, h_2), \ldots, (E_k, N_k, h_k)$ for a nondeterministically chosen $k \in \{1, 2, \ldots, |\text{var}(\alpha)|+1\}$ and $E_i, N_i \subseteq \text{var}(\alpha)$, $1 \leq i \leq k$. The h_i correspond to morphisms $h_i : \mathbb{N}^* \to \mathbb{N}^*$ and can each be given as a list $[x_1, h_i(x_1), x_2, h_i(x_2), \ldots, x_{|\text{var}(\alpha)|}, h_i(x_{|\text{var}(\alpha)|})]$. We additionally restrict the length of the $h_i(x)$ for every $i \in \{1, 2, \ldots, k\}$ and every $x \in \text{var}(\alpha)$ by $|\alpha|$ such that the length of the sequence S is polynomial in $|\alpha|$. Afterwards, we check if S is “compatible” with the definition of the ambiguity partition, which means that $(E_1, N_1) := (\emptyset, \text{var}(\alpha))$ as well as, for every i, $2 \leq i \leq k$, (E_i, N_i) is a partition of $\text{var}(\alpha)$ and $(E, N) := (E_{i-1}, N_{i-1})$, $h = h_i$ and $(E', N') := (E_i, N_i)$ satisfy condition (ii) of Definition 4.4. It can be verified with little effort that this check can be done in polynomial time. We let M go into the accepting state if and only if this check is successful and $(E_k, N_k) = (\text{var}(\alpha), \emptyset)$. Due to point 2 of Proposition 4.5, if the check is successful, $|E_i| > |E_{i+1}|$ holds for every $i \in \{1, 2, \ldots, k-1\}$. Thus, if $(\text{var}(\alpha), \emptyset)$ is an ambiguity partition for α, it can be “reached” by a sequence S of maximal length $|\text{var}(\alpha)|+1$. Consequently, M accepts exactly those patterns α (in polynomial time) such that $(\text{var}(\alpha), \emptyset)$ is an ambiguity partition for α. Due to Theorem 4.22, these are exactly the patterns in $\text{AMB}_{\Sigma_\infty}$.

In order to show that $\text{AMB}_{\Sigma_\infty}$ is NP-hard, we reduce the following problem to $\text{AMB}_{\Sigma_\infty}$:

Morphism Problem/Match Test: The problem of deciding $\text{MATCH}_{\{\mathtt{a},\mathtt{b}\}} := \{(\alpha, w) \mid$ there exists a morphism $\sigma : \mathbb{N}^* \to \{\mathtt{a},\mathtt{b}\}^*$ such that $\sigma(\alpha) = w\}$ is NP-complete (cf. Ehrenfeucht, Rozenberg [4]).

We define a function f for which we shall prove the following:

(a) f is computable in polynomial time.

(b) $(\alpha, w) \in \text{MATCH}_{\{\mathtt{a},\mathtt{b}\}}$ if and only if $f(\alpha, w) \in \text{AMB}_{\Sigma_\infty}$.

In order to define $f(\alpha, w)$, we need the following auxiliary definitions: Let $\alpha \in \mathbb{N}^*$ and $w \in \Sigma^*$. W.l.o.g. let $\text{var}(\alpha) \subseteq \{3, 5, 7, \ldots\}$. Furthermore, let $d : \mathbb{N}^* \to \mathbb{N}^*$ and $\sigma_{\text{inv}} : \Sigma^* \to \mathbb{N}^*$ be morphisms, defined as follows: Let

$$d(x) := x \cdot (x+1),$$

where $\cdot$ refers to the concatenation, and

$$\sigma_{\text{inv}}(c) := \begin{cases} 1, & c = \mathsf{a}, \\ 2, & c = \mathsf{b}. \end{cases}$$

If $\sigma_{\text{inv}}(w)$ is morphically primitive, we set $\beta := \sigma_{\text{inv}}(w)$; otherwise (if $\sigma_{\text{inv}}(w)$ is morphically imprimitive), according to Theorem 2.5, there exists a morphism $g : \mathbb{N}^* \to \mathbb{N}^*$ such that $g(\sigma_{\text{inv}}(w)) = \sigma_{\text{inv}}(w)$ and $g(i) \neq i$ for an $i \in \{1, 2\}$. It particularly follows that $g(x) \neq \varepsilon$ and $g(y) = \varepsilon$ for $\{x, y\} = \{1, 2\}$. In this case, let $\beta := \pi_{\{x\}}(\sigma_{\text{inv}}(w))$.

Finally, let

$$f(\alpha, w) := d(\alpha)\, \beta\, \beta\, d(\alpha).$$

ad (a). It is clear that $d(\alpha)$ and $\sigma_{\text{inv}}(w)$ can be constructed in polynomial time. Furthermore, according to Theorem 4.55, we can also efficiently check if $\sigma_{\text{inv}}(w)$ is morphically imprimitive.

ad (b). We first show the *only if* part. Let $(\alpha, w) \in \text{MATCH}_{\{\mathsf{a},\mathsf{b}\}}$. Hence, there exists a morphism $h' : \mathbb{N}^* \to \Sigma^*$ such that $h'(\alpha) = w$. W.l.o.g., let $h'(x) := \varepsilon$ for every $x \in \{1, 2\} \cup \{4, 6, 8, \ldots\}$. Thus, $h'(\beta) = \varepsilon$ and $h'(d(\alpha)) = h'(\alpha) = w$. Because of the structure of $f(\alpha, w)$ and the fact that $d(\alpha)$ is a pattern with the ambiguity partition $(\text{var}(d(\alpha)), \emptyset)$, we can verify that $(E, N) := (\text{var}(d(\alpha)), \text{var}(\beta))$ is an ambiguity partition for $f(\alpha, w)$. We consider two disjoint cases:

Case 1: $\sigma_{\text{inv}}(w)$ is morphically primitive. Then (E, N) and $h := \sigma_{\text{inv}} \circ h'$ satisfy condition (ii) of Definition 4.4 since

$$\begin{aligned} h(f(\alpha, w)) &= h(d(\alpha)) \cdot h(\beta\beta) \cdot h(d(\alpha)) \\ &= \sigma_{\text{inv}}(h'(d(\alpha))) \cdot \varepsilon \cdot \sigma_{\text{inv}}(h'(d(\alpha))) \\ &= \sigma_{\text{inv}}(w) \cdot \sigma_{\text{inv}}(w) = \beta \cdot \beta = \pi_N(f(\alpha, w)). \end{aligned}$$

Moreover, h is nontrivial for N.

Case 2: $\sigma_{\text{inv}}(w)$ is morphically imprimitive. Then (E, N) and $h := \pi_{\{x\}} \circ \sigma_{\text{inv}} \circ h'$ satisfy condition (ii) of Definition 4.4 since

$$\begin{aligned} h(f(\alpha, w)) &= h(d(\alpha)) \cdot h(\beta\beta) \cdot h(d(\alpha)) \\ &= \pi_{\{x\}}(\sigma_{\text{inv}}(h'(d(\alpha)))) \cdot \varepsilon \cdot \pi_{\{x\}}(\sigma_{\text{inv}}(h'(d(\alpha)))) \\ &= \pi_{\{x\}}(\sigma_{\text{inv}}(w)) \cdot \pi_{\{x\}}(\sigma_{\text{inv}}(w)) = \beta \cdot \beta = \pi_N(f(\alpha, w)). \end{aligned}$$

Furthermore, h is nontrivial for N.

In both cases, $h(x) = \varepsilon$ for every $x \in \text{var}(\beta)$. Thus, $(\text{var}(f(\alpha, w)), \emptyset)$ is an ambiguity partition for $f(\alpha, w)$. Hence, according to Corollary 4.11, there is no unambiguous morphism for $f(\alpha, w)$. This proves the *only if* part.

We now show the *if* part by contraposition. Let $(\alpha, w) \notin \text{MATCH}_{\{\mathsf{a},\mathsf{b}\}}$. Without loss of generality, let $\{\mathsf{a}, \mathsf{b}\} \subseteq \Sigma_\infty$. We shall prove that the morphism $\sigma : \mathbb{N}^* \to \Sigma_\infty^*$, defined by $\sigma(1) := \mathsf{a}$, $\sigma(2) := \mathsf{b}$, $\sigma(x) := \varepsilon$, $x \in \mathbb{N} \setminus \{1, 2\}$, is unambiguous for $f(\alpha, w)$. Assume to the contrary that there exists a morphism $\tau : \mathbb{N}^* \to \Sigma_\infty^*$ satisfying $\sigma(f(\alpha, w)) = \tau(f(\alpha, w))$ and $\sigma(i) \neq \tau(i)$ for an $i \in \text{var}(f(\alpha, w))$. We consider the following cases:

Case 1: $\text{var}(\beta) = \{x\}$. Hence, either $|\text{var}(\sigma_{\text{inv}}(w))| = 1$ or $\sigma_{\text{inv}}(w)$ is morphically imprimitive. In the former case, let g be the identity morphism, in the latter case, let g be the morphism as defined above (below the definition of σ_{inv}).

Case 1.1: $\tau(x) \neq \varepsilon$. Thus, either $\tau(f(\alpha, w)) \neq \sigma(f(\alpha, w))$ or $\tau(f(\alpha, w)) = \sigma(f(\alpha, w))$, $\tau(x) = \sigma(x)$ and, hence, $\tau(i) = \sigma(i)$ for every $i \in \text{var}(f(\alpha, w))$, which contradicts the assumption.

Case 1.2: $\tau(x) = \varepsilon$. Then $\tau(d(\alpha)) = \sigma(\beta)$ and, hence, $\sigma \circ g \circ \sigma_{\text{inv}} \circ \tau \circ d(\alpha) = \sigma \circ g \circ \sigma_{\text{inv}} \circ \sigma(\beta) = w$ since $\sigma_{\text{inv}}(\sigma(\beta)) = \beta$, $g(\beta) = \sigma_{\text{inv}}(w)$ and $\sigma(\sigma_{\text{inv}}(w)) = w$. Thus, $(\alpha, w) \in \text{MATCH}_{\{\mathtt{a},\mathtt{b}\}}$, which is a contradiction.

Case 2: $\text{var}(\beta) = \{x, y\}$. Hence, $\beta = \sigma_{\text{inv}}(w)$ is morphically primitive.

Case 2.1: $\tau(i) = \varepsilon$ for all $i \in \text{var}(d(\alpha))$. Then, $\sigma_{\text{inv}}(\tau(\beta)) = \beta$ and $\sigma_{\text{inv}} \circ \tau$ is nontrivial for $\text{var}(\beta)$ since $\tau(i) \neq \sigma(i)$ for an $i \in \text{var}(f(\alpha, w))$ is required. Thus, β is morphically imprimitive, which contradicts β being morphically primitive.

Case 2.2: $\tau(i) \neq \varepsilon$ for an $i \in \text{var}(d(\alpha))$. Let $\tau(i) = \ldots \mathtt{a} \ldots$ (the case $\tau(i) = \ldots \mathtt{b} \ldots$ is analogous). Then, $\tau(1) = \varepsilon$ since otherwise $|\tau(f(\alpha, w))|_{\mathtt{a}} > |\sigma(f(\alpha, w))|_{\mathtt{a}}$. Assume that $\tau(2) \neq \varepsilon$. With $|\tau(f(\alpha, w))|_{\mathtt{a}} = |\sigma(f(\alpha, w))|_{\mathtt{a}}$ and $|\tau(f(\alpha, w))|_{\mathtt{b}} = |\sigma(f(\alpha, w))|_{\mathtt{b}}$, it follows that $\tau(2) = \mathtt{b}$. Due to the structure of $f(\alpha, w)$, we have $\tau(f(\alpha, w)) = \ldots \sigma(\pi_{\{2\}}(\beta))^2 \ldots$, but $\sigma(\pi_{\{2\}}(\beta))^2 = \mathtt{b}^{2|\beta|_2}$ is not a factor of $\sigma(f(\alpha, w)) = \sigma(\beta)^2$ since $|\sigma(\beta)|_{\mathtt{a}} > 0$. This contradicts the existence of a morphism τ with $\tau(j_1) \neq \varepsilon$ and $\tau(j_2) = \varepsilon$, $\{j_1, j_2\} = \{1, 2\}$. Consequently, $\tau(1) = \tau(2) = \varepsilon$. Thus, $\tau(d(\alpha)) = \sigma(\beta) = w$ and, hence, $(\alpha, w) \in \text{MATCH}_{\{\mathtt{a},\mathtt{b}\}}$, which is again a contradiction.

Consequently, such a morphism τ cannot exist. Hence, σ is unambiguous for α, and this implies $f(\alpha, w) \notin \text{AMB}_{\Sigma_\infty}$. □

The proof of Theorem 4.59 allows us to receive a result on the minimal complexity of the AMB_Σ decision problem for a *finite* alphabet Σ, although it is still open if, in this case, AMB_Σ is decidable at all.

Corollary 4.60. *Let Σ be a finite alphabet, $|\Sigma| \geq 2$. The problem of deciding AMB_Σ is NP-hard.*

Proof. We can use the same reduction function f as in the proof of Theorem 4.59 as it is sufficient to have $\{\mathtt{a}, \mathtt{b}\} \subseteq \Sigma$, which we can assume without loss of generality. □

Consequently, we can conclude our complexity results in the following Corollary.

Corollary 4.61. *The following complexity results hold true:*

- *For any alphabet Σ with $|\Sigma| \geq 2$, $\text{PRIM} = \text{UNAMB}_{\text{NE},\Sigma} = \text{MODAMB}_{\text{NE},\Sigma}$ are decidable in polynomial time.*
- *For any alphabet Σ with $|\Sigma| \geq 2$, the problem of deciding AMB_Σ is NP-hard.*
- *For any infinite alphabet Σ_∞ and any alphabet Σ with $|\Sigma| \geq 2$, the problem of deciding $\text{ERAS} = \text{AMB}_{\Sigma_\infty} = \text{SAMB}_\Sigma$ is NP-complete.*

Proof. Directly from

- Theorem 3.5, Corollary 3.13, Theorem 4.55,
- Corollary 4.60 and
- Theorem 4.22, Theorem 4.59, and Theorem 4.20,

respectively. □

In particular, we receive the following result on the complexity of UNAMB_Σ and MODAMB_Σ.

Corollary 4.62. *Let Σ be an arbitrary alphabet with $|\Sigma| \geq 2$. Unless P=NP, neither* UNAMB_Σ *nor* MODAMB_Σ *are decidable in polynomial time.*

Proof. We argue by contraposition. If UNAMB_Σ is decidable in polynomial time, also its complement AMB_Σ is decidable in polynomial time. Since AMB_Σ is NP-hard (cf. Corollary 4.60), it follows that P=NP. If MODAMB_Σ is decidable in polynomial time, also its complement SAMB_Σ is decidable in polynomial time. Since, for any infinite alphabet Σ_∞, $\mathrm{SAMB}_\Sigma = \mathrm{AMB}_{\Sigma_\infty}$ (cf. Corollary 4.61) which is NP-hard (cf. Theorem 4.59), it follows again that P=NP. □

Thus, depending on the question if there exist unambiguous *nonerasing* or *erasing* morphisms, patterns do not only differ in their structural complexity (morphically primitive vs. morphically unerasable), but also in the computational complexity (P vs. non-P) of the respective decision problems.

We conclude this section with a complexity analysis of k-variable patterns (a pattern subclass introduced in Section 4.4.3).

Definition 4.63 ($\mathrm{UNERAS}_k/\mathrm{UNAMB}_k$). *Let $k \in \mathbb{N}$ and Σ_{k-1} be an alphabet with $k-1$ letters. We define* $\mathrm{UNERAS}_k := \mathrm{UNERAS} \cap \{1,2,\ldots,k\}^+$ *and* $\mathrm{UNAMB}_k := \mathrm{UNAMB}_{\Sigma_{k-1}} \cap \{1,2,\ldots,k\}^+$.

Hence, UNERAS_k and UNAMB_k consist of k-variable patterns only (cf. Definition 4.47). Due to Theorem 4.49, both sets are identical. Additionally, there is a polynomial time decision procedure.

Corollary 4.64. *Let $k \in \mathbb{N}$.* $\mathrm{UNERAS}_k = \mathrm{UNAMB}_k$ *is decidable in polynomial time.*

Proof. Directly from Theorem 4.57 with $|\mathrm{var}(\alpha)| = k$. □

However, although the resulting polynomial degree k is fixed, it can be arbitrarily large and, thus, it can inhibit an effective decision procedure for practical purposes.

Chapter 5

Related problems and topics

In this chapter, we present some results which are closely related to the ambiguity of morphisms.

5.1 Ambiguity of substitutions

As pattern languages are not only defined for patterns $\alpha \in \mathbb{N}^+$, but also for patterns $\alpha \in (\mathbb{N} \cup \Sigma)^+$ with a finite terminal alphabet Σ and $\Sigma \cap \mathbb{N} = \emptyset$, it is a natural approach to analyse the ambiguity of substitutions, i. e. terminal-preserving morphisms $\sigma : (\mathbb{N} \cup \Sigma)^* \to \Sigma^*$. We first define (un)ambiguity of substitutions formally.

Definition 5.1 (Ambiguity and unambiguity of substitutions). *Let Σ be an alphabet, $\alpha \in (\mathbb{N} \cup \Sigma)^+$ and let $\sigma : (\mathbb{N} \cup \Sigma)^* \to \Sigma^*$ be a substitution with $\sigma(x) \neq \varepsilon$ for some $x \in \text{var}(\alpha)$. We call σ* ambiguous *(for α) if and only if there is a substitution $\tau : (\mathbb{N} \cup \Sigma)^* \to \Sigma^*$ satisfying $\tau(\alpha) = \sigma(\alpha)$ and, for some $x \in \text{var}(\alpha)$, $\tau(x) \neq \sigma(x)$. If σ is not ambiguous for α, it is called* unambiguous *(for α).*

We want to note that, as in the case of morphisms, we exclude the trivial case of σ erasing all variables in α.

The study of ambiguous substitutions, as initiated by Reidenbach [25], is not only interesting per se, but allows to draw some very enlightening conclusions on various other topics related to pattern languages as the (non)learnability of pattern languages (cf. Reidenbach [28]), the equivalence problem for erasing pattern languages (cf. Reidenbach [27]) and the classification of pattern languages according to the Chomsky hierarchy of formal languages (cf. Jain et al. [14]). While considering $(\mathbb{N} \cup \Sigma)^+$ enlarges the class of patterns to be analysed, it adds a restriction to the morphisms, namely to map every letter from Σ to itself. Hence, this model can be seen as both a generalisation and a restriction.

We start our examination of the ambiguity of substitutions on patterns from $(\mathbb{N} \cup \Sigma)^+$ with an example pattern for which we can observe a new type of ambiguity that involves the terminal symbols in the pattern.

Example 5.2. Let $\alpha := 1 \cdot \mathtt{a} \cdot 2 \cdot \mathtt{b} \cdot 3$ and let the morphisms $\sigma, \tau : (\mathbb{N} \cup \{\mathtt{a}, \mathtt{b}\})^* \to \{\mathtt{a}, \mathtt{b}\}^*$ be defined by $\sigma(1) := \varepsilon$, $\sigma(2) := \mathtt{a}\,\mathtt{b}$, $\sigma(3) := \varepsilon$, $\tau(1) := \mathtt{a}$, $\tau(2) := \varepsilon$ and $\tau(3) := \mathtt{b}$. σ is ambiguous for α since $\tau(\alpha) = \mathtt{a}\,\mathtt{a}\,\mathtt{b}\,\mathtt{b} = \sigma(\alpha)$ and $\tau(1) \neq \sigma(1)$. ◇

The interesting point with this example is the different "role" that the terminal sequence $\mathtt{a} \ldots \mathtt{b}$ of the pattern α plays depending on whether σ or τ is used to generate $\mathtt{a}\,\mathtt{a}\,\mathtt{b}\,\mathtt{b}$.

With σ, the terminal sequence generates the outer $\mathtt{a}\ldots\mathtt{b}$, with τ, it generates the inner $\mathtt{ab}$. This is a new type of ambiguity, which can only occur for substitutions on patterns in $(\mathbb{N}\cup\Sigma)^+\setminus\mathbb{N}^+$ and is formalised in the following definition.

Definition 5.3 (Terminal comprising ambiguity†). *Let Σ be an alphabet, and let $\alpha := \beta_0\, v_1\, \beta_1\, v_2\, \beta_2\, [\ldots]\, \beta_{n-1}\, v_n\, \beta_n \in (\mathbb{N}\cup\Sigma)^+\setminus\mathbb{N}^+$ with $n\in\mathbb{N}$, $\beta_0,\beta_n\in\mathbb{N}^*$, $\beta_1,\beta_2,\ldots\beta_{n-1}\in\mathbb{N}^+$ and $v_1,v_2,\ldots v_n\in\Sigma^+$. Then a substitution $\sigma:(\mathbb{N}\cup\Sigma)^*\to\Sigma^*$ is called* terminal-comprisingly ambiguous (for α) *if and only if there exists a substitution $\tau:(\mathbb{N}\cup\Sigma)^*\to\Sigma^*$ with $\tau(\alpha)=\sigma(\alpha)$ and, for some k, $0\le k\le n$, $|\tau(\beta_k)|\ne|\sigma(\beta_k)|$.*

For the pattern α from Example 5.2, it is $\alpha=\beta_0\, v_1\, \beta_1\, v_2\, \beta_2$ with $\beta_0:=1$, $v_1:=\mathtt{a}$, $\beta_1:=2$, $v_2:=\mathtt{b}$ and $\beta_2:=3$ and $|\sigma(\beta_0)|=0\ne1=|\tau(\beta_0)|$. Thus, σ (as well as τ) is terminal-comprisingly ambiguous for α.

The conditions of Definition 5.3 imply that there is a letter $c\in\mathrm{term}(\alpha)$ which is mapped to different positions in $\sigma(\alpha)$ and $\tau(\alpha)$. Hence, if k is minimal with $|\sigma(\beta_k)|\ne|\tau(\beta_k)|$, $|\sigma(\beta_k)|<|\tau(\beta_k)|$ and $v_{k+1}=:c\,v'_{k+1}$ with $c\in\Sigma$, we have the following situation

$$\alpha \;=\; \beta_0\, v_1\, \beta_1\, v_2\, \beta_2\, [\ldots]\, \beta_k\, c\, v'_{k+1}\, \beta_{k+1}\, v_{k+2}\, \beta_{k+2}\, [\ldots]\, v_n\, \beta_n,$$

$$\sigma(\alpha) \;=\; \overbrace{\underbrace{w_0\quad c\quad w_1}_{\tau(\beta_0\, v_1\, \beta_1\, v_2\, \beta_2\, [\ldots]\, \beta_k)}}^{\sigma(\beta_0\, v_1\, \beta_1\, v_2\, \beta_2\, [\ldots]\, \beta_k)\ \text{over}\ w_0;\ \sigma(v'_{k+1}\, \beta_{k+1}\, v_{k+2}\, \beta_{k+2}\, [\ldots]\, v_n\, \beta_n)\ \text{over}\ w_1\, c\, w_2}\quad c\quad \underbrace{w_2}_{\tau(v'_{k+1}\, \beta_{k+1}\, v_{k+2}\, \beta_{k+2}\, [\ldots]\, v_n\, \beta_n)} \;=\; \tau(\alpha),$$

for suitable $w_0,w_1,w_2\in\Sigma^*$. This illustrates how the terminal symbol c is *comprised* in the ambiguity of σ.

Regarding Example 5.2, not only σ is terminal-comprisingly ambiguous for α:

Proposition 5.4. *Every morphism $\sigma:(\mathbb{N}\cup\Sigma)^*\to\{\mathtt{a},\mathtt{b}\}^*$ with $\sigma(2)\ne\varepsilon$ is terminal-comprisingly ambiguous for $1\cdot\mathtt{a}\cdot2\cdot\mathtt{b}\cdot3$. This statement does not hold for morphisms $\sigma:(\mathbb{N}\cup\Sigma)^*\to\Sigma^*$ with $\Sigma\supset\{\mathtt{a},\mathtt{b}\}$.*

Proof. Let $\alpha:=\beta_0\, v_1\, \beta_1\, v_2\, \beta_2$ with $\beta_0:=1$, $v_1:=\mathtt{a}$, $\beta_1:=2$, $v_2:=\mathtt{b}$ and $\beta_2:=3$. Thus, $\alpha=1\cdot\mathtt{a}\cdot2\cdot\mathtt{b}\cdot3$. Let $\sigma:(\mathbb{N}\cup\Sigma)^*\to\{\mathtt{a},\mathtt{b}\}^*$ be a morphism with $\sigma(2)\ne\varepsilon$. If $\sigma(2)\in\{\mathtt{a}\}^+$, then the morphism $\tau:(\mathbb{N}\cup\Sigma)^*\to\{\mathtt{a},\mathtt{b}\}^*$ defined by $\tau(1):=\sigma(1)\sigma(2)$, $\tau(2):=\varepsilon$ and $\tau(3):=\sigma(3)$ proves σ being terminal-comprisingly ambiguous since $\tau(\alpha)=\sigma(\alpha)$ and $|\tau(\beta_1)|\ne|\sigma(\beta_1)|$. If $\sigma(2)\in\{\mathtt{a},\mathtt{b}\}^+\setminus\{\mathtt{a}\}^+$, then $\sigma(2)=w_1\mathtt{b}w_2$ for suitable $w_1,w_2\in\{\mathtt{a},\mathtt{b}\}^*$. Hence, the morphism $\tau:(\mathbb{N}\cup\Sigma)^*\to\{\mathtt{a},\mathtt{b}\}^*$ defined by $\tau(1):=\sigma(1)$, $\tau(2):=w_1$ and $\tau(3):=w_2\,\mathtt{b}\,\sigma(3)$ proves σ being terminal-comprisingly ambiguous since $\tau(\alpha)=\sigma(\alpha)$ and $|\tau(\beta_1)|\ne|\sigma(\beta_1)|$.

Let $\Sigma\supset\{\mathtt{a},\mathtt{b}\}$. W.l.o.g., let $\mathtt{c}\in\Sigma$. Then, the morphism $\sigma:(\mathbb{N}\cup\Sigma)^*\to\Sigma^*$ defined by $\sigma(1):=\varepsilon$, $\sigma(2):=\mathtt{c}\ne\varepsilon$ and $\sigma(3):=\varepsilon$ is unambiguous for $1\cdot\mathtt{a}\cdot2\cdot\mathtt{b}\cdot3$. □

As this proposition shows, terminal-comprising ambiguity strongly depends on the size of the terminal alphabet.

In the following, we are mainly interested in ambiguity phenomena, such as terminal-comprising ambiguity, which occur in patterns $(\mathbb{N}\cup\Sigma)^+\setminus\mathbb{N}^+$ only. However, since an

†Note that this definition has been introduced by Reidenbach [25]. In the present thesis, it is slightly modified since we do not use the term "terminal-comprisingly ambiguous word".

$\alpha \in (\mathbb{N} \cup \Sigma)^+ \setminus \mathbb{N}^+$ is the concatenation of words in Σ^+ and (terminal-free) patterns from $\mathbb{N}^+$, ambiguity which merely happens in the $\mathbb{N}^+$-blocks must be taken into account as well. For instance, this includes the case when a morphism is neither unambiguous nor terminal-comprisingly ambiguous for a given pattern. For this case, we can adapt some of the technical concepts of Chapter 4 to analyse this ambiguity, in particular the notion of ambiguity partitions. We generalise Definition 4.4 in the following manner:

Definition 5.5 (Ambiguity partition). *Let $\alpha \in (\mathbb{N} \cup \Sigma)^+$. We inductively define an* ambiguity partition *(for α):*

(i) *$(\emptyset, \mathrm{var}(\alpha))$ is an ambiguity partition for α.*

(ii) *If (E, N) is an ambiguity partition for α and there exists a terminal-preserving morphism $h : (\mathbb{N} \cup \Sigma)^* \to (\mathbb{N} \cup \Sigma)^*$ that is nontrivial for N and satisfies $h(\alpha) = \pi_N(\alpha)$, where $\pi_N : (\mathbb{N} \cup \Sigma)^* \to (\mathbb{N} \cup \Sigma)^*$ is defined by $\pi_N(x) := x$ if $x \in N \cup \Sigma$ and $\pi_N(x) := \varepsilon$ if $x \notin N \cup \Sigma$, then (E', N') is an ambiguity partition for α with*

$$\begin{aligned} E' &:= E \cup \{x \in N \mid h(x) = \varepsilon\}, \\ N' &:= \{x \in N \mid h(x) \neq \varepsilon\}. \end{aligned}$$

We use the terms "*maximal ambiguity partition*", "*morphically erasable*" and "*morphically unerasable*" also for patterns in $(\mathbb{N} \cup \Sigma)^+$ and omit a formal definition at this point (just replace "Let $\alpha \in \mathbb{N}^+$" with "Let Σ be an alphabet and $\alpha \in (\mathbb{N} \cup \Sigma)^+$" in Definitions 4.8 and 4.12).

It is not difficult to prove the same result as Theorem 4.7 for patterns in $(\mathbb{N} \cup \Sigma)^+$.

Theorem 5.6. *Let Σ be an alphabet. Let $\alpha \in (\mathbb{N} \cup \Sigma)^+$ and let (E, N) be an ambiguity partition for α. Then every substitution $\sigma : (\mathbb{N} \cup \Sigma)^* \to \Sigma^*$ satisfying $\sigma(x) \neq \varepsilon$ for an $x \in E$ is ambiguous for α.*

Proof. Replacing "$\mathbb{N}$" with "$(\mathbb{N} \cup \Sigma)$" and "morphism" with "substitution", the proof is verbatim the same as the proof of Theorem 4.7. □

We note that, in the proof of Theorem 4.7 adapted to Theorem 5.6, the substitutions $\sigma : (\mathbb{N} \cup \Sigma)^* \to \Sigma^*$ with $\sigma(e) \neq \varepsilon$ for an $e \in E$ which are proved to be ambiguous for the pattern α do not need to be terminal-comprisingly ambiguous.

We shall now investigate if there are patterns $\alpha := \beta_0 v_1 \beta_1 v_2 \beta_2 [\ldots] \beta_{n-1} v_n \beta_n \in (\mathbb{N} \cup \Sigma)^+ \setminus \mathbb{N}^+$ (cf. Definition 5.3) for which no substitution is unambiguous, but there exists a substitution which is unambiguous for all the terminal-free subpatterns β_i in the pattern. For such a pattern, the fact that no substitution is unambiguous is caused by the terminal-comprising ambiguity of some substitutions as pointed out in the following lemma:

Lemma 5.7. *Let Σ be an alphabet. Furthermore, for an $n \in \mathbb{N}$, let $\alpha := \beta_0\, v_1\, \beta_1\, v_2\, \beta_2\, [\ldots]\, \beta_{n-1}\, v_n\, \beta_n \in (\mathbb{N} \cup \Sigma)^+ \setminus \mathbb{N}^+$ with $v_j \in \Sigma^+$, $1 \leq j \leq n$, $\beta_0, \beta_n \in \mathbb{N}^*$ and $\beta_k \in \mathbb{N}^+$, $1 \leq k \leq n-1$. If there is a substitution $\tau : (\mathbb{N} \cup \Sigma)^* \to \Sigma^*$ with $\tau(x) \neq \varepsilon$ for an $x \in \mathrm{var}(\alpha)$ that is unambiguous for every β_i, $0 \leq i \leq n$, with $\tau(\beta_i) \neq \varepsilon$ and there is no unambiguous substitution $\sigma : (\mathbb{N} \cup \Sigma)^* \to \Sigma^*$ for α, then τ is terminal-comprisingly ambiguous for α.*

Proof. Since no substitution is unambiguous for α, also τ is ambiguous for α . Thus, there exists a substitution $\tau' : (\mathbb{N} \cup \Sigma)^* \to (\mathbb{N} \cup \Sigma)^*$ with $\tau'(\alpha) = \tau(\alpha)$ and $\tau'(j) \neq \tau(j)$ for a $j \in \text{var}(\alpha)$. Assume that τ is not terminal-comprisingly ambiguous. Hence, $|\tau'(\beta_i)| = |\tau(\beta_i)|$ and, thus, $\tau'(\beta_i) = \tau(\beta_i)$ for every $i \in \{0, 1, \ldots, n\}$. Let $k \in \{0, 1, \ldots, n\}$ with $j \in \text{var}(\beta_k)$. Since $\tau'(j) \neq \tau(j)$ and $\tau'(\beta_k) = \tau(\beta_k)$, τ is not unambiguous for β_k, which contradicts the choice of τ. Thus, τ is terminal-comprisingly ambiguous for α, which proves the lemma. We note that since $\tau'(j) \neq \tau(j)$, it is $|\tau'(j)| \geq 1$ or $|\tau(j)| \geq 1$ and, thus, since $\tau'(\beta_k) = \tau(\beta_k)$, $\tau(\beta_k) \neq \varepsilon$. □

Consequently, if we find patterns that satisfy the conditions of Lemma 5.7, we can identify a new ambiguity phenomenon solely occurring for patterns in $(\mathbb{N}\cup\Sigma)^+ \setminus \mathbb{N}^+$. As pointed out by Proposition 5.4, all considerations concerning terminal-comprising ambiguity depend on the size of Σ. Therefore, we start our observations for a binary terminal alphabet.

Example 5.8. Let $\Sigma := \{\mathtt{a}, \mathtt{b}\}$ and $\alpha := 1 \cdot 2 \cdot \mathtt{a} \cdot 3 \cdot \mathtt{b} \cdot 4 \cdot 5 \in (\mathbb{N} \cup \Sigma)^+$. We can use the same reasoning as in the proof of Proposition 5.4 to show that every substitution $\sigma : (\mathbb{N} \cup \Sigma)^* \to \Sigma^*$ with $\sigma(3) \neq \varepsilon$ is terminal-comprisingly ambiguous for α. Furthermore, since $(\{1, 2, 4, 5\}, \{3\})$ is an ambiguity partition for α, no substitution $\sigma : (\mathbb{N}\cup\Sigma)^* \to \{\mathtt{a}, \mathtt{b}\}^*$ with $\sigma(e) \neq \varepsilon$ for an $e \in \{1, 2, 4, 5\}$ is unambiguous for α (cf. Theorem 5.6). Hence, no substitution $\sigma : (\mathbb{N} \cup \Sigma)^* \to \{\mathtt{a}, \mathtt{b}\}^*$ is unambiguous for α. However, for $\alpha = \beta_0\, v_1\, \beta_1\, v_2\, \beta_2$ with $\beta_0 := 1 \cdot 2$, $v_1 := \mathtt{a}$, $\beta_1 := 3$, $v_2 := \mathtt{b}$ and $\beta_2 := 4 \cdot 5$, it is easy to see that the substitution $\tau : (\mathbb{N} \cup \Sigma)^* \to \{\mathtt{a}, \mathtt{b}\}^*$, defined by $\tau(3) := \mathtt{a}$ and $\tau(x) := \varepsilon$ for $x \neq 3$, erases β_0, β_2 and is unambiguous for β_1. Thus, τ meets the requirements of Lemma 5.7. Consequently, the fact that there is no unambiguous substitution for α is co-caused by terminal-comprising ambiguity of morphisms like τ.

The following theorem states that suchlike example patterns exist for every alphabet Σ.

Theorem 5.9. *For every alphabet Σ, there is a pattern $\alpha := \beta_0\, v_1\, \beta_1\, v_2\, \beta_2\, [\ldots]\, \beta_{m-1}\, v_m\, \beta_m \in (\mathbb{N} \cup \Sigma)^+ \setminus \mathbb{N}^+$ with $m \in \mathbb{N}$, $\beta_0, \beta_m \in \mathbb{N}^*$, $\beta_1, \beta_2, \ldots \beta_{m-1} \in \mathbb{N}^+$ and $v_1, v_2, \ldots v_m \in \Sigma^+$ such that*

1. *no substitution $\sigma : (\mathbb{N} \cup \Sigma)^* \to \Sigma^*$ is unambiguous for α and*
2. *there exists a substitution $\tau : (\mathbb{N} \cup \Sigma)^* \to \Sigma^*$ with $\tau(x) \neq \varepsilon$ for an $x \in \text{var}(\alpha)$ that is unambiguous for every β_i, $0 \leq i \leq n$, with $\tau(\beta_i) \neq \varepsilon$.*

Proof. Let $k \in \mathbb{N} \cup \{0\}$ and let Σ be an alphabet with $k + 1$ letters and $\mathtt{a} \in \Sigma$. Let α_k be the pattern from the proof of Theorem 4.43 and $(E, N) := (\text{var}(\alpha_k) \setminus \{1, 2, \ldots, k + 1\}, \{1, 2, \ldots, k+1\})$ be its maximal ambiguity partition. The following claims shall support our proof.

Claim 1. Let $\sigma : \mathbb{N}^* \to \Sigma^*$ be a morphism. It is $\sigma(\alpha_k) \in \text{UNAMB}_\Sigma(\alpha_k)$ if and only if $|\sigma(x)| = 1$ for every $x \in N$ and $|\sigma(x)| = 0$ for every $x \in E$.

Proof (Claim 1). Directly from the proof of Theorem 4.43. *q.e.d. (Claim 1)*

Claim 2. For every morphism $\sigma : \mathbb{N}^* \to \Sigma^*$ with $\sigma(\alpha_k) \in \text{UNAMB}_\Sigma(\alpha_k)$, there exists an $n \in N$ with $\sigma(n) = \mathtt{a}$.

Proof (Claim 2). Let $\sigma(\alpha_k) \in \text{UNAMB}_\Sigma(\alpha_k)$. Assume to the contrary, that $\sigma(n) \neq \mathtt{a}$ for every $n \in \mathbb{N}$. Since $|\Sigma \setminus \{\mathtt{a}\}| = k$ and $|N| = k + 1$, it follows from Claim 1 that there are variables $n_1, n_2 \in N$, $n_1 \neq n_2$, with $\sigma(n_1) = \sigma(n_2)$. Let $\tau : \mathbb{N}^* \to \Sigma^*$ be the morphism defined by $\tau(n) := \sigma(n)$ for every $n \in N \setminus \{n_1, n_2\}$, $\tau(x_{\{(n_1,\text{le}),(n_2,\text{le})\}}) := \sigma(n_1)(= \sigma(n_2))$ and $\tau(x) = \varepsilon$ for all other variables x. Hence, $\tau(\alpha_k) = \sigma(\alpha_k)$ and, thus, σ is not unambiguous for α_k, which contradicts $\sigma(\alpha_k) \in \text{UNAMB}_\Sigma(\alpha_k)$. *q.e.d. (Claim 2)*

Finally, we proof the points 1 and 2 of Theorem 5.9. To this purpose, we define the pattern α as follows:

$$\alpha := z_1 \cdot z_2 \cdot \mathtt{a} \cdot \alpha_k \cdot \mathtt{a} \cdot z_3 \cdot z_4,$$

with pairwise different variables $z_1, z_2, z_3, z_4 \in \mathbb{N} \setminus \text{var}(\alpha_k)$. Thus, $\alpha = \beta_0\, v_1\, \beta_1\, v_2 \beta_2$ with $\beta_0 := z_1 \cdot z_2$, $v_1 = \mathtt{a}$, $\beta_1 := \alpha_k$, $v_2 := \mathtt{a}$, $\beta_2 := z_3 \cdot z_4$.

ad 1. Let $\sigma : (\mathbb{N} \cup \Sigma)^* \to \Sigma^*$ be a substitution. Assume that σ is unambiguous for α. Since $(E \cup \{z_1, z_2, z_3, z_4\}, N)$ is an ambiguity partition for α, it is $\sigma(x) = \varepsilon$ for every $x \in E \cup \{z_1, z_2, z_3, z_4\}$ (cf. Theorem 5.6). Moreover, if $|\sigma(n)| \geq 2$ for an $n \in N$, σ is not unambiguous for α_k by Claim 1 and, thus, not unambiguous for α. Furthermore, according to Claim 2, there exists an $n \in N$ with $\sigma(n) = \mathtt{a}$. Summarising our insights so far, we have

$$\begin{aligned}\sigma(\alpha) &= \mathtt{a}\,\sigma(1)\,\sigma(2)[\ldots]\,\sigma(n-1)\,\sigma(n)\,\sigma(n+1)[\ldots]\,\sigma(k+1)\\ &\quad\ \sigma(k+1)\,\sigma(k)[\ldots]\,\sigma(n+1)\,\sigma(n)\,\sigma(n-1)[\ldots]\,\sigma(1)\,\mathtt{a}\\ &= \mathtt{a}\,\sigma(1)\,\sigma(2)[\ldots]\,\sigma(n-1)\,\mathtt{a}\,\sigma(n+1)[\ldots]\,\sigma(k+1)\\ &\quad\ \sigma(k+1)\,\sigma(k)[\ldots]\,\sigma(n+1)\,\mathtt{a}\,\sigma(n-1)[\ldots]\,\sigma(1)\,\mathtt{a}\,.\end{aligned}$$

We can verify with little effort that the substitution $\tau : (\mathbb{N} \cup \Sigma)^* \to \Sigma^*$, defined by $\tau(z_1) := \mathtt{a}\,\sigma(1)\,\sigma(2)[\ldots]\,\sigma(n-1)$, $\tau(z_3) := \sigma(n-1)[\ldots]\,\sigma(1)\,\mathtt{a}$, $\tau(x) := \sigma(x)$ for every $x \in \{n+1, \ldots, k+1\}$ and $\tau(x) := \varepsilon$ for all other variables x, satisfies $\tau(\alpha) = \sigma(\alpha)$ and, hence, contradicts σ being unambiguous for α. Consequently, there is no unambiguous substitution for α.

ad 2. Let $\tau : (\mathbb{N} \cup \Sigma)^* \to \Sigma^*$ be a substitution with $\tau(z_1 \cdot z_2 \cdot z_3 \cdot z_4) = \varepsilon$ and $\tau(\alpha_k) \in \text{UNAMB}_\Sigma(\alpha_k)$. Hence, $\tau(x) \neq \varepsilon$ for an $x \in \text{var}(\alpha_k) \subseteq \text{var}(\alpha)$. Assume to the contrary that τ is ambiguous for a β_i, $0 \leq i \leq 2$, with $\tau(\beta_i) \neq \varepsilon$. Thus, τ is ambiguous for $\beta_1 = \alpha_k$, which contradicts the choice of $\tau(\alpha_k)$. Consequently, τ is unambiguous for β_1. □

From Theorem 5.9 and Lemma 5.7, we can conclude that, for every alphabet Σ, there exist patterns α for which no substitution $\sigma : (\mathbb{N} \cup \Sigma)^* \to \Sigma^*$ is unambiguous because certain morphisms are terminal-comprisingly ambiguous. This situation is caused by the interplay of substituted variables $\sigma(\beta_i)$ and terminal sequences v_i in the pattern – for the variable sequences β_i alone, there is an unambiguous morphism τ. The pattern from the proof of Theorem 5.9 is not the only type of pattern showing this behaviour, as demonstrated by the following example.

Example 5.10. Let $\alpha \in (\mathbb{N} \cup \{\mathtt{a}, \mathtt{b}, \mathtt{c}\})^+$ be given by

$$\alpha := 1 \cdot 2 \cdot \mathtt{a} \cdot \mathbf{3} \cdot 4 \cdot 5 \cdot 6 \cdot 7 \cdot \mathtt{a} \cdot 8 \cdot 9 \cdot \mathtt{b} \cdot \mathbf{3} \cdot 6 \cdot 7 \cdot 10 \cdot 11 \cdot \mathtt{b} \cdot 12 \cdot 13 \cdot \mathtt{c} \cdot \mathbf{3} \cdot 4 \cdot 5 \cdot 10 \cdot 11 \cdot \mathtt{c} \cdot 14 \cdot 15\,.$$

We note that this pattern can be seen as renaming of the "union" of the patterns α and β from the proof of Theorem 6 in Freydenberger and Reidenbach [7]. We can verify that $(E, N) := (\text{var}(\alpha) \setminus \{3\}, \{3\})$ is an ambiguity partition for α. Hence, no substitution $\sigma : (\mathbb{N} \cup \{\mathtt{a}, \mathtt{b}, \mathtt{c}\})^* \to \{\mathtt{a}, \mathtt{b}, \mathtt{c}\}^*$ with $\sigma(e) \neq \varepsilon$ for an $e \in E$ is unambiguous for α (cf.

Theorem 5.6). Let $\sigma(e) = \varepsilon$ for every $e \in E$ and $\sigma(3) \neq \varepsilon$. If $\sigma(3) = \mathtt{a}u$ for a $u \in \{\mathtt{a}, \mathtt{b}, \mathtt{c}\}^*$, we define a substitution $\tau : (\mathbb{N} \cup \{\mathtt{a}, \mathtt{b}, \mathtt{c}\})^* \to \{\mathtt{a}, \mathtt{b}, \mathtt{c}\}^*$ by $\tau(8) := u\,\mathtt{a}$, $\tau(10) := \mathtt{a}\,u$ and $\tau(x) := \varepsilon$ for all other variables x. We can verify that $\tau(\alpha) = \sigma(\alpha)$ and, thus, σ is not unambiguous for α.

If $\sigma(3) = \mathtt{b}\,u$ for a $u \in \{\mathtt{a}, \mathtt{b}, \mathtt{c}\}^*$, we define $\tau(12) := u\,\mathtt{b}$, $\tau(4) := \mathtt{b}\,u$ and $\tau(x) := \varepsilon$ for all other variables x. Thus, $\tau(\alpha) = \sigma(\alpha)$ and, hence, σ is not unambiguous for α.

If $\sigma(3) = \mathtt{c}\,u$ for a $u \in \{\mathtt{a}, \mathtt{b}, \mathtt{c}\}^*$, we define $\tau(14) := u\,\mathtt{c}$, $\tau(6) := \mathtt{c}\,u$ and $\tau(x) := \varepsilon$ for all other variables x. Again, $\tau(\alpha) = \sigma(\alpha)$ and, thus, σ is not unambiguous for α.

Consequently, there is no unambiguous substitution for α. However, the substitution $\sigma(3) := \mathtt{a}$ and $\sigma(x) := \varepsilon$ for every $x \in \mathbb{N} \setminus \{3\}$ can be verified to satisfy condition 2 of Theorem 5.9. ◇

The pattern α from the above example can be easily generalised for arbitrary alphabets Σ different from $\{\mathtt{a}, \mathtt{b}, \mathtt{c}\}$.

Summarising the insights of this section, we can conclude that even a potential characterisation of patterns in $\mathbb{N}^+$ with an unambiguous (erasing) morphism is of limited use when considering the class of patterns with terminal symbols $(\mathbb{N} \cup \Sigma)^+$ since Theorem 5.9 and Example 5.10 show that there are patterns with an unambiguous morphism for all the variable sequences $\beta_i \in \mathbb{N}^+$ in the pattern, but without an unambiguous substitution for the entire pattern $\alpha \in (\mathbb{N} \cup \Sigma)^+$, which is caused by terminal-comprising ambiguity. Nevertheless, the given (generic) example patterns in the proof of Theorem 5.9 and Example 5.10 can serve as a good starting point for future research on the topic of unambiguous substitutions.

In the following subsection, we will follow Section 4.4.2 by counting the number of unambiguous morphic images of a pattern in $(\mathbb{N} \cup \Sigma)^+$.

5.1.1 Finitely many unambiguous substitutions

As shown in Section 4.4.2, there are patterns $\alpha \in \mathbb{N}^+$ and suitable target alphabets Σ such that $\mathrm{UNAMB}_\Sigma(\alpha)$ is finite. We first define UNAMB for patterns $\alpha \in (\mathbb{N} \cup \Sigma)^+$ formally.

Definition 5.11 (UNAMB_Σ). *Let Σ be an alphabet and $\alpha \in (\mathbb{N} \cup \Sigma)^+$. Then $\mathrm{UNAMB}_\Sigma(\alpha)$ is the set of all $\sigma(\alpha)$, where $\sigma : (\mathbb{N} \cup \Sigma)^* \to \Sigma^*$ is a substitution that is unambiguous for α.*

All of the example patterns $\alpha \in \mathbb{N}^+$ from Section 4.4.2 with a finite set $\mathrm{UNAMB}_\Sigma(\alpha)$ for some alphabet Σ show the same behaviour in terms of maximal substitution length for each variable of α. To be specific, for every $\sigma : \mathbb{N}^* \to \Sigma^*$ with $\sigma(\alpha) \in \mathrm{UNAMB}_\Sigma(\alpha)$ and every $x \in \mathrm{var}(\alpha)$, it is $|\sigma(x)| \leq 2$. For $|\Sigma| \geq 3$, only examples with $|\sigma(x)| \leq 1$ are known. The following proposition shows that, for alphabet size 2 and 3, arbitrary substitution lengths are possible, i. e., for any $n \in \mathbb{N}$, we can find an example pattern α and an unambiguous substitution σ for α with $|\sigma(x)| = n$ for some $x \in \mathrm{var}(\alpha)$.

Proposition 5.12. *Let $n \in \mathbb{N}$, $\alpha_{\mathtt{ab}} := 1 \cdot 2 \cdot \mathtt{a} \cdot 3 \cdot \mathtt{b} \cdot (4 \cdot 5)^{n+1}$ and $\alpha_{\mathtt{abc}} := 1 \cdot 2 \cdot \mathtt{a} \cdot 3 \cdot 4^{n+1} \cdot \mathtt{b} \cdot 5 \cdot 6$.*

A substitution $\sigma : (\mathbb{N} \cup \{\mathtt{a}, \mathtt{b}\})^* \to \{\mathtt{a}, \mathtt{b}\}^*$ is unambiguous for $\alpha_{\mathtt{ab}}$ if and only if $\sigma(3) \in \{\mathtt{b}, \mathtt{b}^2, \dots, \mathtt{b}^n\}$ and $\sigma(x) := \varepsilon$ for every $x \in \mathbb{N} \setminus \{3\}$.

A substitution $\sigma : (\mathbb{N} \cup \{\mathtt{a}, \mathtt{b}, \mathtt{c}\})^* \to \{\mathtt{a}, \mathtt{b}, \mathtt{c}\}^*$ is unambiguous for $\alpha_{\mathtt{abc}}$ if and only if $\sigma(3) \in \{\mathtt{c}, \mathtt{c}^2, \dots, \mathtt{c}^n\}$ and $\sigma(x) := \varepsilon$ for every $x \in \mathbb{N} \setminus \{3\}$.

Hence, it is $\mathrm{UNAMB}_{\{\mathtt{a},\mathtt{b}\}}(\alpha_{\mathtt{ab}}) = \{\mathtt{a}\,\mathtt{b}^2, \mathtt{a}\,\mathtt{b}^3, \dots, \mathtt{a}\,\mathtt{b}^{n+1}\}$ and $\mathrm{UNAMB}_{\{\mathtt{a},\mathtt{b},\mathtt{c}\}}(\alpha_{\mathtt{abc}}) = \{\mathtt{a}\,\mathtt{c}\,\mathtt{b}, \mathtt{a}\,\mathtt{c}^2\,\mathtt{b}, \dots, \mathtt{a}\,\mathtt{c}^n\,\mathtt{b}\}$.

Proof. Let us consider $\alpha_{\mathtt{ab}}$ first. Since $(E,N) := (\{1,2,4,5\},\{3\})$ is an ambiguity partition for $\alpha_{\mathtt{ab}}$, no substitution $\sigma : (\mathbb{N} \cup \{\mathtt{a},\mathtt{b}\})^* \to \{\mathtt{a},\mathtt{b}\}^*$ with $\sigma(e) \neq \varepsilon$ for an $e \in E$ is unambiguous for $\alpha_{\mathtt{ab}}$ (cf. Theorem 5.6). Let $\sigma(e) = \varepsilon$ for every $e \in E$ and $\sigma(3) \neq \varepsilon$. Assume that σ is unambiguous for $\alpha_{\mathtt{ab}}$. If $\sigma(3) \in \{\mathtt{a},\mathtt{b}\}^+ \setminus \{\mathtt{b}\}^+$, it is $\sigma(3) = u\,\mathtt{a}\,v$ for suitable $u, v \in \{\mathtt{a},\mathtt{b}\}^*$. We define a substitution $\tau : (\mathbb{N} \cup \{\mathtt{a},\mathtt{b}\})^* \to \{\mathtt{a},\mathtt{b}\}^*$ by $\tau(1) := \mathtt{a}\,u$, $\tau(3) := v$ and $\tau(x) := \varepsilon$ for all other variables $x \in \mathbb{N}$. Hence, $\tau(\alpha_{\mathtt{ab}}) = \mathtt{a}\,u\,\mathtt{a}\,v\,\mathtt{b} = \sigma(\alpha_{\mathtt{ab}})$, which contradicts σ being unambiguous for α.

If $\sigma(3) = \mathtt{b}^m$ with $m \geq n+1$, we define a substitution $\tau : (\mathbb{N} \cup \{\mathtt{a},\mathtt{b}\})^* \to \{\mathtt{a},\mathtt{b}\}^*$ by $\tau(3) := \mathtt{b}^{m-(n+1)}$, $\tau(4) := \mathtt{b}$ and $\tau(x) := \varepsilon$ for all other variables $x \in \mathbb{N}$. Hence, $\tau(\alpha_{\mathtt{ab}}) = \mathtt{a}\,\mathtt{b}^{m-(n+1)}\,\mathtt{b}\,\mathtt{b}^{n+1} = \mathtt{a}\,\mathtt{b}^m\,\mathtt{b} = \sigma(\alpha_{\mathtt{ab}})$, which contradicts σ being unambiguous for α.

If $\sigma(3) = \mathtt{b}^m$ with $m \leq n$, σ is unambiguous for $\alpha_{\mathtt{ab}}$, which proves the first statement of the proposition.

Let us now consider $\alpha_{\mathtt{abc}}$. Since $(E,N) := (\{1,2,4,5,6\},\{3\})$ is an ambiguity partition for $\alpha_{\mathtt{abc}}$, no substitution $\sigma : (\mathbb{N} \cup \{\mathtt{a},\mathtt{b},\mathtt{c}\})^* \to \{\mathtt{a},\mathtt{b},\mathtt{c}\}^*$ with $\sigma(e) \neq \varepsilon$ for an $e \in E$ is unambiguous for $\alpha_{\mathtt{abc}}$ (cf. Theorem 5.6). Let $\sigma(e) = \varepsilon$ for every $e \in E$ and $\sigma(3) \neq \varepsilon$. Assume that σ is unambiguous for $\alpha_{\mathtt{abc}}$. If $\sigma(3) \in \{\mathtt{a},\mathtt{b},\mathtt{c}\}^+ \setminus \{\mathtt{b},\mathtt{c}\}^+$, it is $\sigma(3) = u\,\mathtt{a}\,v$ for suitable $u, v \in \{\mathtt{a},\mathtt{b}\}^*$. We define a substitution $\tau : (\mathbb{N} \cup \{\mathtt{a},\mathtt{b},\mathtt{c}\})^* \to \{\mathtt{a},\mathtt{b},\mathtt{c}\}^*$ by $\tau(1) := \mathtt{a}\,u$, $\tau(3) := v$ and $\tau(x) := \varepsilon$ for all other variables $x \in \mathbb{N}$. Hence, $\tau(\alpha_{\mathtt{abc}}) = \mathtt{a}\,u\,\mathtt{a}\,v\,\mathtt{b} = \sigma(\alpha_{\mathtt{abc}})$, which contradicts σ being unambiguous for $\alpha_{\mathtt{abc}}$.

If $\sigma(3) \in \{\mathtt{b},\mathtt{c}\}^+ \setminus \{\mathtt{c}\}^+$, it is $\sigma(3) = u\,\mathtt{b}\,v$ for suitable $u, v \in \{\mathtt{a},\mathtt{b}\}^*$. We define a substitution $\tau : (\mathbb{N} \cup \{\mathtt{a},\mathtt{b},\mathtt{c}\})^* \to \{\mathtt{a},\mathtt{b},\mathtt{c}\}^*$ by $\tau(3) := u$, $\tau(5) := v\,\mathtt{b}$ and $\tau(x) := \varepsilon$ for all other variables $x \in \mathbb{N}$. Hence, $\tau(\alpha_{\mathtt{abc}}) = \mathtt{a}\,u\,\mathtt{b}\,v\,\mathtt{b} = \sigma(\alpha_{\mathtt{abc}})$, which contradicts σ being unambiguous for $\alpha_{\mathtt{abc}}$.

If $\sigma(3) = \mathtt{c}^m$ with $m \geq n+1$, we define a substitution $\tau : (\mathbb{N} \cup \{\mathtt{a},\mathtt{b},\mathtt{c}\})^* \to \{\mathtt{a},\mathtt{b},\mathtt{c}\}^*$ by $\tau(3) := \mathtt{c}^{m-(n+1)}$, $\tau(4) := \mathtt{c}$ and $\tau(x) := \varepsilon$ for all other variables $x \in \mathbb{N}$. Hence, $\tau(\alpha_{\mathtt{abc}}) = \mathtt{a}\,\mathtt{c}^{m-(n+1)}\,\mathtt{c}^{n+1}\,\mathtt{b} = \mathtt{a}\,\mathtt{c}^m\,\mathtt{b} = \sigma(\alpha_{\mathtt{abc}})$, which contradicts σ being unambiguous for $\alpha_{\mathtt{abc}}$.

If $\sigma(3) = \mathtt{c}^m$ with $m \leq n$, σ is unambiguous for α, which proves the second statement of the proposition. □

It is an interesting open questions if there exist patterns with similar properties as $\alpha_{\mathtt{ab}}$ and $\alpha_{\mathtt{abc}}$ for larger alphabets.

5.2 Nonerasing multi-pattern languages

In this section, we focus again on terminal-free patterns $\alpha \in \mathbb{N}^+$ and morphisms $\sigma : \mathbb{N}^* \to \Sigma^*$. In the following, we illustrate how questions concerning the ambiguity of erasing morphisms relate to problems for nonerasing multi-pattern languages. A multipattern language is simply the union of several pattern languages (cf. Kari et al. [18]), i.e., for $\star \in \{\mathrm{E}, \mathrm{NE}\}$, an alphabet Σ and a finite set $P \subseteq (\mathbb{N} \cup \Sigma)^+$,

$$L_{\star,\Sigma}(P) := \bigcup_{\alpha \in P} L_{\star,\Sigma}(\alpha).$$

From a language theoretic point of view, it is an interesting question if a union of pattern languages is a pattern language again. In terms of multipattern languages, is $L_{\star,\Sigma}(P) =$

$L_{\star,\Sigma}(\beta)$ for $|P| \geq 2$ and some $\beta \in (\mathbb{N} \cup \Sigma)^+$? The ambiguity of morphisms reveals interesting, nontrivial examples having this property.

Example 5.13. Let $\Sigma := \{\mathtt{a}, \mathtt{b}\}$ and $\beta := 2 \cdot 2 \cdot 4 \cdot 1 \cdot 3 \cdot 3 \cdot 4$. In Example 4.44, it is demonstrated that all words in $\Sigma^+ \setminus \{\mathtt{a}, \mathtt{b}, \mathtt{ab}, \mathtt{ba}\}$ can be generated by one of the patterns in $P := \{2 \cdot 2,\ 2 \cdot 2 \cdot 1,\ 1 \cdot 3 \cdot 3,\ 4 \cdot 1 \cdot 4\}$. Thus, $\Sigma^+ \setminus \{\mathtt{a}, \mathtt{b}, \mathtt{ab}, \mathtt{ba}\} = L_{\mathrm{NE},\Sigma}(P)$ and, therefore, the following equivalences hold:

$$L_{\mathrm{NE},\Sigma}(1 \cdot 2) = L_{\mathrm{NE},\Sigma}(\{\mathtt{ab},\ \mathtt{ba},\ 2 \cdot 2,\ 2 \cdot 2 \cdot 1,\ 1 \cdot 3 \cdot 3,\ 4 \cdot 1 \cdot 4\}),$$

and

$$L_{\mathrm{NE},\Sigma}(1) = L_{\mathrm{NE},\Sigma}(\{\mathtt{a},\ \mathtt{b},\ \mathtt{ab},\ \mathtt{ba},\ 2 \cdot 2,\ 2 \cdot 2 \cdot 1,\ 1 \cdot 3 \cdot 3,\ 4 \cdot 1 \cdot 4\}).$$

◇

On the other hand, the ambiguity of morphisms can be expressed by certain vital properties of multi-pattern languages. For a more succinct formulation of the following results, we introduce the notion of unambiguous words:

Definition 5.14 (Unambiguous word). *Let Σ be an alphabet, let $w \in \Sigma^+$ and $\alpha \in \mathbb{N}^+$. We call w* unambiguous *for α if and only if there is an unambiguous morphism $\sigma : \mathbb{N}^* \to \Sigma^*$ satisfying $\sigma(\alpha) = w$.*

With the help of multi-pattern languages, we can even present a characterisation of those patterns that have an unambiguous erasing morphism. However, the immediate usefulness of the result is limited. Nevertheless, our examinations reveal some enlightening and rather counter-intuitive insights that might be relevant for further investigations.

Our characterisation shall demonstrate deep connections between the main subject of the present thesis and vital properties of *NE*-pattern languages. It reads as follows:

Theorem 5.15. *Let Σ be an alphabet, and let $\alpha \in \mathbb{N}^+$. For any partition (U, V) of $\mathcal{P}(\mathrm{var}(\alpha)) \setminus \{\emptyset\}$, let*

$$L_{\alpha,U,V} := \bigcup_{u \in U} L_{\mathrm{NE},\Sigma}(\pi_u(\alpha)) \cap \bigcup_{v \in V} L_{\mathrm{NE},\Sigma}(\pi_v(\alpha)).$$

There is no unambiguous word for α in $L_{\mathrm{E},\Sigma}(\alpha)$ if and only if there is no unambiguous word for α in $L_{\mathrm{E},\Sigma}(\alpha) \setminus L_{\alpha,U,V}$.

Proof. It is sufficient to show that every word in $L_{\alpha,U,V}$ is not unambiguous for α. Hence, for any $u \in U$, let w be any word in $L_{\mathrm{NE},\Sigma}(\pi_u(\alpha))$. Thus, there is a nonerasing morphism $\sigma : \mathbb{N}^* \to \Sigma^*$ with $\sigma(\pi_u(\alpha)) = w$. If, for a $v \in V$, $w \in L_{\mathrm{NE},\Sigma}(\pi_v(\alpha))$, then there additionally is a nonerasing morphism $\tau : \mathbb{N}^* \to \Sigma^*$ with $\tau(\pi_v(\alpha)) = w$. We define a morphism $\sigma' : \mathbb{N}^* \to \Sigma^*$ by, for every $x \in \mathbb{N}$,

$$\sigma'(x) := \begin{cases} \sigma(x) & , x \in \mathrm{var}(\pi_u(\alpha)), \\ \varepsilon & , \text{else}, \end{cases}$$

and a morphism $\tau' : \mathbb{N}^* \to \Sigma^*$ by, again for every $x \in \mathbb{N}$,

$$\tau'(x) := \begin{cases} \tau(x) & , x \in \mathrm{var}(\pi_v(\alpha)), \\ \varepsilon & , \text{else}. \end{cases}$$

Then $\sigma'(\alpha) = \sigma(\pi_u(\alpha)) = w = \tau(\pi_v(\alpha)) = \tau'(\alpha)$. Furthermore, because of the fact that (U, V) is a partition of $\mathcal{P}(\mathrm{var}(\alpha)) \setminus \{\emptyset\}$, it directly follows that $u \neq v$ and, thus, $\{x \in \mathrm{var}(\alpha) \mid \sigma'(x) \neq \varepsilon\} \neq \{x \in \mathrm{var}(\alpha) \mid \tau'(x) \neq \varepsilon\}$. Consequently, w is ambiguous for α. Since w, u and v were arbitrarily chosen, this directly implies that every word $w \in L_{\alpha,U,V}$ is ambiguous for α. □

It is a noteworthy property of Theorem 5.15 that it covers the ambiguity of both erasing and nonerasing morphisms and, hence, allows a unified view on both topics. However, for the latter case, Corollary 3.14 already gives a definite answer, indirectly stating that, for every *morphically primitive* pattern α, there is *no* partition (U, V) of $\mathcal{P}(\mathrm{var}(\alpha)) \setminus \{\emptyset\}$ such that every word in $L_{\mathrm{E},\Sigma}(\alpha) \setminus (\{\varepsilon\} \cup L_{\alpha,U,V})$ is ambiguous for α. Thus, we can completely concentrate on morphically imprimitive patterns when investigating the applicability and the consequences of Theorem 5.15.

From a practical point of view, Theorem 5.15 is only helpful when it notably reduces the number of words that need to be examined with regard to their ambiguity, i. e., when $L_{\alpha,U,V}$ has a large size. The following example shows how an adequate choice of (U, V) can drastically reduce the number of words that need to be examined with regard to their ambiguity.

Example 5.16. Let $\Sigma := \{\mathtt{a}, \mathtt{b}\}$ and $\beta := 2{\cdot}2{\cdot}4{\cdot}1{\cdot}3{\cdot}3{\cdot}4$. Let $U := (\{2\}, \{1, 2\}, \{1, 3\}, \{1, 4\})$ and $V := \mathcal{P}(\mathrm{var}(\beta)) \setminus U$. Clearly, (U, V) is a partition of $\mathcal{P}(\mathrm{var}(\beta))$. Furthermore, $\bigcup_{u\in U} L_{\mathrm{NE},\Sigma}(\pi_u(\beta)) = L_{\mathrm{NE},\Sigma}(2 \cdot 2,\ 2 \cdot 2 \cdot 1,\ 1 \cdot 3 \cdot 3,\ 4 \cdot 1 \cdot 4) = \Sigma^+ \setminus \{\mathtt{a}, \mathtt{b}, \mathtt{ab}, \mathtt{ba}\}$ (cf. Example 5.13) and, since $\{1\} \in V$, $\bigcup_{v\in V} L_{\mathrm{NE},\Sigma}(\pi_v(\beta)) = \Sigma^+$. Thus, $L_{\beta,U,V} = \Sigma^+ \setminus \{\mathtt{a}, \mathtt{b}, \mathtt{ab}, \mathtt{ba}\}$ and, according to Theorem 5.15, there is no unambiguous word for β in $L_{\mathrm{E},\Sigma}(\beta) \setminus \{\varepsilon\}$ if and only if there is no unambiguous word for β in $L_{\mathrm{E},\Sigma}(\beta) \setminus (\{\varepsilon\} \cup L_{\beta,U,V}) = \{\mathtt{a}, \mathtt{b}, \mathtt{ab}, \mathtt{ba}\}$. This is true since $\mathtt{a}, \mathtt{b}, \mathtt{ab}, \mathtt{ba}$ are the only unambiguous words for β. ◇

However, so far, Theorem 5.15 cannot be seen as an applicable characterisation of those patterns that have an unambiguous erasing morphism since it is not clear how U and V have to be chosen such that $L_{\alpha,U,V}$ has maximal size and what a maximal $L_{\alpha,U,V}$ looks like for a given α. Nevertheless, we consider this an interesting task for further research.

Moreover, since, for any pattern α, $L_{\mathrm{E},\Sigma}(\alpha)$ is equivalent to a finite union of NE-pattern languages (see Theorem 2.1 by Jiang et al. [15]), Theorem 5.15 shows that the existence of unambiguous *erasing* morphisms strongly depends on equivalence and inclusion of nonerasing multi-pattern languages. This is not only a rather counter-intuitive insight, but it also gives an idea of how difficult the problem of the existence of unambiguous erasing morphisms might be. More precisely, even the decidability of the inclusion problem for ordinary terminal-free NE-pattern languages is open and includes some prominent open problems on pattern avoidability (cf. [15]). The inclusion of terminal-free NE-pattern languages is also known to depend on the size of the target alphabet, which fits very well with what is known for the ambiguity of erasing morphisms with a finite target alphabet (see, e. g., Theorem 4.43).

The following sufficient condition illustrates how Theorem 5.15 can be used to find criteria on the nonexistence of unambiguous erasing morphisms:

Corollary 5.17. *Let Σ be an alphabet, and let $\alpha \in \mathbb{N}^+$. If there exists a partition (U, V) of $\mathcal{P}(\mathrm{var}(\alpha)) \setminus \{\emptyset\}$ with*

$$L_{\mathrm{E},\Sigma}(\alpha) \setminus \{\varepsilon\} = \bigcup_{u\in U} L_{\mathrm{NE},\Sigma}(\pi_u(\alpha)) = \bigcup_{v\in V} L_{\mathrm{NE},\Sigma}(\pi_v(\alpha)),$$

then there is no unambiguous word for α in $L_{\mathrm{E},\Sigma}(\alpha) \setminus \{\varepsilon\}$.

Proof. Directly from Theorem 5.15. □

Corollary 5.17 is indeed applicable to certain patterns like, for example, $\alpha = 1 \cdot 2$ with $(U, V) := (\{\{1\}, \{1, 2\}\}, \{\{2\}\})$. However, it is an open question whether or not the condition of Corollary 5.17 is characteristic.

We finally want to mention that Theorem 5.15 and Corollary 5.17 do not need to be based on a *partition* (U, V) of $\mathcal{P}(\mathrm{var}(\alpha)) \setminus \{\emptyset\}$. Alternatively, they could refer to *arbitrary* disjoint subsets U and V of $\mathcal{P}(\mathrm{var}(\alpha)) \setminus \{\emptyset\}$.

5.3 A variation of the problem setting

In this section, we reverse our problem setting: Instead of asking for which patterns there are unambiguous words (cf. Definition 5.14), we shall investigate which words qualify as unambiguous words. Thus, our question is: Given Σ and $w \in \Sigma^+$, is there a pattern α for which w is unambiguous?

It is clear that every w is unambiguous for $\alpha_1 = 1$. Furthermore, every w is unambiguous for any pattern α_2 with $|\alpha_2|_x = 1$ for an $x \in \mathbb{N}$ and $|\alpha_2|_y > |w|$ for all $y \in \mathrm{var}(\alpha_2) \setminus \{x\}$. If $|w|_c = 1$ for a $c \in \Sigma$, then α_1 and α_2 are the only types of patterns for which w is unambiguous. In order to exclude these trivial cases, we require $|\mathrm{var}(\alpha)| \geq 2$ and $\sigma(\alpha) = w$ for a *nonerasing* morphism σ.

In the following, we use the notion of morphic primitivity for words over arbitrary alphabets Σ as well, although it is only formally defined for patterns $\alpha \in \mathbb{N}^+$ in Definition 2.3. However, the respective modification of Definition 2.3 is straight-forward. We first note that there are patterns for which a morphically primitive word is unambiguous.

Corollary 5.18. *Let Σ be an alphabet, let $w \in \Sigma^+$ and let $k := |\mathrm{symb}(w)|$. There is an $\alpha \in \mathbb{N}^+$ with $|\mathrm{var}(\alpha)| = k$ and an unambiguous nonerasing morphism $\sigma : \mathbb{N}^* \to \Sigma^*$ with $\sigma(\alpha) = w$ if w is morphically primitive.*

Proof. Without loss of generality, let $\Sigma \supseteq \{1, 2, \ldots, k\}$ and $w \in \{1, 2, \ldots, k\}^+$. With $\alpha := w$, w is unambiguous for α (cf. Theorem 2.10 with any nonerasing morphism σ satisfying $\sigma(i) = i$ for every $i \in \{1, 2, \ldots, k\}$). □

Now we characterise the case of words over a binary alphabet:

Theorem 5.19. *Let $w \in \{\mathtt{a}, \mathtt{b}\}^+$. There are an $\alpha \in \mathbb{N}^+$ with $|\mathrm{var}(\alpha)| \geq 2$ and an unambiguous nonerasing morphism $\sigma : \mathbb{N}^* \to \{\mathtt{a}, \mathtt{b}\}^*$ for α with $\sigma(\alpha) = w$ if and only if*

$$\begin{aligned} w \;\notin\; & \{(\mathtt{b}^s\mathtt{a}\mathtt{b}^t)^n \mid s, t \in \mathbb{N} \cup \{0\} \text{ and } n \in \{1, 2, 3, 4, 6\}\} \cup \\ & \{(\mathtt{a}^s\mathtt{b}\mathtt{a}^t)^n \mid s, t \in \mathbb{N} \cup \{0\} \text{ and } n \in \{1, 2, 3, 4, 6\}\}. \end{aligned}$$

Proof. We show the *only if* part by contraposition: Let $w = (\mathtt{b}^s\mathtt{a}\mathtt{b}^t)^n$ with $s, t \in \mathbb{N} \cup \{0\}$ and $n \in \{1, 2, 3, 4, 6\}$ (the case $w = (\mathtt{a}^s\mathtt{b}\mathtt{a}^t)^n$ is analogous). Let $\alpha \in \mathbb{N}^+$ with $|\mathrm{var}(\alpha)| \geq 2$ and $\sigma : \mathbb{N}^* \to \Sigma^*$ be a nonerasing morphism with $\sigma(\alpha) = w$. W.l.o.g., let $\mathrm{var}(\alpha) = \{1, 2, \ldots, k\}$ for a $k \in \mathbb{N} \setminus \{1\}$. Since every such pattern α with $|\alpha|_x = 1$ for an $x \in \mathrm{var}(\alpha)$ is morphically imprimitive (cf. Definition 2.6 with $f(\alpha) = (x; \alpha)$ and Corollary 2.7), exactly one of the following cases is satisfied:

1. α is morphically imprimitive,
2. α is morphically primitive, $\mathrm{var}(\alpha) = \{1, 2\}$ and $|\alpha|_1 = |\alpha|_2 = 2$,
3. α is morphically primitive, $\mathrm{var}(\alpha) = \{1, 2\}$ and $|\alpha|_1 = |\alpha|_2 = 3$,
4. α is morphically primitive, $\mathrm{var}(\alpha) = \{1, 2, 3\}$ and $|\alpha|_1 = |\alpha|_2 = |\alpha|_3 = 2$,
5. α is morphically primitive, $\mathrm{var}(\alpha) = \{1, 2\}$, $|\alpha|_1 = 2$ and $|\alpha|_2 = 4$, or
6. α is morphically primitive, $\mathrm{var}(\alpha) = \{1, 2\}$, $|\alpha|_1 = 4$ and $|\alpha|_2 = 2$.

Ad 1. If α is morphically imprimitive, the nonerasing morphism σ is not unambiguous for α according to Theorem 2.9.

Ad 2–5. Since for all patterns corresponding to the cases 2, 3, 4 and 5, the number of occurences of every variable in the pattern has even length, it is $\sigma(\alpha) = (\mathtt{b}^s\mathtt{a}\mathtt{b}^t)^n$ with n even. Thus, the erasing morphism $\tau : \mathbb{N}^* \to \{\mathtt{a}, \mathtt{b}\}^*$, defined by $\tau(1) := (\mathtt{b}^s\mathtt{a}\mathtt{b}^t)^{\frac{n}{2}}$ and $\tau(x) := \varepsilon$ for all other variables x, satisfies $\tau(\alpha) = \sigma(\alpha)$. Furthermore, $\tau(2) = \varepsilon \neq \sigma(2)$. Hence, σ is not unambiguous for α.

Ad 6. Here, we define the morphism $\tau : \mathbb{N}^* \to \{\mathtt{a}, \mathtt{b}\}^*$ by $\tau(1) := \varepsilon$ and $\tau(2) := (\mathtt{b}^s\mathtt{a}\mathtt{b}^t)^{\frac{n}{2}}$ and use a similar argumentation as in the cases 2–5 to show that τ contradicts σ being unambiguous for α.

Consequently, σ is ambiguous for α, which proves the *only if* part.

To prove the *if* part, let $w \neq (\mathtt{b}^s\mathtt{a}\mathtt{b}^t)^n$ and $w \neq (\mathtt{a}^s\mathtt{b}\mathtt{a}^t)^n$ for any $s, t \in \mathbb{N} \cup \{0\}$ and any $n \in \{1, 2, 3, 4, 6\}$. We first state the following claim, which can be verified with help of Definition 2.6 and Corollary 2.7.

Claim. A word $w \in \{\mathtt{a}, \mathtt{b}\}^+$ is morphically imprimitive if and only if $w = (\mathtt{b}^s\mathtt{a}\mathtt{b}^t)^n$ or $w = (\mathtt{b}^s\mathtt{a}\mathtt{b}^t)^n$ with $s + t > 0$ and $n \in \mathbb{N}$.

Now, we consider the following cases:

Case 1: w is morphically primitive and $w \neq c^n$ for any $c \in \{\mathtt{a}, \mathtt{b}\}$. There is an $\alpha \in \mathbb{N}^+$ and an unambiguous nonerasing morphism $\sigma : \mathbb{N}^* \to \{\mathtt{a}, \mathtt{b}\}^*$ for α with $\sigma(\alpha) = w$ according to Corollary 5.18.

Case 2: w is morphically imprimitive or $w = c^n$ for a $c \in \{\mathtt{a}, \mathtt{b}\}$. Thus, $w = (\mathtt{b}^s\mathtt{a}\mathtt{b}^t)^n$ or $w = (\mathtt{a}^s\mathtt{b}\mathtt{a}^t)^n$ for an $n \in \mathbb{N} \setminus \{1, 2, 3, 4, 6\}$ (cf. the above claim). Let $w = (\mathtt{b}^s\mathtt{a}\mathtt{b}^t)^n$ (the other case is analogous). We define $l := \frac{n-1}{2}$ and $r := \frac{n-1}{2} + 1$ if n is odd, and $\ell := \frac{n}{2} - 1$ and $r := \frac{n}{2} + 1$ if n is even. Thus, in both cases, $n = \ell + r$. Furthermore, let $\alpha := 1^\ell \cdot 2^r$. Let $\sigma : \mathbb{N}^* \to \{\mathtt{a}, \mathtt{b}\}^*$ be a nonerasing morphism satisfying $\sigma(1) = \sigma(2) = \mathtt{b}^s\mathtt{a}\mathtt{b}^t$. Clearly, $\sigma(\alpha) = w$. Now, assume that there is another morphism $\tau : \mathbb{N}^* \to \{\mathtt{a}, \mathtt{b}\}^*$ with $\tau(\alpha) = \sigma(\alpha)$. Due to the structure of α, it is $\tau(1), \tau(2) \in \{\mathtt{b}^s\mathtt{a}\mathtt{b}^t\}^*$. Let $\tau(1) = (\mathtt{b}^s\mathtt{a}\mathtt{b}^t)^{q_1}$ and $\tau(2) = (\mathtt{b}^s\mathtt{a}\mathtt{b}^t)^{q_2}$ with $q_1, q_2 \in \mathbb{N} \cup \{0\}$.

Case 2.1: $q_1 = 0$. If $q_2 < 2$, $|\tau(\alpha)| < |\sigma(\alpha)|$. If $q_2 \geq 2$, $|\tau(\alpha)| > |\sigma(\alpha)|$.

Case 2.2: $q_1 = 1$. If $q_2 = 0$, $|\tau(\alpha)| < |\sigma(\alpha)|$. If $q_2 \geq 2$, $|\tau(\alpha)| > |\sigma(\alpha)|$. If $q_2 = 1$, then τ is not different from σ on the variables 1, 2.

Case 2.3: $q_1 = 2$. If n is odd, we have $\tau(1^\ell) = (\mathtt{b}^s\mathtt{a}\mathtt{b}^t)^{q_1(\frac{n-1}{2})} = (\mathtt{b}^s\mathtt{a}\mathtt{b}^t)^{n-1}$. Thus, $\tau(2^r)$ must equal $\mathtt{b}^s\mathtt{a}\mathtt{b}^t$, which is not possible since $n \geq 5$ and, thus, $r = \frac{n-1}{2} + 1 > 2$. If n is even, we have $\tau(1^\ell) = (\mathtt{b}^s\mathtt{a}\mathtt{b}^t)^{q_1(\frac{n}{2}-1)} = (\mathtt{b}^s\mathtt{a}\mathtt{b}^t)^{n-2}$. Thus, $\tau(2^r)$ must equal $(\mathtt{b}^s\mathtt{a}\mathtt{b}^t)^2$, which is not possible since $n \geq 8$ and, thus, $r = \frac{n}{2} + 1 > 2$.

Case 2.4: $q_1 \geq 3$. If n is odd, we have $|(\mathtt{b}^s\mathtt{ab}^t)^{q_1(\frac{n-1}{2})}| = |\tau(1^\ell)| \leq |\tau(\alpha)| = |(\mathtt{b}^s\mathtt{ab}^t)^n|$ and, thus, $q_1(\frac{n-1}{2}) \leq n$. Furthermore, since $q_1 \geq 3$, it is $3(\frac{n-1}{2}) \leq q_1(\frac{n-1}{2})$, which leads to $3(\frac{n-1}{2}) \leq n$. Solving this inequality shows $n \leq 3$, which contradicts the choice of $n \notin \{1, 2, 3, 4, 6\}$. If n is even, we have $|(\mathtt{b}^s\mathtt{ab}^t)^{q_1(\frac{n}{2}-1)}| = |\tau(1^\ell)| \leq |\tau(\alpha)| = |(\mathtt{b}^s\mathtt{ab}^t)^n|$ and, thus, $q_1(\frac{n}{2} - 1) \leq n$. Furthermore, since $q_1 \geq 3$, it is $3(\frac{n}{2} - 1) \leq q_1(\frac{n}{2} - 1)$, which leads to $3(\frac{n}{2} - 1) \leq n$. Solving this inequality shows $n \leq 6$, which contradicts the choice of an even $n \notin \{1, 2, 3, 4, 6\}$.

It follows from the Cases 2.1–2.4 that another morphism τ cannot exist and, hence, σ (and w) is unambiguous for α.

This case-by-case analysis is exhaustive and, hence, we have proved Theorem 5.19. □

Theorem 5.19 specifically addresses words over a binary alphabet. For words over a larger alphabet, a condition as simple as in Theorem 5.19 cannot be found since there is no such simple description as $w = (\mathtt{b}^s\mathtt{ab}^t)^n$ or $w = (\mathtt{b}^s\mathtt{ab}^t)^n$, expressing that w is morphically imprimitive. Hence, we expect a characterising theorem for $w \in \{\mathtt{a}, \mathtt{b}, \mathtt{c}\}^+$ to be technically more involved, but, nevertheless, not much more complicated. The case that w is morphically primitive is already answered by Corollary 5.18 for any alphabet size.

Chapter 6

Conclusion and open problems

In this thesis, we have systematically examined the ambiguity of erasing morphisms. As our main results, we have given a characterisation of patterns with a moderately ambiguous morphism (cf. Theorem 4.20) and characterised the ambiguity of morphisms with an infinite target alphabet Σ (cf. Theorem 4.22). Additionally, we have shown that the respective decision problems are NP-complete (cf. Theorem 4.59 and Corollary 4.61). For these results, the partition of $\mathbb{N}^+$ into morphically erasable and unerasable patterns (cf. Definition 4.12) is of major importance. This partition is solely based on the structure of the pattern. Contrary to this, when we consider finite target alphabets Σ, we have discovered that the question if, for a given pattern α, there exists an unambiguous erasing morphism with target alphabet Σ for α does not depend on the structure of α only, but also on the size of Σ (cf. Theorem 4.24), which is a novel and rather unexpected phenomenon in the theory of ambiguity of morphisms. To analyse unambiguity of morphisms, ambiguity partitions and, thus, the property of a pattern being morphically erasable or unerasable is a helpful tool, although this property has turned out not to be characteristic (as also pointed out in Theorem 4.24). In Section 4.4.1, we identify one phenomenon that causes target alphabet dependent ambiguity and investigate this phenomenon in detail. Even though this phenomenon covers many example patterns of different structures, it is not the only phenomenon that can cause ambiguity even for morphically unerasable patterns, which has been demonstrated in Section 4.4.2. This section also covers another interesting phenomenon which occurs for erasing morphisms only, namely the fact that there are patterns with only finitely many unambiguous morphic images.

Finally, we have discussed some related topics. Therefore, we have extended our analysis of ambiguity to substitutions (cf. Section 5.1), where many concepts can be adapted and a new type of ambiguity, terminal-comprising ambiguity, can be observed. Furthermore, we have shown connections to nonerasing multi-pattern languages. Ambiguity of morphisms does not only lead to interesting examples for equivalent nonerasing multi-pattern languages generated by disjoint sets of patterns, but it can even be characterised with help of basic properties of multi-pattern languages (cf. Theorem 5.15 and Corollary 5.17). The immediate use of these results is limited (see the explanations after Theorem 5.15), although they deliver a promising approach for further research. Finally, Section 5.3 is dedicated to the question which words are suited for unambiguous morphic images at all. A characterisation for words over a binary alphabet is given.

In the following, we shall discuss the question why the situation is more complex when considering erasing morphisms rather than only nonerasing morphisms. Compared to the

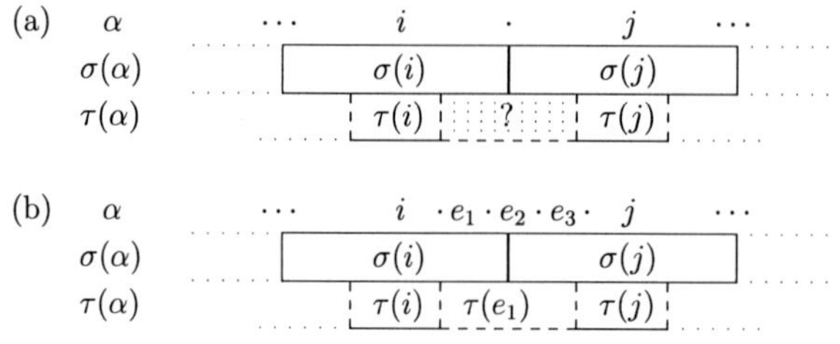

Figure 6.1: (a) nonerasing morphisms, (b) erasing morphisms

theory of nonerasing morphisms, we have discovered numerous novel phenomena that occur only for patterns for which no *nonerasing* morphism is unambiguous, but for which there exist unambiguous *erasing* morphisms. Thus, some variables in such a pattern *must* be erased by a potentially unambiguous morphism and, hence, it is fairly challenging to find an unambiguous morphism that maps certain variables to nonempty words since the arbitrarily complex structure of the erased variables can regenerate parts of the morphic image – a situation which directly leads to an ambiguous morphism. An immediate example for this context is given in Proposition 4.52. Also, the patterns in the proofs of Theorem 4.24 and Theorem 4.43 are based on a very complex structure of variables that must be erased by any potentially unambiguous morphism.

In Figure 6.1, the different settings (nonerasing vs. erasing morphisms) are illustrated. For nonerasing morphisms (a) and for every morphically primitive pattern α, moderate ambiguity can be achieved through any three-segmented nonerasing morphism σ (cf. Theorem 3.7). Thus, we know that every morphism τ with $\tau(\alpha) = \sigma(\alpha)$ covers a certain factor of $\sigma(i)$ at a certain position with $\tau(i)$ (the dashed box around $\tau(i)$) and a certain factor of $\sigma(j)$ at a certain position with $\tau(j)$ (the dashed box around $\tau(j)$). The dotted area around the question mark can be generated by the end of $\tau(i)$ or the beginning of $\tau(j)$ (or by both of it). However, if we can assure that α ends with i, begins with j or there is at least one occurrence of a variable k, $k \neq j$, in α such that $\alpha = \dots i \cdot k \dots$ and $\sigma(k)$ begins with a different letter than $\sigma(j)$, then the question mark exactly separates $\tau(i)$ from $\tau(j)$ and, thus, no ambiguity is caused at this point. As shown in the proof of Theorem 3.12 (see Freydenberger et al. [8]), this is indeed possible for every variable pair $i \cdot j$ in a morphically primitive pattern. For the resulting unambiguous morphisms, two letters in the target alphabet are sufficient.

Now, consider the pattern α in (b). If α is morphically imprimitive, certain variables must be erased (cf. Theorem 2.9) and the tools of Section 4.1 provide concrete information which variables these are at least. Let us assume that e_1, e_2, e_3 are such variables, whereas i, j may be mapped to nonempty words. Again, we can achieve moderate ambiguity (cf. Theorem 4.20), but now the factor between $\tau(i)$ and $\tau(j)$ does not need to be generated by $\tau(i)$ or $\tau(j)$ since there are other variables e_1, e_2, e_3 between i and j that can potentially be used to generate this factor – in the illustration, e_1 is being used. This substantial degree of freedom caused by the interplay of arbitrarily many erased variables does not only make the situation more involved, it is also responsible for the fact that ambiguity of erasing morphisms is dependent on the size of the target alphabet (cf. Theorem 4.24) and for various other interesting differences as well that we shall summarise in the following.

Difference 1. There is a pattern for which every nonerasing morphism is ambiguous, but for which there exists an unambiguous erasing morphism.

Difference 2. Let Σ be an alphabet with $|\Sigma| \geq 2$. There exists an unambiguous nonerasing morphism $\sigma : \mathbb{N}^* \to \Sigma^*$ for a pattern $\alpha \in \mathbb{N}^+$ if and only if there exists a moderately ambiguous nonerasing morphism $\sigma : \mathbb{N}^* \to \Sigma^*$ for α. However, there exists a pattern $\beta \in \mathbb{N}^+$ such that no morphism $\sigma : \mathbb{N}^* \to \Sigma^*$ is unambiguous for β, but there exists a moderately ambiguous erasing morphism $\sigma : \mathbb{N}^* \to \Sigma^*$ for β.

Difference 3. Let Σ and Σ' be alphabets with $2 \leq |\Sigma| < |\Sigma'|$. There exists an unambiguous nonerasing morphism $\sigma : \mathbb{N}^* \to \Sigma^*$ for a pattern $\alpha \in \mathbb{N}^+$ if and only if there exists an unambiguous nonerasing morphism $\sigma : \mathbb{N}^* \to \Sigma'^*$ for α. However, there exists a pattern $\beta \in \mathbb{N}^+$ such that no morphism $\sigma : \mathbb{N}^* \to \Sigma^*$ is unambiguous for β, but there exists an unambiguous erasing morphism $\sigma : \mathbb{N}^* \to \Sigma'^*$ for β.

Difference 4. Let Σ be an alphabet. The set of images of unambiguous nonerasing morphisms for a pattern $\alpha \in \mathbb{N}^+$ is either empty or infinite. However, there is a pattern $\beta \in \mathbb{N}^+$ such that the set of images of unambiguous erasing morphisms for β is nonempty and finite.

Difference 1 is shown by Example 4.1, Difference 2 follows from Theorem 3.5 and Corollary 4.28, Difference 3 can be concluded from Corollary 3.13 and Theorem 4.24, and Difference 4 is proved by Theorem 4.42 and Theorem 4.43.

We conclude this thesis by presenting some open problems and further tasks of research. Obviously, the most prominent open problem is the following.

Open Problem 1. *Let Σ be a finite alphabet and let $\alpha \in \mathbb{N}^+$. Does there exist an unambiguous morphism $\sigma : \mathbb{N}^* \to \Sigma^*$ for α?*

A characterisation for one special size of Σ (for example, a binary target alphabet) would already be very desirable. Various examples and considerations in Section 4.4 suggest that an answer to Open Problem 1 is quite intricate and difficult. However, we feel that Theorem 5.15 and Corollary 5.17 might be a promising approach. Moreover, we consider the search for further natural subclasses of $\mathbb{N}^+$ for which Open Problem 1 can be solved or even becomes decidable to be an interesting task.

Furthermore, since we can observe that, for some patterns, we need a certain number of symbols in the target alphabet of an unambiguous morphism (cf. Difference 3 and Theorem 4.24), we can formulate the following problem.

Open Problem 2. *Let $\alpha \in \mathbb{N}^+$. What is the minimal size of the alphabet Σ such that there exists an unambiguous morphisms $\sigma : \mathbb{N}^* \to \Sigma^*$ for α if such a morphisms exists at all?*

We know from Corollary 4.13 that a pattern for which there exists an unambiguous morphism must be morphically unerasable. Thus, Corollary 4.27 and Proposition 4.48 give a first upper bound to the size of Σ. Hence, if Open Problem 1 can be answered and, hence, AMB_Σ turns out to be uniformly decidable for every Σ, then we can also algorithmically solve Open Problem 2.

Bibliography

[1] D. Angluin. Finding patterns common to a set of strings. *Journal of Computer and System Sciences*, 21:46–62, 1980.

[2] D. Angluin. Inductive inference of formal languages from positive data. *Information and Control*, 45:117–135, 1980.

[3] K. Culik II and J. Karhumäki. On the equality sets for homomorphisms on free monoids with two generators. *Theoretical Informatics and Applications (RAIRO)*, 14:349–369, 1980.

[4] A. Ehrenfeucht and G. Rozenberg. Finding a homomorphism between two words is NP-complete. *Information Processing Letters*, 9:86–88, 1979.

[5] D.D. Freydenberger, H. Nevisi, and D. Reidenbach. Weakly unambiguous morphisms. In *Proc. 28th Annual Symposium on Theoretical Aspects of Computer Science, STACS 2011*, 2011.

[6] D.D. Freydenberger and D. Reidenbach. The unambiguity of segmented morphisms. *Discrete Applied Mathematics*, 157:3055–3068, 2009.

[7] D.D. Freydenberger and D. Reidenbach. Bad news on decision problems for patterns. *Information and Computation*, 208:83–96, 2010.

[8] D.D. Freydenberger, D. Reidenbach, and J.C. Schneider. Unambiguous morphic images of strings. *International Journal of Foundations of Computer Science*, 17:601–628, 2006.

[9] M.R. Garey and D.S. Johnson. *Computers and Intractability – A Guide to the Theory of NP-Completeness.* W.H. Freeman and Company, New York, 1979.

[10] E.M. Gold. Language identification in the limit. *Information and Control*, 10:447–474, 1967.

[11] T. Harju and J. Karhumäki. Morphisms. In G. Rozenberg and A. Salomaa, editors, *Handbook of Formal Languages*, volume 1, chapter 7, pages 439–510. Springer, 1997.

[12] T. Head. Fixed languages and the adult languages of 0L schemes. *International Journal of Computer Mathematics*, 10:103–107, 1981.

[13] Š. Holub. Polynomial-time algorithm for fixed points of nontrivial morphisms. *Discrete Mathematics*, 309:5069–5076, 2009.

[14] S. Jain, Y.S. Ong, and F. Stephan. Regular patterns, regular languages and context-free languages. *Information Processing Letters*, 110:1114–1119, 2010.

[15] T. Jiang, E. Kinber, A. Salomaa, K. Salomaa, and S. Yu. Pattern languages with and without erasing. *International Journal of Computer Mathematics*, 50:147–163, 1994.

[16] T. Jiang, A. Salomaa, K. Salomaa, and S. Yu. Decision problems for patterns. *Journal of Computer and System Sciences*, 50:53–63, 1995.

[17] J. Karhumäki. On cube-free ω-words generated by binary morphisms. *Discrete Applied Mathematics*, 5:279–297, 1983.

[18] L. Kari, A. Mateescu, G. Păun, and A. Salomaa. Multi-pattern languages. *Theoretical Computer Science*, 141:253–268, 1995.

[19] L. Kari, G. Rozenberg, and A. Salomaa. L systems. In G. Rozenberg and A. Salomaa, editors, *Handbook of Formal Languages*, volume 1, chapter 5, pages 253–328. Springer, 1997.

[20] M. Lothaire. *Combinatorics on Words.* Addison-Wesley, Reading, MA, 1983.

[21] A. de Luca. A combinatorial property of the Fibonacci words. *Information Processing Letters*, 12:193–195, 1981.

[22] A. Mateescu and A. Salomaa. Patterns. In G. Rozenberg and A. Salomaa, editors, *Handbook of Formal Languages*, volume 1, chapter 4.6, pages 230–242. Springer, 1997.

[23] A. Mateescu, A. Salomaa, K. Salomaa, and S. Yu. P, NP, and the Post Correspondence Problem. *Information and Computation*, 121:135–142, 1995.

[24] E.L. Post. A variant of a recursively unsolvable problem. *Bulletin of the American Mathematical Society*, 52:264–268, 1946.

[25] D. Reidenbach. *The Ambiguity of Morphisms in Free Monoids and its Impact on Algorithmic Properties of Pattern Languages.* PhD thesis, Fachbereich Informatik, Technische Universität Kaiserslautern, 2006. Logos Verlag, Berlin.

[26] D. Reidenbach. A non-learnable class of E-pattern languages. *Theoretical Computer Science*, 350:91–102, 2006.

[27] D. Reidenbach. An examination of Ohlebusch and Ukkonen's conjecture on the equivalence problem for E-pattern languages. *Journal of Automata, Languages and Combinatorics*, 12:407–426, 2007.

[28] D. Reidenbach. Discontinuities in pattern inference. *Theoretical Computer Science*, 397:166–193, 2008.

[29] D. Reidenbach and J.C. Schneider. Morphically primitive words. *Theoretical Computer Science*, 410:2148–2161, 2009.

[30] D. Reidenbach and J.C. Schneider. Restricted ambiguity of erasing morphisms. In *Proc. 14th International Conference on Developments in Language Theory, DLT 2010*, volume 6224 of *Lecture Notes in Computer Science*, pages 387–398, 2010.

[31] D. Reidenbach and J.C. Schneider. Restricted ambiguity of erasing morphisms. *Theoretical Computer Science*, 412:3510–3523, 2011.

[32] G. Rozenberg and A. Salomaa. *Handbook of Formal Languages*, volume 1. Springer, Berlin, 1997.

[33] K. Saari. Periods of factors of the Fibonacci word. In *Proc. 6th International Conference on Words, WORDS 2007*, pages 273–279, 2007.

[34] A. Salomaa. Equality sets for homomorphisms of free monoids. *Acta Cybernetica*, 4:127–139, 1978.

[35] J.C. Schneider. Unambiguous erasing morphisms in free monoids. In *Proc. SOFSEM 2009: Theorie and Practice of Computer Science*, volume 5404 of *Lecture Notes in Computer Science*, pages 473–484, 2009.

[36] J.C. Schneider. Unambiguous erasing morphisms in free monoids. *RAIRO – Theoretical Informatics and Applications*, 44:193–208, 2010.

[37] T. Shinohara. Polynomial time inference of extended regular pattern languages. In *Proc. RIMS Symposia on Software Science and Engineering, Kyoto*, volume 147 of *Lecture Notes in Computer Science*, pages 115–127, 1982.

[38] A. Thue. Über unendliche Zeichenreihen. *Norske Videnskaps-Selskabets Skrifter (Mat.-Nat. Klasse)*, 7:1–22, 1906.

Index

Curriculum Vitae

Name:	Johannes C. Schneider
Address:	Werschweilerstr. 18 67657 Kaiserslautern Germany
Date of Birth:	February 1, 1980
Place of Birth:	Speyer, Germany
Marital Status:	married

1986-1990	Zeppelin-Grundschule, Speyer, Germany
1990-1999	Gymnasium am Kaiserdom, Speyer
1999-2000	Civilian service
2000-2006	Studies at the University of Kaiserslautern, Germany, Diploma in Computer Science, 2006
2005	Studies at Lunds Tekniska Högskola in Lund, Sweden
since December 2006	Research associate at the Department of Computer Science, University of Kaiserslautern, Germany